MARK & METHOD

MARK &

METHOD

NEW APPROACHES IN
BIBLICAL STUDIES

EDITED BY

Janice Capel Anderson

AND Stephen D. Moore

FORTRESS PRESS ✳ MINNEAPOLIS

MARK AND METHOD
New Approaches in Biblical Studies

Cover and text design by James F. Brisson
Cover art reproduced from the *Lindisfarne Gospel* by permission of the British Library
Chapter opening art by Elizabeth Foster
Herod's Banquet by Filippo Lippi reproduced by permission of Alinari/Art Resource
L'apparition by Gustave Moreau reproduced by permission of Giraudon/Art Resource
The Dancer's Reward by Aubrey Beardsley reproduced by permission of Dover Publications, Inc.
"Atta Troll" is from *The Complete Poems of Heinrich Heine: A Modern English Version*, tr. Hal Draper, copyright © 1982 Suhrkamp Verlag. Used by permission.

Library of Congress Cataloging-in-Publication Data

Mark and method : new approaches in biblical studies / edited by
   Janice Capel Anderson and Stephen D. Moore.
        p.   cm.
   Includes bibliographical references and indexes.
   ISBN 0-8006-2655-9 (alk. paper)
      1. Bible.   N.T.   Mark—Criticism, interpretation, etc.
   I. Anderson, Janice Capel, 1952–   . II. Moore, Stephen D., 1954–   .
   BS2585.2.M2397   1992
   226.3'06'01—dc20   92-17158
                                                                          CIP

The paper used in this publication meets the minimum requirements of American National Standard for Information Sciences—Permanence of Paper for Printed Library Materials, ANSI Z329.48-1984. ∞™

Manufactured in the U.S.A.   AF 1-2655

96   95   94   93   92   1   2   3   4   5   6   7   8   9   10

CONTENTS

PREFACE

The purpose of this book is to introduce students and teachers to new approaches in the interpretation of the Gospels, using the Gospel of Mark as a case study. The introductory chapter traces the career(s) of the evangelist Mark, and Gospel interpretation generally, through history. The remaining chapters are devoted to some of the more exciting contemporary approaches to Mark—narrative criticism, reader-response criticism, deconstruction, feminist criticism, and social criticism—a five-sided prism through which the Gospel is refracted. We have striven to keep our language clear, to define terms, and to limit footnotes. A glossary of technical terms is provided. It is our hope that anyone who has completed a basic introductory course in biblical studies will be able to benefit from *Mark and Method*, and that it will also hold some surprises for those who are veterans of such study. Those who have little familiarity with gospel criticism may wish to read the chapter on narrative criticism first. The chapter on deconstruction is perhaps the most difficult. All the chapters should be read with a good modern translation of Mark in hand. This book can be used in courses on Mark, the Gospels, biblical hermeneutics, New Testament introduction, and the Bible as literature. It can supplement standard introductory textbooks as well as stand on its own. Scholars who are trying to keep abreast of new developments in the field may also find it useful.

Producing this book has been a rewarding collaborative venture. All of the contributors have read and commented upon each other's work. We have benefited from one another's strengths and, we hope, reduced some of our weaknesses. Working together has decreased the sense of isolation that scholars sometimes feel. The joy of having a cowriter who cares as passionately as you do about your subject matter should not be underestimated. This does not mean that we have reached—or want to reach—unanimity on Mark or method. In fact, one conviction that we share in common is the importance of multiple angles of vision. We value one another for our differences as well as our similarities.

There are many persons to whom we owe a debt of gratitude. We wish to thank the American Academy of Religion for a Collaborative Research Grant in 1989–90 that facilitated our initial efforts. We would also like to thank

Elizabeth Struthers Malbon, chairwoman of the Society of Biblical Literature's section on Biblical Criticism and Literary Criticism, who made it possible for us to present portions of our chapters to a stimulating and challenging audience at the 1991 annual meeting in Kansas City. All of the contributors to this volume are members of the Society of Biblical Literature's Group on the Literarary Aspects of the Gospels and Acts, and we have learned much from our colleagues in the group over the years. We also thank our students and our families who frequently provided jaded critics with fresh perspectives. Finally, we wish to thank Fortress Press's editorial director Marshall D. Johnson and editors Charles B. Puskas, Pam McClanahan, and Julie Odland for understanding our purposes so well and seeing our project through to completion.

1

Introduction:

The Lives of Mark

JANICE CAPEL ANDERSON AND STEPHEN D. MOORE

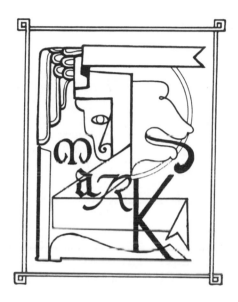

It is not uncommon for a New Testament professor to begin an introductory lecture on the Gospels by asking students, Have you ever read an entire Gospel straight through? "If you have not," the teacher will continue, "you may not realize that each of the four evangelists is a full-fledged author in his own right. Each paints a unique portrait of Jesus." If students are familiar with the Gospels at all, they will likely have read, or heard read, only short passages taken out of their contexts. Here the classroom has parted company with the church. Short passages are read aloud in church services and expounded in sermons. They regularly form the basis for Sunday school lessons. Before hearing that gently accusing voice (How many of you have ever read a Gospel in one sitting?) most of us unconsciously combined passages from all four Gospels into a kind of mishmash or harmony.

Tradition is firmly on the side of the student here. As early as the second century of the Common Era, a Syrian Christian named Tatian produced a highly influential harmony of all four Gospels known as the *Diatessaron*. Tatian had his work cut out for him. Hard-to-reconcile details abound in the Gospels. You can quickly establish this by comparing the accounts that the evangelists give of Jesus' resurrection, for example (Matt 28:1-10; Mark 16:1-8; Luke 24:1-12; John 20:1-10), or of Jesus' death (Matt 27:45-56; Mark 15:33-41; Luke 23:44-49; John 19:28-37), transfiguration (Matt 17:1-8; Mark 9:2-8; Luke 9:28-36), or baptism (Matt 3:13-17; Mark 1:9-11; Luke 3:21-22; cf. John 1:24ff.).

Oddly enough, the modern New Testament scholar tends to be someone who seizes gleefully on discrepancies among the four Gospels. Such discrepancies, far from closing the door to understanding, are instead the keys that he or she hopes to use to unlock the particular theological viewpoint of each evangelist. For example, Mark's Jesus dies with a cry of desolation (15:34ff.) in sharp contrast to Luke's Jesus, who expires on a note of serene confidence (23:46; cf. 23:34, 43). Typically the scholar will explain this discrepancy with reference to Mark's theology, which is said to be a theology of the cross. Jesus' cross casts a longer and darker shadow over the Markan landscape than over the Lukan landscape, which helps to explain the bleak manner in which Jesus dies in Mark.

Like evangelists, New Testament professors are mediators of a tradition. An oral tradition of some thirty or forty years is thought to lie behind Mark. The teacher who takes pains to unlock Mark's theological slant is likewise the bearer of a thirty- or forty-year-old tradition. In the 1950s the German New Testament scholar Willi Marxsen insisted more emphatically than anyone before him that the evangelist Mark should be viewed as a full-fledged author.[1] The approach that Marxsen pioneered on Mark, and that certain of his colleagues pioneered on Luke and Matthew, came to be known as *redaction criticism*. Mark was said to be a redactor or editor who exercised creative control in his reworking of the traditions he inherited concerning Jesus. Marxsen insisted that Mark is "an individual, an author personality who pursues a definite goal with his work."[2] But if Mark was *not* an individual, or even an author in the strict sense of the term, in the period before Marxsen and redaction criticism—a rather lengthy period, to be sure—what then was he? What follows is a highly selective and greatly simplified résumé of the two-thousand-year career of the first evangelist.

How Mark Became an Author

Mark as Peter's Scribe

"Mark" was probably not his real name. At first the Gospels circulated anonymously. Later the shortest Gospel came to be titled *Kata Markon*, "(the Gospel) according to Mark." Most likely the name was lifted from certain other

---

1. Willi Marxsen, *Mark the Evangelist: Studies in the Redaction History of the Gospel*, trans. James Boyce et al. (Nashville: Abingdon Press, 1959), 15–22.
2. Ibid., 18.

texts, also on their way to becoming New Testament texts. These feature a (John) Mark who is associated with Paul and Peter (Acts 12:12, 25; 15:37-39; 2 Tim 4:11; 1 Pet 5:13). By the second century the church was increasingly anxious to keep Gospel authorship in the family. Mark's relationship to Peter is the topic of the earliest "biographical" statement on the evangelist that has come down to us. It is attributed to Papias, Bishop of Hieropolis (in what is now Turkey). Eusebius (c. 260–340 C.E.), one of the earliest church historians, reports that Papias (c. 140 C.E.) wrote:

> And the Presbyter used to say this, "Mark became Peter's interpreter and wrote accurately all that he remembered, not, indeed, in order, of the things said or done by the Lord. For he had not heard the Lord, nor had he followed him, but later on, as I said, followed Peter, who used to give teaching as necessity demanded but not making, as it were, an arrangement of the Lord's oracles, so that Mark did nothing wrong in thus writing down single points as he remembered them. For to one thing he gave attention, to leave out nothing of what he had heard and to make no false statements in them."[3]

This early snapshot of Mark presents him as a scribe—an accurate scribe, but one whose talents are otherwise limited. The towering figure of Peter overshadows him. Indeed, Mark is mentioned primarily because he has been enlisted in a battle. Certain second-century groups, struggling for control of the church, want to show that their teaching goes back unerringly to Jesus Christ by way of the apostles, the evangelists, and their legitimate successors. Mark has become a link in a chain of authority—although he has not gained any real authority for himself in the process.

Mark as Matthew's Summarizer

If Mark was overshadowed by Peter, on the one hand, he soon came to be overshadowed by Matthew, on the other. St. Augustine is especially associated with the influential view of Mark as Matthew's less illustrious cousin. Writing in about 400 C.E. Augustine declares: "Mark followed him [Matthew] like a slave and seems his summarizer."[4] Partly as a result of Augustine's pronouncement, Mark would labor in Matthew's shadow down to the nineteenth century.

Mark as the Holy Spirit's Writing Instrument

Of course, Matthew no less than Mark was eclipsed by the Holy Spirit, the real author of Scripture as far as the church was concerned. So long as the evangelists'

3. Eusebius, *Ecclesiastical History,* Loeb translation, 3.39.15, quoting from Papias, *Expositions of the Words of the Lord.* The latter work, which we know only through Eusebius, seems to date from about 140 C.E.
4. Augustine, *On the Agreement of the Evangelists,* 1.2.4; Seán P. Kealy's translation (*Mark's Gospel: A History, of Its Interpretation* [Ramsey, N.J.: Paulist Press, 1982], 27).

pens were in the firm grip of the Holy Spirit, there could be no real contradictions between their accounts. The Spirit was the guarantee not only of the Bible's authority but also of its consistency. Apparent contradictions could always be resolved on some higher, more sublime level. For example, in Matthew, Mark, and Luke, Jesus is tempted soon after his baptism (Matt 4:1-11; Mark 1:12-13; Luke 4:1-13) and cleanses the Temple near the end of his ministry (Matt 21:12-17; Mark 11:15-19; Luke 19:45-48). In John, however, there is no account at all of the temptation, and the Temple cleansing occurs near the *beginning* of Jesus' ministry (2:13-22). Writing in about 200 C.E. Origen, an early Christian theologian and author of the first technical work on Christian interpretation theory, tried to resolve such discrepancies between the Gospels by turning to allegory or spiritual interpretation. The Holy Spirit was not so much concerned with chronology or literal accuracy as with higher meaning: "The truth of these matters must lie in that which is seen by the mind."[5] What Origen's mind sees is that the Temple can represent the church, Judaism, or even the rational soul, which is higher than the body just as the earthly Jerusalem to which Jesus ascends is higher than Capernaum (see John 2:12-13), a lower region of less dignity.[6] The student of Scripture, "staggered" at finding discrepancies in the Gospel accounts, "will either renounce the attempt to find all the Gospels true . . . or he will accept the four, and will consider that their truth is not to be sought for in the outward and material letter."[7] In addition to solving the problem of contradictions, the authorship of the Holy Spirit and spiritual interpretation also solved the problem of passages that did not seem to make sense or that were offensive when taken literally. Origen gives the example of the devil showing Jesus all the kingdoms of the world from a high mountain during his temptation as a story that should not be taken literally: "Now who but the most superficial reader of a story like this would not laugh at those who think that the kingdoms of the Persians, the Scythians, the Indians, and the Parthians . . . can be seen with the eye of the flesh."[8]

For Origen, scanning Scripture with the eye of the Spirit, "innumerable instances afford nothing more than a fleeting glimpse, a view as through a tiny hole, of a host of most sublime thoughts."[9] But these thoughts are not necessarily those of the biblical writers. Rather, they are those of the Holy Spirit. What the biblical writer seems to be saying on the literal level is less important than what the Holy Spirit means to say. If the writer's own limited intentions thereby lessen in interest, so too do the historical circumstances in which he wrote.

Mark would remain the Holy Spirit's stenographer down to the Reformation and beyond. In 1555 Calvin's *Commentary on a Harmony of the Evangelists* appeared. A crisis of authority in the second-century church had required that

---

5. Origen, *Commentary on John,* trans. Allan Menzies, in *The Ante-Nicene Fathers,* vol. 10, ed. Allan Menzies (Grand Rapids; Wm. B. Eerdmans, n.d.), book 10, sect. 2, p. 382.

6. Ibid., book 10, sect. 16, pp. 393–94.

7. Ibid., book 10, sect. 2, p. 382.

8. Origen, *On First Principles,* trans. Karlfried Froelich, in *Biblical Interpretation in the Early Church,* ed. Karlfried Froelich (Philadelphia: Fortress Press, 1984), 4.3.1.

9. Ibid., 4.2.3.

Mark sit faithfully at Peter's feet and accurately transcribe Peter's eyewitness testimony, as we have seen. But Calvin has other problems, and whether Mark was Peter's scribe or not is no longer of any great consequence:

> *Mark* is generally supposed to have been the private friend and disciple of Peter. It is even believed that he wrote the Gospel, as it was dictated to him by Peter, and thus merely performed the office of an amanuensis or clerk. But on this subject we need not give ourselves much trouble, for it is of little importance to us, provided only we believe that he is a properly qualified and divinely appointed witness, who committed nothing to writing, but as the Holy Spirit directed him and guided his pen.[10]

The pen would soon be snatched from the Holy Spirit's grasp, or at any rate Mark would tighten his grip. The seventeenth and eighteenth centuries saw the advent of the Enlightenment, with its emphasis on reason at the expense of tradition and its emphasis on scientific observation at the expense of divine revelation. "The Gospel under four aspects, but bound together by one Spirit," Irenaeus had pronounced in the second century.[11] But what had held together for so long now threatened to come apart with the irruption of the scientific worldview. The problem of the fourfold Gospel began to elicit radical new solutions.

Mark as Reporter

From Origen to Calvin, commentators had noted that Matthew, Mark, and Luke were similar to each other but different from John. In the eighteenth century the first three Gospels came to be called the Synoptic Gospels: they saw as with (*syn*) one eye (*ōps*). But if they did they were wearing differently tinted spectacles, for there were striking differences among them as well. How could one explain these similarities and differences without recourse to the Holy Spirit? Either all three relied on a common earlier written or oral Gospel, or else they relied on each other. Some scholars still held the view, popularized by Augustine, that Mark abbreviated Matthew. The view that eventually won out, however, and that continues to be the majority view today, was that Mark is the earliest Gospel. Matthew and Luke had used Mark along with another source called Q. Q stood for the German word *Quelle*, meaning "source." This two-source hypothesis, as it came to be called, attributed passages common to all three Gospels to Mark. Passages that appeared only in Matthew and Luke stemmed from the Q source that they shared in common. To round things out, many scholars spoke of M and L sources to indicate material unique to Matthew or Luke. The quest for the Gospels' sources was called *source criticism*.

10. John Calvin, *Commentary on a Harmony of the Evangelists Matthew, Mark, and Luke*, trans. William Pringle (Grand Rapids; Wm. B. Eerdmans, 1949), vol. 1, p. xxxviii.
11. Irenaeus, *Against Heresies*, trans. A. Cleveland Coxe, in *The Ante-Nicene Fathers*, vol. 1, ed. Alexander Roberts and James Donaldson (Grand Rapids; Wm. B. Eerdmans, n.d.), 3.11.8.

What did source criticism mean for our elusive evangelist? It elevated Mark to center stage. If Mark is indeed the earliest Gospel, was it not likely that the life of Jesus was preserved with greater historical accuracy in Mark than in the other Gospels? Mark's plot became the privileged framework for reconstructions of the ministry of Jesus. Mark appeared to be the most realistic Gospel, the least theological, the least shaped by the needs and concerns of the early church. This view of the first Gospel and its author was called the Markan hypothesis.

Mark was now thrust into the limelight, not for his theological and authorial creativity, but for the lack of it. What was most important about Mark's Gospel was not its author's intentions, or even the text itself, but the text as a window on history. Mark was more a chronicler or reporter than a full-fledged author. Paradoxically, despite his newfound acclaim, Mark was reappointed to the same position that he had begun to occupy in the second century—that of unobtrusive recorder.

Mark as Theologian

Clearly, Mark was overdue for a promotion. In 1901 William Wrede published *The Messianic Secret.* "Exegesis must appreciably modify its previous view of the type of authorship that we have in Mark," Wrede insisted.[12] He added: "Present-day investigation of the Gospels is entirely governed by the idea that Mark in his narrative had more or less clearly before his eyes the actual circumstances of the life of Jesus, even if not without gaps."[13] For Wrede, Mark's narrative reflects the circumstances in which Mark wrote as much as the circumstances of Jesus' ministry. Wrede makes much of Mark 9:9. There Jesus directs his disciples "to tell no one what they have seen, until the Son of Man should have risen from the dead." Similar injunctions to secrecy occur elsewhere in Mark (1:34, 43-45; 3:12; 5:43; 7:36; 8:26, 30). This pattern arouses Wrede's suspicions. If "Jesus had really kept himself strictly concealed then [his] life would hardly have been worth relating."[14] Moreover, Jesus' trial and execution would then have had nothing to do with his messiahship, for no one would have known of it.[15] For Wrede the messianic secret is not a historical fact so much as a theological idea, the idea that Jesus became Messiah through his resurrection.[16] However, Jesus' "previous life was only worthy of the Easter morning if the splendour of this day itself shone back upon it."[17] Mark tries to resolve the tension between Jesus' resurrected glory and his earthly existence by asserting that Jesus "really was messiah already on earth"—and he knew it—but he did not yet wish it to be generally known.[18]

12. William Wrede, *The Messianic Secret,* trans. J. C. G. Greig (Greenwood, S.C.: Attic Press, 1971), 129, his emphasis.
13. Ibid.
14. Ibid., 125–26.
15. Ibid., 69.
16. Ibid., 72, 215.
17. Ibid., 229.
18. Ibid.

Interestingly, the relationship between Jesus' glory and his earthly existence is also a central problem in the Gospel of John. In the scholarly tradition that Wrede was opposing, John and Mark had conveniently been set at opposite poles, the "theologian" among the evangelists at one end, the "historian" at the other end. Wrede's daring thesis was that "Mark too is already very far removed from the actual life of Jesus and is dominated by views of a dogmatic kind. If we look at Mark through a large magnifying-glass, it may well be that we find a type of authorship such as is exhibited in John."[19]

Thanks to Wrede, Mark became not only an author but also a theologian. Still, Mark would have to wait another sixty years before his talents would be widely recognized. The intervening years would be lean ones for the evangelist.

Mark as Scissors-and-Paste Man

Form criticism rose to prominence in Germany in the period immediately following the First World War. Its aims were twofold: first, to classify the units of tradition of which the Gospels were thought to be composed into appropriate categories or "forms," such as parables, legends, myths, exhortations, proverbs, and controversy stories; and second, to assign each of these units a *Sitz im Leben*, a setting and function in the life of the early Christian communities, such as preaching, teaching, and baptismal ceremony. With the rise of form criticism, Mark became a scissors-and-paste man. Martin Dibelius, one of the pioneers of the approach, wrote in 1919:

> The literary understanding of the Synoptic Gospels begins with recognition of the fact that they are made up of collections of traditional material. Only in the smallest degree are the writers of the Gospels authors; they are in the main collectors, transmitters, editors. Their activity consists in the handing on, grouping and working over the material that has come down to them, and their theological apprehension of the material, insofar as one can speak of an apprehension at all, finds expression only in this secondary and mediated form. Their attitude to their work is far less independent than of the author of the Fourth Gospel, far less than that of the writer of the Acts of the Apostles.[20]

For Rudolf Bultmann, the second major figure associated with form criticism, the theological creativity of the early church was such that the historical Jesus disappears altogether behind the Gospels. But if Jesus vanishes, so do the evangelists—they disappear behind their texts. The Gospels do not "let the personalities of their author appear."[21] *Das Volk*, "the people," the anonymous

---

19. Ibid., 145.
20. Martin Dibelius, *From Tradition to Gospel*, trans. Bertram Lee Woolf (New York: Charles Scribner's Sons, 1935), 3.
21. Rudolf Bultmann, *The History of the Synoptic Tradition*, trans. John Marsh (New York: Harper & Row, 1965), 372. Karl Ludwig Schmidt, the third figure most often associated with the form-critical study of the Gospels, pronounces a judgment similar to Bultmann's, but with particular reference to Mark (*Der Rahmen der Geschichte Jesu* [Berlin: Trowitzsch, 1919]).

oral tradition of the early church, becomes the true author of the Gospels. The unity and authority of the Gospels is located in the faith of the early church, not in the Gospels themselves or in their authors.

Mark as Redactor and Author

And so we return to Willi Marxsen, with whom we began. Against the backdrop of statements such as those of Dibelius and Bultmann is situated Marxsen's plea for an appreciation of Mark as "an individual, an author personality who pursues a definite goal with his work."[22] Marxsen bases his case on the relative unity of Mark itself. This unity is no longer a direct effect of divine authorship, as in the precritical period. The unifying power once ascribed to the Holy Spirit is transferred to the evangelist himself.

For Marxsen, form criticism's emphasis on the small traditional units that make up the Gospels fails to explain how "this totally disparate material should finally find its way into the unity of a Gospel."[23] The unity evident in Mark "cannot be understood as the 'termination' of the anonymous transmission of material." Such a process would lead "rather to ultimate 'fragmentation.'" Mark's own contribution to the tradition has "counteracted" its drive toward fragmentation, and this countermovement can be explained only with reference to "an individual, an author personality."[24]

Not for the first time in his career, Mark is dragged into the spotlight and declared superior to his fellow evangelists:

> From the outset, Matthew and Luke had access to a presentation [Mark's] which somehow was already formed. It consisted of an enlarged sketch which formed a unity created by one individual. In addition, Matthew and Luke used anonymous tradition. . . . Mark, on the other hand, has at his disposal only anonymous individual traditions, except for certain complexes and a passion narrative. Mark's achievement in shaping the tradition is thus incomparably greater. As far as we can tell, Mark is the first to bring the individualistic element to the forming and shaping of the tradition.[25]

Mark's preeminence among the evangelists no longer derives from his self-effacement, however. It does not stem from his role as a humble recorder of tradition, as for Papias and Eusebius, or as a fairly reliable chronicler of facts, as for the life of Jesus researchers of the nineteenth century. For Marxsen, Mark is first among the evangelists precisely because he is the most individual and the most creative. He is the most original author of the four.

22. Marxsen, *Mark the Evangelist*, 18.
23. Ibid., 17.
24. Ibid., 18.
25. Ibid., 19.

How Mark Became a Narrator

Mark as Allegorist

Marxsen completed what Wrede had started. With the subsequent popularization of redaction criticism, Mark finally came into his own, no longer eclipsed by Peter, Matthew, or even the Holy Spirit. Nevertheless, Mark's *text* continued to remain in the wings. Redaction criticism was interested in the text only as a means to an end. Marxsen wrote: "The form of the Gospels [i.e., the text] should help us to draw inferences as to the author's point of view and the situation of his community."[26] To see Mark's point of view, to see as he sees, we must look through his text. "First we shall go back behind Mark," writes Marxsen, "and separate tradition from redaction"—what Mark received from his tradition as distinct from what he added to it. Recall Origen's statement that innumerable instances in Scripture "afford nothing more than a fleeting glimpse, a view as through a tiny hole, of a host of most sublime thoughts,"[27] those of the Holy Spirit. For the redaction critics the Gospel text would likewise afford a glimpse, as through a hole or window, of a host of other thoughts—those of the Gospel writers. Once again a theological notion has gone underground to reemerge in secular guise.

Marxsen's approach to Mark is also reminiscent of patristic and medieval allegory. To read Scripture allegorically was to read it for hidden meanings—meanings metaphorically implied but not expressly stated. Interpreters often identified four levels of meaning in Scripture: the literal, the allegorical, the moral, and the anagogical. This fourfold approach is conveniently summarized in this memory verse common as late as the sixteenth century:

> The letter shows what God and our fathers did;
> The allegory shows us where our faith is hid;
> The moral meaning gives us rules of daily life;
> The anagogy shows us where we end our strife.[28]

For example, Jerusalem was literally the historical city, but allegorically it was the church, morally it was the human soul, and anagogically (in terms of last things) it was the heavenly city.[29] Allegory freed the Gospels to speak to the needs of individuals and the church in ever-changing contexts. It helped to make relevant what, on the surface, seemed irrelevant or downright problematic.

Compare Marxsen's treatment of geographical references in Mark. The wilderness in which John's ministry begins, for example, is not a real place. "We ought not to speculate as to its location," advises Marxsen. Rather, because of

---

26. Ibid., 25.
27. Origin, *On First Principles*, 4.2.3.
28. Quoted in Kealy, *Mark's Gospel*, 33. The verse is atrributed to Augustine of Dacia (d. 1282).
29. Kealy, *Mark's Gospel*, 36.

the well-established link between the wilderness and Old Testament prophecy, the phrase "in the desert" is introduced in Mark 1:4 merely to qualify "the Baptist as the fulfiller of Old Testament predictive prophecy. Put in exaggerated form, the Baptist would still be the one who appears 'in the wilderness' even if he had never been there in all his life."[30] Similarly for Marxsen, although for more complex reasons, Galilee is not primarily a geographical locale in Mark. Its significance is first and foremost theological.[31]

Indeed, redaction criticism's resemblance to allegory is general and far-reaching. For redaction criticism in the classic German mold, each evangelist's theology assumed its particular form in response to the specific situation in which the evangelist was writing. In retelling the story of Jesus, the evangelist had one foot in the past and the other one firmly in the present. Dimly mirrored in the details of each Gospel narrative, then, are circumstances contemporary with the evangelist that he means to address. The Gospel becomes an "allegory" of the situation that occasioned it.

Theodore Weeden's important study of the Markan disciples, *Mark: Traditions in Conflict*, offers an especially striking example of such allegory.[32] Why are Jesus' disciples presented so "negatively" in Mark? Why do they have such difficulty understanding? Why do they fail so miserably (8:32-33; 9:5-6, 18, 32, 33-34; 10:13-14, 35ff.; 14:27-31, 37ff., 50; 16:8)? Weeden's answer is that the disciples in Mark are essentially stand-ins, cardboard cutouts, for Mark's opponents. In attempting to get beyond the literal sense of Mark to unveil its hidden senses, Marxsen, Weeden, and other redaction critics have reactivated the role of the patristic and medieval diviner of allegories.

Catena and Commentary

Another premodern device that has reemerged in a new guise in modern biblical scholarship is the catena. Catenae were collections of authoritative pronounce-ments on biblical passages and interpretive problems. In the medieval period, for example, Thomas Aquinas produced the *Catena Aurea*, which contained opinions from fifty-four Greek and Latin church fathers and other church writers. We no longer appeal to the pronouncements of the church fathers when confronted with a difficult passage of Scripture. We do invoke other authorities, however, especially in our footnotes or endnotes. To write as a scholar is scrupulously to keep track of one's debts to the "fathers" of one's discipline and to their less illustrious sons and daughters.

With the passage of time these debts have grown monstrous. The Gospel texts creak beneath their dreadful weight. Scholars regularly worry that we are losing sight of the texts in a dense forest of commentaries. Then, too, there is

30. Marxsen, *Mark the Evangelist*, 37–38.
31. Ibid., 92; cf. 54–116 passim. Kealy, too, notes that "symbolic exegesis . . . has become popular among several modern interpreters of Mark's gospel" (*Mark's Gospel*, 36).
32. Theodore J. Weeden, *Mark: Traditions in Conflict* (Philadelphia: Fortress Press, 1971).

the redaction critic's habit of peering over the shoulders of the evangelists while addressing them. The fascination with background is still very strong. Increasingly over the past two decades, however, other scholars have been complaining that whereas the Gospels have been endlessly read through, or read around, they have all too seldom been read on their own terms.

The winds of change have again been blowing in Gospel studies. A recent review in the *Journal of Biblical Literature* will serve as a wind sock to show the direction of that change. Jack Dean Kingsbury, a well-known Matthean scholar, is reviewing the first volume of W. D. Davies and Dale C. Allison's *Critical and Exegetical Commentary on the Gospel according to Saint Matthew*.[33] Increasingly, as Kingsbury notes, biblical commentaries "are assuming encyclopedic proportions"; this one devotes some eight hundred pages to the first seven chapters of Matthew.[34] As such they are predestined to "be consulted on a piecemeal basis" only.[35] By design, this particular commentary "is quintessentially redaction-critical in nature: the steady focus is on questions of tradition history, the situation of Matthew's community, and the intention of Matthew as [the authors] believe this comes to expression in various aspects of his Gospel."[36]

Kingsbury's main objection to Davies and Allison's approach echoes a concern that has been mounting in Gospel studies since the late 1970s, especially in the United States. According to Kingsbury,

> [Davies and Allison] ignore "plot development" in Matthew's Gospel and hence fail totally to convey to the reader any sense of the narrative and dramatic movement of Matthew's Gospel-story. Two consequences flow from this. The first is that the reader often, and sometimes for pages at a time, loses all sense of the fact that any story whatever is being narrated. Or to put it another way, because Davies and Allison pay no attention to plot development, the welter of scholarly observations they make serves not to highlight the story Matthew narrates but to obscure and suppress it. And the second consequence is that in this absence of concern for plot development, the reader gets the distinct impression that Matthew's "theology" becomes the element that Davies and Allison regard as binding the whole of the Gospel together. . . . Without question, one can abstract from Matthew's story a "theology." Still, it dare not happen that recognition of this be permitted to blur the fact that the story Matthew narrates does not turn on "theology" but on "conflict" [e.g., between Jesus and the religious authorities]. Abstracting from Matthew's Gospel-story its

33. W. D. Davies and Dale C. Allison, *Critical and Exegetical Commentary on the Gospel according to Saint Matthew*. Volume I: *Introduction and Commentary on Matthew I-VII* (Edinburgh: T. & T. Clark, 1988), reviewed in the *Journal of Biblical Literature* 110 (1991): 344–46.

34. Ibid., 344.

35. Ibid.

36. Ibid.

"theology" can never be a substitute for analyzing the development of the plot of this story.[37]

Kingsbury, along with many others, is arguing that an approach that would tear the theology of a Gospel away from its moorings in the evangelist's narrative is necessarily inadequate. A Gospel is not reducible to a set of theological propositions. Redaction criticism seeks to distill the evangelist's overarching theological perspective from his story. For critics such as Kingsbury, however, the Gospels are not simply the vehicles or instruments of a detachable theology. The evangelists are narrative thinkers, narrative theologians. The thought of an evangelist consists in the mediation of an enigmatic set of events centered on Jesus of Nazareth. It transmits those events through emphasizing certain details and repressing others, through plotting, characterization, point of view, and so forth. It renders those events in the form of structured, coherent narrative. Critics who read the Gospels as story, as narrative, are called *narrative critics*. All the contributors to the present volume are, or have been called at one time or another, narrative critics.

How Mark Lost His Grip on the Text

Narrative Criticism and Reader-Response Criticism

Marxsen's case against form criticism began with an appeal to the unity of Mark's creation, as we noted earlier. But Marxsen saw the unity of Mark as residing in the intention of the evangelist, his overarching theological purpose. For the narrative critics, in contrast, the locus of unity is more in the text itself, in the internal organization of its story world (the artful arrangement of its plot, for example). The author does not vanish from the scene, although his relationship to his creation does become more distant; it is conducted through intermediaries such as the implied author and the narrator, as Elizabeth Struthers Malbon explains in chapter 2.

Narrative criticism easily shades over into a preoccupation with readers and reading. The current interest in the Gospel reader also has its roots in redaction criticism. Once the idea began to take hold that the evangelists were authors as well as collectors, the critic's task became more than ever one of trying to put himself or herself in the position of the original readers or hearers of the Gospels. Implicitly the task became one of reenacting the roles scripted for these original audiences, of recreating the responses to the story that the evangelist might have anticipated or intended, and of becoming attuned even to the subtler nuances of the Gospel writer's intentions. But what if the critic were to take the reading experience as his or her explicit focus and examine the complex interaction between story and audience? Then the critic would be fully into the realm of *reader-response criticism*, as Robert M. Fowler explains in chapter 3.

37. Ibid., 346.

From the vantage point of the present (ever precarious), source criticism, form criticism, redaction criticism, and narrative criticism all appear to have "evolved" out of each other. To do redaction criticism on Mark, for example, one must be able to distinguish what Mark contributed from what he inherited, redaction from tradition. Redaction criticism builds on source and form criticism, and frequently narrative criticism and reader-response criticism build on redaction criticism. This bears out the claim of the late Norman Perrin that redaction criticism was "mutating" into a true literary criticism. (Actually it was mutating right before his eyes; two of the contributors to the present volume, Fowler and Anderson, are former students of Perrin.)

The "author personality" that Willi Marxsen claimed to glimpse behind the Gospel of Mark grew ever more dominant as form criticism gave way to redaction criticism. The advent of narrative criticism has done nothing to retard Mark's personality development. Mark's text assumes an even higher degree of unity and coherence for narrative critics than for redaction critics, as we have seen. Implicitly, the evangelist's masterful purpose, expressed in his narrative creation, remains the ultimate source of that unity. He retains a powerful hold on his text.

Does he retain a corresponding grip on the reader? Is the reader whose responses are the domain of reader-response criticism a puppet in the hands of the evangelist? Or does the reader cocreate the meaning of the text together with the evangelist, as Robert Fowler suggests in his chapter? Mark's control over his text appears to weaken once we venture into the territory of reader response. Traditionally that control has been bound up with the concept of the "author's intention." How has that concept been used in biblical studies? Mary Ann Tolbert explains:

> modern biblical scholars often tend to use a claim of "authorial intention" to argue for the superiority of their interpretations. . . . And this claim is effective because "authorial intention" is currently accepted by the guild as a conventional criterion of "truthful" research. So, although there may be a variety of texts in the Bible, each text reflects only its own author's intention, thereby giving the illusion, if not in fact the reality, of limitation to the process. The singular Word of God is not restored, but the cacophany is sharply reduced.[38]

In other words, the authority that was once the Holy Spirit's has passed to the biblical authors. Or has it passed instead to those scholars who claim to discern these authors' hidden intentions?

For the form critics, the Gospel of Mark was essentially a community product. The evangelist himself played a modest role as compiler or collector of traditions. With the advent of redaction criticism, the Gospel of Mark was declared to be the product of a bona fide author. It was a creative retelling of the story of

38. Mary Ann Tolbert, "Reading the Bible with Authority: Feminist Interrogation of the Canon" (paper delivered at the Feminist Hermeneutics Consultation at the Society of Biblical Literature Annual Meeting, Anaheim, 1989), 11.

Jesus designed to deliver a forceful message to the community to which it was addressed. With the arrival of literary criticism, Mark's narrative creativity is celebrated still further, and the attempt to reconstruct the situation for which he was writing recedes in importance. Over a period of some fifty years, then, the author of the First Gospel has emerged into ever sharper focus. Strange to say, however, in the neighboring field of secular literary studies, the figure of the author in general has receded steadily into the background over the same period. In this respect, biblical studies and literary studies have been like two trains traveling on parallel tracks in opposite directions. In literary studies, an initial preoccupation with the biographies of authors and other background factors gradually gave way in the 1930s and 1940s to the New Criticism, which eventually declared the author's intention irrelevant to the task of interpretation. The New Criticism was gradually superseded in its turn in the 1960s and 1970s by structuralism and deconstruction. In the process, the text slipped out of the author's grasp—and the author slipped on the text and began to dissolve into it.

Deconstruction

Deconstruction is suspicious of the power often attributed to authors to bend the language of texts to their will, to use language only and not be used by it. For deconstruction, language is an extremely slippery, infinitely resourceful element that refuses to limit itself to what its user intends it to say. There is always an unpredictable and uncontrollable excess of meaning that simmers within every text, always ready to spill over, as Stephen D. Moore explains (and attempts to demonstrate) in chapter 4. In a deconstructive perspective, therefore, Mark himself would be in the powerful grip of something that operates through him and exceeds his abilities to control it, just as he was for the patristic and medieval commentators—although that something is no longer the Holy Spirit.

The question inevitably arises, If interpretation is no longer answerable to the author's intentions, to what does it answer instead? Here again the history of biblical interpretation can be usefully consulted, a history in which the (human) author's intentions have played but a minor role. In Gospel studies, for example, only in the last thirty years or so have the evangelists' intentions come to play a central role, and for nonacademic Bible readers they continue to count for very little. For much of Christian history the arbiter of conflicting interpretations was the so-called rule of faith—what the church had "always and everywhere" taught, as guaranteed by the apostolic succession. Interestingly, the erosion of the authority of authors in our time, coupled with the disintegration of the unified literary text, has resulted in an unprecedented upsurge of interest in the rules and regulations that govern interpretation. Increasingly, literary critics have shifted their attention to the network of conflicting interests whose complex interaction determines what may and may not be read in(to) a given text in a given period. Rules governing what one may say and the ways in which it may be said permeate academic life at every level, from the undergraduate term paper on Mark to the weightiest scholarly tome.

The academy functions like a secularized church in this regard, the rule of faith having been displaced by other rules, notably the rule of fact.

The modern biblical scholar respects the rule of fact. Davies and Allison's massive Matthean commentary, mentioned earlier, for example, aims to be a "disinterested and objective study in biblical criticism."[39] However, the widespread philosophical and political turn in recent literary studies has had the effect of discrediting terms such as *disinterested* and *objective*. As long as the text was viewed as a stable container of meaning—meaning that its author had put into it and that the critic could extract from it—the critic could claim an effaced and neutral role in relation to the text, somewhat like Papias's Mark at Peter's feet. Once the contribution of the reader to the creation of textual meaning came to be emphasized, however, the critic's role took on a rather different aspect.

Reader-response critics have argued that meaning is not something that one extracts from a text, like a nut from its shell or a nugget from a streambed. Meaning occurs not between the covers of a book or between the margins of a page but in the consciousness of the one who reads.[40] Prior to the creative engagement of a reader who "activates" it, the Bible, like any other text, remains a partial or unfinished object. Criticism is an inescapably creative activity. Prior to the interpretive act, there is nothing definitive in the text to be discovered.

But if meaning is in part the creation of the critic, then criticism can never be "disinterested." The disinterested critic is like Mark before redaction criticism—a neutral recorder or compiler. With the shift of attention to the reader, however, the critic, like Marxsen's Mark, comes to be seen as a creative writer in his or her own right. The critic reworks the textual data in the interests of a particular agenda. As deconstructionists in particular see it, criticism is not qualitatively different from literature. Markan criticism becomes a unconscious reenactment of the text it sets out to master.

Feminist Criticism

Feminist critics, too, have been acutely aware that scholarship is always "interested" and never neutral. They point out that gender shapes readings of the Gospels, just as it has shaped the Gospels themselves. It is no accident that female characters in the Bible, female imagery for God, and the role of women in the early church have only recently become significant areas of investigation for biblical scholars. How reading a Gospel from a feminist or misogynist position affects one's interpretation is only now being explored. Appeals to the Holy Spirit, the author's intention, or the historical Jesus (as one reconstructs him) have often authorized oppression. Such appeals have often masked misogyny. Christian feminists focus less on the perennial problems of the unity of the Gospels and discrepancies between them than on the problems of offensive passages, multiple interpretations, and authority.

39. Davies and Allison, *Critical and Exegetical Commentary*, xi.
40. See Jane P. Tompkins, "An Introduction to Reader-Response Criticism," in *Reader-Response Criticism: From Formalism to Post-Structuralism*, ed. Jane P. Tompkins (Baltimore: Johns Hopkins University Press, 1980), xvi–xvii.

Which texts belong in the canon? Which interpretations should govern faith and practice? Where is the locus of authority? How is a person of faith to come to terms with an authoritative text or interpretation that is androcentric (male-centered) and patriarchal (sanctioning male authority over females and children, especially the authority of males of dominant races and classes)? What institutional interests, whether of church or academy, are involved in our interpretations?

From a feminist perspective, whether Mark is an author in his own right or merely a collector is less important than the views of gender relations that the Gospel and its interpreters embody. Religious and nonreligious feminist critics care about how the social construction of gender shaped and shapes lives past and present. Feminists are concerned with the symbolic meanings of gender in the texts and in the cultures that produced and read the Gospels. They are also concerned with the actual behavior of men and women. These concerns unite historical and theological interests of the past fifty years with the more recent narrative and reader-oriented approaches.

A text reflects the culture that produced it, and culture is a "text" to be interpreted. Feminists are aware that gender relations have taken different forms in different historical and cultural circumstances. Race, class, and other factors have given rise to multiple forms and ideologies of oppression as well as female agency and power. If culture is a text, a script, that assigns gender roles to each of its participants, it is also a text that can be rewritten. If gender relations are at least in part culturally constructed, if they are not always and everywhere the same, then they can be reconstructed through a critique of culture. The feminist attempt to situate interpretations culturally (see Janice Capel Anderson's investigation in chapter 5 of the interpretive history of the "Salome" story) arises out of a desire to rewrite the scripts of our culture. Feminists seek to write scripts that call for equality, for the celebration of female difference, or for a new world beyond the two.

How Mark Became Increasingly Distant

Social Criticism

The feminist concern to place Mark and his interpreters culturally also finds expression in another new direction in Markan studies, the turn to social history and the social sciences, especially anthropology and sociology. Courses on the Gospels sometimes begin with a suggestion that students try reading a Gospel straight through, as a narrative whole, as we noted earlier. Mark, as the shortest Gospel, is the obvious choice for such an experiment. Gospel courses can also begin with cautions about ethnocentrism (reading the Gospels through the lenses of one's own culture) and anachronism (reading the Gospels through the lenses of one's own time). Social criticism of the Gospels insists that the proper reading lenses are those tinted by the first-century Mediterranean cultures in which these texts took shape. One should avoid being an "ugly American" (or Canadian, Peruvian, or whatever) as one journeys through the Gospel narratives.

Concern for the original historical context is, of course, nothing new in biblical scholarship. Beginning with the revival during the Renaissance of the practice of reading the Bible in the original languages and the cry of *sola scriptura* during the Reformation, church tradition came to be placed increasingly in question as an adequate resource for interpreting Scripture. Exegesis of the biblical text (reading its meaning *out* of it) as opposed to eisegesis (reading *into* it) became the ideal. With the rise of historical criticism in the eighteenth and nineteenth centuries, scholars began to see the Gospels more and more as artifacts from the past. The Gospels offered windows on an ancient world that grew stranger the longer one peered into it.

For some scholars the Gospels also represented a primitive or quaint stage in an evolution toward the enlightened European culture of their own day. What such scholars viewed as irrational in the Gospels had to be decoded into acceptable scientific or historical terms. At the beginning of the nineteenth century, for example, the German critic H.E.G. Paulus explained Jesus walking on the water as the result of the disciples' confusion when Jesus walked on a sandbar in a mist, whereas the "miraculous" feedings of the multitudes simply involved the rich sharing with the poor. A later critic, D. F. Strauss, rejected both naturalistic and supernaturalistic interpretations of miracles and other such phenomena in the Gospels; such elements should be understood as myth, the primitive narrative expression of ideas.

The evolutionary and comparative approach was typical of the rise of the social sciences in general. In New Testament studies, the views of myth that this approach entailed have since been criticized for being simplistic and misleading. Some have also argued that the rationalist, evolutionary approach served a hidden theological agenda: the rationality of Christianity would be shown to be independent of the historical accuracy of the New Testament. The primitive presentations and mythic forms of the Gospels, for example, would be shown to house eternal truths acceptable to reason. It would fall to a later historical critic, Rudolf Bultmann, to "demythologize" the New Testament for twentieth-century theology. He sought to translate the three-story universe and myths of the New Testament into existentialist expressions about the truth of what it means to live as an authentic human being in this world. Bultmann's emphasis, however, was less on reason than on faith, which he likewise declared to be independent of the historical accuracy of the Gospels. Christian faith was based on the Christ of faith rather than the Jesus of history.

The movement of Europeans into all parts of the globe in the nineteenth century as traders, missionaries, travelers, and colonizers stimulated research not only into contemporary primitive peoples but also into Greco-Roman and Middle Eastern history. Attempts to trace the origins and diffusion of Indo-European folklore fueled attempts in biblical studies to trace the history of the oral traditions that lay behind the Bible. Folklore studies, emerging from the social sciences of the late nineteenth and early twentieth centuries, had a significant impact on the development of form criticism.

The turn of the nineteenth century also saw the rise in Germany of a more encompassing movement called the History of Religions School. Historians such as Gunkel, Heitmueller, and Bousset insisted that New Testament scholars pay closer attention to the religions of the Hellenistic world, especially Judaism, Gnosticism, and the mystery religions. Christianity was a syncretistic religion, meaning that it combined many elements of preexisting religions, both Hellenistic and Oriental. Along with religion, other aspects of ancient history and culture would shed light on the Gospels. In the United States, Shirley Jackson Case, F. C. Grant, and the Chicago school produced a number of studies of the social world of the New Testament. These movements can be seen as forerunners of recent social criticism.

However, there are also certain discontinuities between social criticism and historical criticism as traditionally practiced. Today's social historians and scientists are less optimistic than their predecessors that history can be reconstructed "as it actually was." They are also more sensitive to cultural diversity. Seeming parallels between events or symbols from different groups in the Greco-Roman world can be misleading. Phenomena such as miracles or dying and rising gods do not always have the same meaning in different social contexts, and as the term *social* indicates, there is less concern with the individual or the unique than with the general and the group. (Mark again begins to fade into his community, his tradition, and his culture.)

In chapter 6 David Rhoads identifies four types of social criticism of the Gospels. The first is *social description*, which reconstructs the material culture, customs, and everyday life of the first-century Mediterranean world. The second is *social history*, which attempts to chart sweeping historical changes. It focuses on the history of groups, movements, and institutions rather than individual persons or events. The activities of women and other marginalized groups frequently come to the fore, in marked contrast to earlier historians' focus on Great Men, great battles, and political elites. Frequently, too, social history highlights struggles for power, sometimes from the perspective of liberation theology. A third area is *sociology of knowledge*, which studies the relationship between a group's worldview and its social organization. It seeks to reconstruct a culture's basic assumptions or common sense. It then correlates this information with the culture's social order. In seeking the fit between worldview and social order, sociology of knowledge often homes in on the function of certain beliefs and practices in the maintenance of the group's social equilibrium or stability. It can also document clashes of worldviews and corresponding conflicts in the social order. A fourth type of social scientific work on the Gospels involves the use of models from *cultural anthropology*. Such models organize information about a single culture, such as a culture's family structure. They also enable cross-cultural comparisons. One can construct a model, for example, of a culture's kinship system or family structure and then compare it to those of other cultures. Many New Testament scholars now turn to such models as aids to interpretation. Constructing a model of one's own culture can help one to avoid ethnocentrism in the study of other cultures. Models can help to fill in the gaps created by the limited information we have about the first century. Models developed from the study of current Mediterranean culture, for example, may shed light on ancient Mediterranean culture. The roles of women in an isolated farm community in Greece may shed light on the roles of women in early Christianity. The responses of contemporary sects to the failure of prophecy may shed light on early Christian responses to the delay of Jesus' second coming, and vice versa. Rhoads particularly shows how a cross-cultural model of purity and pollution can shed light on Mark.

In some ways, then, Mark has become an informant for an ethnography. An *ethnography* is the description and interpretation of a culture that an anthropologist produces. The Gospel ethnographer looks for mentions of tools, for example, and clues concerning agricultural or marriage practices. He or she looks for references to political and economic institutions and marks of social status. Key terms and assumptions of Mark's worldview are sought. His symbolic and mythic universe is mapped.

There are, however, complications. A modern ethnographer is typically a "participant-observer" who lives with the group being studied. He or she can ask questions and can question more than one member of the group. "Mark" can no longer be questioned, needless to say, and his community cannot be observed over the course of several years. Furthermore, *he* is only one informant. Archeology, other texts, and models must fill in the gaps. Moreover, as the term *participant-observer* indicates, the scholar is always a cocreator of meaning.

The twin goals of social criticism of Mark are to understand the first-century Mediterranean world and to understand the Gospel narrative as a first-century hearer or reader might. Social criticism remains the heir of historical criticism and redaction criticism in viewing the text of Mark as a window on the first-century Mediterranean world. Its second goal, that of understanding the Gospel narrative as a first-century hearer or reader might, suggests the potential impact of narrative criticism and reader-response criticism on this approach.

Of course, deconstruction has also had a good deal to say about reading (see chapter 4), and so has feminism, as we noted earlier. Anthropology, deconstruction, political criticism—mix them all together and what do you get? An explosion in the kitchen or the basis for a new menu? Significantly, during the 1980s, the New Historicism emerged from the oven of American literary studies as a result of combining these very ingredients.[41] Somewhat surprisingly, it has yet to be sampled by biblical scholars. *Mark and Method* can be said to contain, then, separately packaged and as yet unmixed, the ingredients for an unorthodox but potent recipe that literary critics have been following for some years with very interesting results.

"Mark" and "Method"

From Peter's scribe, to a writing instrument in the hand of the Holy Spirit, to a reliable chronicler, to a front for an anonymous Christian community, to an editor, to a full-fledged author of a unified narrative, to a provoker of reader response, to an embodier of gender ideology, to an ethnographic informant—

41. See H. Aram Veeser, ed., *The New Historicism* (New York: Routledge, 1989). The anthropology in question tends to be that of Clifford Geertz, the deconstruction (or better, the poststructuralism) tends to be that of Michel Foucault, and the political ingredients tend to be Marxist as well as feminist.

Mark has had many careers. He has been promoted and demoted more times than we can count. Future bosses, future interpreters, will undoubtedly find many other uses for his invention, his Gospel, and Mark's responsibilities will once again diminish or increase.

What factors have determined Mark's more recent careers? The primary stimuli to new approaches in Gospel studies over the past twenty years have come from extrabiblical literary studies and the social sciences. There are signs of convergence between these two new developments, as we have seen. Feminist criticism, for example, is interested in the interplay of the "literary" and the "cultural." That interplay is becoming ever more charged. Literary criticism, cultural studies, and the social sciences in the nonbiblical arena all share one thing in common: they have all been infected by the "postmodern condition," of which deconstruction is but one manifestation. Some have embraced this condition, others have attempted to ward it off.

Prophecy is not our forte, but we suspect that the next few years will see increased attempts to forge links between literary and social criticism. At the same time literary criticism of the Gospels will have to reckon more and more with deconstruction. A still more important challenge will come from biblical interpreters who have not generally been admitted to the scholarly club. The exegesis and exegetical traditions of women and men of color and of the Two-Thirds World will offer powerful new insights.

Whatever the new developments may be, they will both echo and contest previous ways of looking at Mark. The essays in this volume also involve such challenges and echoes. The contributors are as passionate about the approaches they describe as they are about Mark. We, too, have our favorite axes to grind. One of our key motivations in writing this textbook was to disseminate our ideas and interests to students and those who teach them. When we were students, textbooks provided our initial contact with biblical scholarship. They excited us and colored our views, sometimes indelibly. Some of us can never view the Hebrew Scriptures without being influenced by the emphasis on the covenant put forward in Bernard Anderson's *Understanding the Old Testament*. Norman Perrin's brief *What Is Redaction Criticism?* unlocked the mysteries of form criticism and redaction criticism for us. As teachers we have found we have limited time to keep up with all of the developments in New Testament study. We have learned that there is no better way to come to terms with a new approach than to teach it. So this book is unapologetically for students and teachers.

Finally, in fairness to the students and teachers who read this book, we should say something about ourselves. All of us are white, middle class, and thirty or forty something. One of us, Moore, comes out of the Roman Catholic tradition. Anderson, Fowler, Malbon, and Rhoads are mainline Protestants. All except Moore, who hails from Ireland, are Americans who received their graduate training at American graduate schools. Three of us, Anderson, Malbon, and Moore, now teach at American state universities. Rhoads teaches at a seminary and Fowler at a private college. All of us are card-carrying members of the Society of Biblical Literature and the American Academy of Religion.

We are members of the critical guild, in other words, overtrained readers who need to unlearn as well as to learn.

We hope that the interplay between our readings will shed light both on Mark and on recent trends in Gospel study. The "method" in our title is somewhat misleading, admittedly. None of us gives you a concise, three-step method to apply to Mark or some other biblical text. Few of the approaches we survey would be comfortable with being handled in quite this fashion. At most we hope to stimulate you to bring new questions to the Gospel texts and to create readings of your own that are richer for having read ours.

FURTHER READING

ALTER, Robert, and Frank Kermode, eds. *The Literary Guide to the Bible*. Cambridge: Harvard University Press, 1987. Bracketing deconstruction, feminism, and other controversial approaches, various contributors offer readings of each book of the Bible. Also contains some general essays on such topics as midrash and allegory.

BRUCE, F. F. "The History of New Testament Study." In *New Testament Interpretation: Essays on Principles and Methods*, edited by I. Howard Marshall, 21–59. Grand Rapids; Wm. B. Eerdmans, 1977. A brief review by a conservative scholar.

COGGINS, R. J., and J. L. Houlden, eds. *A Dictionary of Biblical Interpretation*. Philadelphia: Trinity Press International, 1990. This is the place to look up terms, persons, schools, and methods of interpretation. There are entries on allegorical interpretation, Calvin, source criticism, narrative criticism, and reader-response criticism, for example.

EPP, Eldon Jay, and George W. MacRae, S.J., eds. *The New Testament and Its Modern Interpreters*. Atlanta: Scholars Press, 1989. Surveys New Testament scholarship from 1945 to approximately 1980. Contains four sections: The World of the New Testament, Methods of New Testament Study, The Literature of the New Testament, and New Testament Interpretation. Also contains a good review of textual criticism, a topic we have not discussed.

FROEHLICH, Karlfried, ed. and trans. *Biblical Interpretation in the Early Church*. Philadelphia: Fortress Press, 1984. A useful introduction to the history of exegesis in the first four centuries C.E., with translated excerpts from works by Irenaeus, Origen, and other commentators

GRANT, Robert M., with David Tracy. *A Short History of the Interpretation of the Bible*. 2d ed. Philadelphia: Fortress Press, 1984. Contains chapters on various periods and schools of interpretation. A section on theological interpretation by Tracy is added to the chapters by Grant that made up the original edition.

KEALY, Seán P., C.S.Sp. *Mark's Gospel: A History of Its Interpretation*. Ramsey, N.J.: Paulist Press, 1982. An indispensable summary of the history of interpretation of Mark from the early centuries through 1979. Includes bibliographic references to commentators in each historical period.

KEEGAN, Terence J. *Interpreting the Bible: A Popular Introduction to Biblical Hermeneutics*. Mahwah, N.J.: Paulist Press, 1985. The focus is primarily on the New Testament. Contains chapters on several of the new methods, including structuralism, narrative criticism, and reader-response criticism.

KÜMMEL, Werner Georg. *The New Testament: The History of the Investigation of Its Problems*. Translated by S. McLean Gilmour and Howard Clark Kee. Nashville: Abingdon Press, 1972. A weighty tome that traces New Testament criticism from its inception down to 1930. Focuses primarily on German scholarship.

MOORE, Stephen D. *Literary Criticism and the Gospels: The Theoretical Challenge.* New Haven: Yale University Press, 1989. Includes chapters on narrative criticism, reader-response criticism, and deconstruction.

MORGAN, Robert, with John Barton. *Biblical Interpretation.* Oxford: Oxford University Press, 1988. Includes a survey of the development of historical criticism during the past 150 years and of recent developments in the use of social scientific and literary critical methods for biblical study.

NEILL, Stephen, and Tom Wright. *The Interpretation of the New Testament 1861–1986.* 2d ed. Oxford: Oxford University Press, 1988. An engaging account, although oddly silent on important developments in Gospel studies in the 1970s and 1980s.

PERRIN, Norman. *What Is Redaction Criticism?* Philadelphia: Fortress Press, 1969. In addition to providing an answer to the title question, this book also does a good job of describing form criticism and the Markan hypothesis.

PETERSEN, Norman R. *Literary Criticism for New Testament Critics.* Philadelphia: Fortress Press, 1978. Usefully charts the development from form criticism and redaction criticism to literary criticism. Provides literary readings of Mark and Luke-Acts.

SCHWARTZ, Regina M. "Introduction: On Biblical Criticism." In *The Book and the Text*, edited by Regina M. Schwartz, 1–15. Oxford: Basil Blackwell, 1990. Discusses many of the issues that we cover in the present chapter. Schwartz fills in vital gaps in our own discussion, however, in her coverage of the Hebrew Scriptures and Jewish exegetical traditions.

SCHWEITZER, Albert. *The Quest for the Historical Jesus.* 2d English ed. Translated by W. Montgomery. London: A & C Black, 1911. Traces the history of Jesus research from Reimarus to Wrede. A landmark in the modern study of the Gospels.

2

Narrative Criticism:

How Does the Story Mean?

ELIZABETH STRUTHERS MALBON

The questions we ask of the texts we read are as important as the answers we are led to. Most readers of the New Testament for almost two thousand years have asked religious questions. What does the text mean? What does it mean to me? to us? to our faith and our lives? The answers have reflected not only the different individual readers but also broader cultural shifts. The time and place of the readers or communities of readers have influenced their answers. What other types of questions have been asked by New Testament readers—especially scholarly readers?

Since the nineteenth century, most New Testament scholars have asked, What *did* the text mean? What did it mean in its original context? for its author? to its first hearers or readers? Chapter 1 discusses three chief ways the question, What *did* the text mean? has been asked: source criticism, form criticism, and redaction criticism. Source, form, and redaction criticism might seem to be asking literary questions. Source criticism was first called literary criticism because it approached Matthew, Mark, and Luke as literary documents. However, source criticism is a search for literary sources and relationships in history. Which Gospel was written first? Which Gospel was the historical source for the others? These questions are primarily historical. Form criticism is concerned with the literary form of the small stories. However, form criticism is a search for the sources behind the sources in history. What do the individual stories tell us about the history of the earliest churches? What may we attribute to the historical Jesus? Redaction criticism certainly has literary aspects. As the study of the theological motivation of the editing of earlier traditions, it is concerned with the Gospels as literary wholes. However, redaction criticism is a search for the theology of the churches of the Gospel writers in history. What *did* the text mean? To ask *what* did the text mean is to seek referential meaning. The text's meaning is found in what it refers to—what it refers to other than and outside itself.

In the past two decades an increasing number of biblical scholars (especially in the United States) have been asking a different question: *How* does the text mean? This question is literary; it represents a search for internal meaning rather than external (or referential) meaning. How do various literary patterns enable the text to communicate meaning to its hearers and readers? How do the interrelated characters, settings, and actions of the plot contribute to a narrative's meaning for a reader? The move from historical to literary questions represents a paradigm shift in biblical studies. A paradigm gives us our basic way of understanding things. When there is a paradigm shift, we are challenged to think of the old and familiar in a new way. The writer of Mark is no longer a cut-and-paste editor but an author with control over the story he narrates. The Jesus of Mark is no longer a shadowy historical personage but a lively character. Galilee and Jerusalem are no longer simply geographical references but settings for dramatic action. The account of Jesus' passion (suffering and death) is no longer the source of theological doctrine but the culmination of a dramatic and engaging plot.

The New Criticism and Structuralism

The shift to a literary paradigm by some biblical interpreters echoed a similar and earlier shift among interpreters of secular literature. In the 1940s the New Criticism argued that the key to reading a poem, play, novel, or short story is to be found in the work itself. Historical information about the culture and biographical information about the author were pushed aside as external to the work. The New Criticism must be understood as a reaction to previous literary studies that gave such information primary importance. A similar re-action in biblical studies led many to move from redaction criticism to literary criticism. The final lines of a poem by Archibald MacLeish may be understood almost as a slogan for the New Critics: "A poem should not mean/But be."[1] A critic or reader must not be concerned with a poem's referential meaning, that

1. Archibald MacLeish, "Ars Poetica," in *Collected Poems 1917–1954* (Boston: Houghton Mifflin, 1962), 50–51.

is, its reference to some external world. She or he must attend to its being, its presence, its metaphoric power. The poem's power to speak to us depends neither on the author's intention nor on the reader's knowledge of the author's circumstances. It depends on the poem itself—its words, its rhythms, its images.

The New Criticism made its initial impact in New Testament studies on interpretations of the sayings and parables of Jesus. The "significance of forceful and imaginative language" in the Synoptic sayings of Jesus was explored by Robert Tannehill.[2] Robert Funk considered "language as event and theology" in parable and letter.[3] Dan Via reflected on the "literary and existential dimension" of the parables.[4] The surprising, challenging, world-shattering potential of the parables was the theme of John Dominic Crossan's work.[5] "A poem should not mean/But be"—and a parable should not refer but impel.

Structuralism is another critical approach that has influenced biblical literary criticism. Structuralism was born in linguistics and grew up in anthropology, literature, and other areas. Central to structuralism are three affirmations about language. First, language is communication. Language as communication involves a sender giving a message to a receiver; literature as communication means an author giving a text to a reader. Redaction critics focus on the sender or author, and reader-response critics (see chap. 3) focus on the receiver or reader. Structuralist critics in particular, like literary critics in general, focus on the text. By analogy, structuralist critics note that within a narrative text a "sender" gives an "object" to a "receiver." For example, in a traditional fairy tale the king gives his daughter in marriage to the most worthy suitor. (Much of the tale works out which suitor is most worthy.) In a Synoptic parable a king gives a feast to—surprisingly—the poor and the outcast. This model of language as communication and narrative as language has been worked out by French structuralist A. J. Greimas.[6]

Second, structuralism stresses that language is a system of signs. No sign has meaning on its own. Signs have meaning in relation to other signs. Analogously, no element of a literary work has meaning in isolation. Everything has meaning as part of a system of relationships. A narrative, that is, a literary work that

2. Robert C. Tannehill, *The Sword of His Mouth* (Semeia Supplements 1; Philadelphia: Fortress Press; Missoula, Mont.: Scholars Press, 1975).

3. Robert W. Funk, *Language, Hermeneutic, and Word of God: The Problem of Language in the New Testament and Contemporary Theology* (New York: Harper & Row, 1966).

4. Dan Otto Via, Jr., *The Parables: Their Literary and Existential Dimension* (Philadelphia: Fortress Press, 1967).

5. John Dominic Crossan, *In Parables: The Challenge of the Historical Jesus* (New York: Harper & Row, 1973); idem, *The Dark Interval: Towards a Theology of Story* (Niles, Ill.: Argus Communications, 1975; Sonoma, Calif.: Polebridge Press, 1988).

6. A. J. Greimas, "Elements of a Narrative Grammar," trans. Catherine Porter, *Diacritics* 7 (1977): 23–40. For an explanation see Daniel Patte, *What is Structural Exegesis?* (Guides to Biblical Scholarship; Philadelphia: Fortress Press, 1976), 41–43. For an adaptation and application to the parables, see Crossan, *Dark Interval.*

tells a story, must be read in two ways to disclose its system of relations. It must be read diachronically, that is, through time, from beginning to end. It must also be read (understood) synchronically, that is, as if everything happened at the same time. For a synchronic reading, logical categories (good versus evil, order versus chaos, etc.) are more important than chronological categories. The interrelation of parts within a whole is the key. This approach has been worked out by French structural anthropologist Claude Lévi-Strauss and applied in detail to the spatial settings of Mark's Gospel.[7]

Third, structuralism focuses on language as a cultural code. This understanding of language builds on the other two. Through careful analysis of the oppositions expressed in a text, the even more basic oppositions implicitly supporting it are revealed. Daniel Patte, the foremost biblical structuralist, has illustrated this and other aspects of structuralism in relation to Paul's letters and Matthew's Gospel. Patte seeks to uncover the "system of convictions" of Paul and of Matthew.[8]

Both the New Criticism and structuralism focus on the text itself—the language of the text and the text as language. Biblical literary criticism has been influenced by both approaches and shares this focus on the text. The first texts examined in detail by New Testament literary critics were the sayings and parables of Jesus. These short and powerful texts are in some ways comparable to the poems that intrigued the New Critics. The Gospels are the texts most explored by current New Testament literary critics. The Gospels are narratives, stories, in many ways not unlike the myths and folktales that structuralists often analyzed. New Testament literary criticism has become largely narrative criticism, a label employed by biblical critics but not by secular critics. To understand narrative criticism, we must consider the essential elements or aspects of narratives.

Narrative Elements

The distinction between story and discourse that was highlighted by literary critic Seymour Chatman has proved very useful to narrative critics. Story is the *what* of a narrative; discourse is the *how*. Story indicates the content of the narrative, including events, characters, and settings, and their interaction as

7. Claude Lévi-Strauss, "The Structural Study of Myth," *Journal of American Folklore* 68 (1955): 428–44; idem, "The Story of Asdiwal," trans. Nicholas Mann, in *The Structural Study of Myth and Totemism*, ed. Edmund Leach (Association of Social Anthropologists Monographs 5; London: Tavistock, 1967), 1–47. Elizabeth Struthers Malbon, *Narrative Space and Mythic Meaning in Mark* (New Voices in Biblical Studies; San Francisco: Harper & Row, 1986; The Biblical Seminar 13; Sheffield, Eng.: Sheffield Academic Press, 1991).
8. Daniel Patte, *Paul's Faith and the Power of the Gospel: A Structural Introduction to the Pauline Letters* (Philadelphia: Fortress Press, 1983); idem, *The Gospel according to Matthew: A Structural Commentary on Matthew's Faith* (Philadelphia: Fortress Press, 1987). See also idem, *Structural Exegesis for New Testament Critics* (Guides to Biblical Scholarship; Minneapolis: Fortress Press, 1990).

the plot. Discourse indicates the rhetoric of the narrative, how the story is told. The four canonical Gospels, for example, share a similar (although not identical) story of Jesus, but the discourse of each Gospel is distinctive. The story is where the characters interact; the discourse is where the implied author and implied reader interact. Story and discourse are not really separable. What we have, in Chatman's words, is the story-as-discoursed. It is this about which narrative critics ask, How does the text mean?

The following elements or aspects of narrative (story-as-discoursed), although overlapping, are frequently distinguished by narrative critics: implied author and implied reader, characters, settings, plot, rhetoric. We will look at each in turn.

Implied Author and Implied Reader

The communication model of sender-message-receiver gives narrative critics a framework for approaching texts: author-text-reader. This simple model, however, soon proves inadequate for narrative analysis. Recent literary criticism has taught us to conceive of the author and the reader not as isolated entities but as poles of a continuum of communication. A real author writes a text for a real reader. An implied author, a creation of the real author that is implied in his or her text, presents a narrative to an implied reader, a parallel creation of the real author that is embedded in the text, and a narrator tells a story to a narratee. Of course, within a story a character may narrate another story to another character. This expanded model is often diagramed like this:[9]

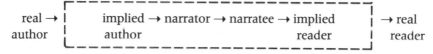

real → | implied → narrator → narratee → implied | → real
author | author   reader | reader

TEXT or NARRATIVE

Narrative criticism focuses on the narrative, but the implied author and the implied reader are understood as aspects of the narrative in this model. The implied author is a hypothetical construction based on the requirements of knowledge and belief presupposed in the narrative. The same is true of the implied reader. The implied author is the one who would be necessary for this narrative to be told or written. The implied reader is the one who would be necessary for this narrative to be heard or read.

The distinctions between the real and implied author and the real and implied reader are important for narrative critics, who wish to interpret the narrative without reliance on biographical information about the real author and cultural information about the real reader. Of course, basic information about the cultural context is essential to any interpretation. The implied author and implied reader of Mark's Gospel, for example, were literate in *koine* (common) Greek and knew the Hebrew Bible (later to become the Old Testament for Christians) in the

---

9. This diagram is based on that of Seymour Chatman, *Story and Discourse: Narrative Structure in Fiction and Film* (Ithaca, N.Y.: Cornell University Press, 1978), 151.

form of its Greek translation in the Septuagint. Narrative critics are eager to know as much as possible about the cultural contexts—especially of ancient works—in order to understand more completely the implied author and the implied reader of the narrative. However, narrative critics are wary of interpretations based on elements external to the narrative—including the intentions (known or supposed) of the real author.

The distinctions between the implied author and the narrator and between the narratee and the implied reader were developed in secular literary criticism for the close analysis of nineteenth- and twentieth-century novels. Ishmael is the narrator of *Moby Dick*, but he is the creation of the implied author. Most narrative critics of the first-century Gospels have not found these distinctions as useful. Most narrative critics have observed little or no difference between the implied author and narrator or between the narratee and implied reader of Matthew, Mark, Luke, and John. The implied author of *Moby Dick* knows more than Ishmael, but a similar separation is not obvious in Mark. Thus some narrative critics use the terms *narrator* and *narratee,* and others employ *implied author* and *implied reader.*

The implied author/narrator may be characterized in various ways, according to the particular nature of the narrative. The implied authors/narrators of the Gospels are generally described as omniscient (all knowing), omnipresent (present everywhere), or unlimited. The implied author/narrator of Mark, for example, is able to narrate events involving any character or group of characters, including Jesus when alone. This implied author/ narrator knows past, present, and future, as well as the inner thoughts and feelings of the characters. The Markan implied author/narrator is also reliable. The narratee/implied reader may trust him (probably him) as a nondeceptive guide to the action and safely believe that what he foreshadows will be fulfilled. (Even a reliable implied author/narrator may be ironic, however.) In addition, the point of view of the implied author/narrator of Mark is aligned not only with the point of view of the main character, Jesus, but also with the point of view of God. From the point of view of the implied reader/narratee, you can't get any more reliable than that! The implied author/narrator begins: "The beginning of the good news of Jesus Christ (Messiah), the Son of God" (1:1). Ten verses later, God concurs, saying to Jesus, "You are my Son" (1:11). The interaction of the implied author and the implied reader is part of the discourse. The interaction of the characters is part of the story.

Characters

Characters are an obvious narrative element. A story is about someone—the characters. The actions are carried out by someone—the characters. Narrative analysis of characters is intertwined with narrative analysis of plot. The implied reader of the story-as-discoursed is frequently invited to admire, judge, or identify with the characters. Characters are brought to life for the implied reader by the implied author through narrating words and actions. These words and actions may be those of the character himself or herself, those of another character, or those of the narrator. A character can be known by what she says and does; a character can be known by what other characters say to or about her and by what they do in relation to or because of her. A character can be known by what the narrator says about him—including names, epithets, and descriptions—or by what the narrator does in relation to him—including comparative or contrasting juxtapositions with other characters and the unfolding of the plot.

For example, the first mention of Judas Iscariot in Mark, at Jesus' appointing of the Twelve, is followed immediately by the narrator's comment, "who betrayed him" (3:19). At the point when Judas's betrayal is being narrated, however, the narrator calls him "Judas Iscariot, who was one of the twelve" (14:10). This is characterization by the narrator's words *and actions*, that is, the ironic placement of these descriptions at moments of greatest contrast. The ironic contrast is extended by the immediate juxtaposition of the story of the unnamed woman who gives up money for Jesus (the anointing woman, 14:3-9) and the story of one of the twelve specially named men who gives up Jesus for money (Judas's betrayal, 14:10-11).

Some narrative critics distinguish characterization by "telling" and characterization by "showing." "Telling" involves the explicit words of a reliable narrator about a character. Anything else is "showing." "Showing" requires more from the narratee and implied reader and is thus more engaging. Most of the characterization in the Gospels is by "showing."

Some narrative critics find it helpful to identify the dominant traits of characters. A trait is a personal quality that persists over time. Sometimes such traits are explicitly named in a narrative. Frequently they are inferred from words and actions, as suggested previously. Some characters are portrayed with only one trait. Others are given a number of traits, or developing traits, or even conflicting traits.

E. M. Forster, novelist and literary critic, called these two types of characters "flat" and "round."[10] The distinction, which is sometimes elaborated, has proved to be extremely helpful for narrative critics. Flat characters are simple and consistent. Some flat characters appear but once, others again and again, but their actions and words are predictable. Round characters are complex or dynamic. They may reveal new aspects of themselves or even change. The distinction between flat and round characters is not the same as the distinction between "minor" and "major" characters. The Jewish leaders are hardly minor characters in Mark but they are flat. Nor is the flat/round distinction equivalent to negative versus positive. The Jewish leaders in Mark are flat and negative; the anointing woman is flat and positive. The disciples are round and both positive and negative; the Markan Jesus alone is a round, positive character. The flatness or roundness of characters, however, does affect the implied reader's response in praise, judgment, or identification. Round characters elicit identification in a way that flat characters do not.

Just as the point of view of the implied author/narrator is aligned and takes on a positive or negative value, so the point of view of each character or group

10. E. M. Forster, *Aspects of the Novel* (New York: Harcourt, Brace & World, 1927, 1954), 103–118.

of characters is given an evaluative point of view by the implied author. Norman Petersen has argued that the two evaluative points of view among Markan characters are "thinking the things of God" and "thinking the things of men."[11] The implied author, narrator, Jesus, and several minor exemplary characters represent the first (positive) point of view. The Jewish leaders and sometimes the disciples represent the second (negative) one.

New Testament narrative critics are generally aware of the differences in characterization between nineteenth- and twentieth-century psychological novels, for example, and the Gospels. The secular literary theory on which biblical narrative critics so often lean is not particularly supportive at this point. Ways of analyzing characterization in the Gospels are still being developed. Perhaps the current debate about the portrayal of the disciples of Jesus in Mark (Are they "fallible followers" or final failures?[12]) will settle down somewhat as interpreters explore more thoroughly the techniques of characterization in use in the ancient world. Vernon Robbins has instructively compared the portrayal of the Markan disciples of Jesus with the portrayal of the disciples of Apollonius of Tyana by Philostratus.[13] I have pointed out that characterization by "types" was conventional in ancient literature, including history as well as epic, drama, and other forms. Mark seems to continue this convention by presenting contrasting groups—exemplars to emulate and enemies to eschew. But perhaps Mark challenges this convention as well by presenting fallible followers with whom to identify.[14] More research remains to be done in this area.

Settings

Characters are the "who" of the narrative; settings are the "where" and "when." The shift from historical questions to literary questions has made a significant impact on the way interpreters think about the spatial and temporal settings of the Gospels.[15] The original questers for the historical Jesus combed the Gospels for information about the geography and chronology of Jesus' ministry. Early

11. Norman R. Petersen, " 'Point of View' in Mark's Narrative," *Semeia* 12 (1978): 97–121.
12. For the now classic exposition of the disciples as failed followers, see Theodore J. Weeden, Jr., *Mark: Traditions in Conflict* (Philadelphia: Fortress Press, 1971). See also Werner H. Kelber, *Mark's Story of Jesus* (Philadelphia: Fortress Press, 1979). For the view of the disciples as "fallible followers," see Robert C. Tannehill, "The Disciples in Mark: The Function of a Narrative Role," *Journal of Religion* 57 (1977): 386–405, and Elizabeth Struthers Malbon, "Fallible Followers: Women and Men in the Gospel of Mark," *Semeia* 28 (1983): 29–48.
13. Vernon K. Robbins, *Jesus the Teacher: A Socio-Rhetorical Interpretation of Mark*, rev. ed. (Philadelphia: Fortress Press, 1992).
14. Elizabeth Struthers Malbon, "The Jewish Leaders in the Gospel of Mark: A Literary Study of Marcan Characterization," *Journal of Biblical Literature* 108 (1989): 259–81, esp. 275–81.
15. Elizabeth Struthers Malbon, "Galilee and Jerusalem: History and Literature in Marcan Interpretation," *Catholic Biblical Quarterly* 44 (1982): 242–55.

redaction critics of Mark argued that its confused geographical references indicate an author writing outside Galilee and Israel, probably in Rome. Later redaction critics speculated that the positive connotations of Galilee in Mark indicate Galilee as the locale of the community for which the Gospel was written.[16] The prediction of the destruction of the Jewish Temple in chapter 13 of Mark—especially with its cryptic parenthetical phrase: "(let the reader understand)," 13:14—has been cited as evidence that Mark was written prior to 70 C.E. (the date of the Temple's actual destruction by the Romans) *and* as evidence that it was written after 70 C.E.! The spatial and temporal settings of Mark give a clear picture of neither Jesus' time and place in history nor Mark's.

Literary critics, especially narrative critics, interpret these spatial and temporal references internally rather than externally. Together they form the background for the dramatic action of Mark's Gospel. In fact, settings often participate in the drama of the narrative. Places and times are rich in connotational, or associative, values, and these values contribute to the meaning of the narrative for the implied reader. For example, the Markan narrator says that Jesus "went up the mountain" (3:13) to appoint the Twelve. Historical critics have searched in vain for a mountain in Galilee. For the implied author and implied reader, who know their Bible, "the mountain" is where God comes to meet leaders of the people of God. Similarly, "the sea" is where God manifests divine power, and "the wilderness" is where God manifests divine care in miraculously feeding the people of God. Thus the implied reader is shown (not told) that Jesus' power over the sea (4:35-41; 6:45-52) and miraculous feedings in the wilderness (6:31-44; 8:1-10) are divine manifestations.

Markan temporal settings also contribute significantly to the implied reader's appreciation of the narrative. Some temporal references are clearly allusive or symbolic. Jesus' testing in the wilderness for forty days (1:13) is an allusion to Israel's forty years of testing in the wilderness during the Exodus. The twelve years of age of Jairus's daughter and the twelve years of suffering of the hemorrhaging woman intensify the Jewish flavor of the interwoven stories (5:21-43). Twelve is a number symbolic of Israel, with its twelve tribes.

In other cases the implied author uses temporal markers to pace the unfolding of the story. The first several chapters of Mark are peppered with the Greek adverb *euthus*, "immediately." (In English translation this effect is clearer in the Revised Standard Version than in the New Revised Standard Version.) The Markan Jesus rushes around—from baptism in the Jordan, to testing in the wilderness, to preaching and exorcising a demon in the Capernaum synagogue, to healing in Simon's house, to healing throughout Galilee. The Markan Jesus' first words tell of the urgency of the present time: "The time is fulfilled, and the kingdom of God has come near; repent and believe in the good news"

16. Willi Marxsen, *Mark the Evangelist: Studies on the Redaction History of the Gospel*, trans. James Boyce et al. (Nashville and New York: Abingdon Press, 1969). Werner H. Kelber, *The Kingdom in Mark: A New Place and a New Time* (Philadelphia: Fortress Press, 1974).

(1:15). The Markan narrator's first series of scenes *shows* this urgency. Immediately Jesus acts; immediately the implied reader is to respond.[17]

The pace of the Markan story-as-discoursed is dramatically different in the passion narrative, the story of Jesus' suffering and death. Everything slows down. Story time for the first ten chapters is months and months, perhaps a year. Story time for the last six chapters is about a week. Moreover, everything becomes more specific. Instead of the "in those days" or "in the morning" of the first ten chapters, we now read "two days before the Passover and the festival of Unleavened Bread" (14:1) or "nine o'clock in the morning" (15:25, "the third hour [or watch]," RSV). The same specificity occurs spatially. Instead of "in the house," we find "at Bethany in the house of Simon the leper, . . . at the table" (14:3). A modern-day analogy would be a filmmaker's skillful use of slow motion photography to suggest the profound significance of a climaxing series of scenes. The more detailed setting of scenes in time and space of the Markan passion narrative is the implied author's plea to the implied reader: slow down; take this in; to understand anything of the story, you must understand this. It is another form of urgency.

Spatial and temporal settings need to be mapped out in correlation with the plot of the narrative, just as characters need to be interpreted in terms of their roles in the plot. For the implied author and the implied reader, the elements of narrative—characters, settings, plot, rhetoric—are essentially integrated.

Plot

The plot is the "what" and the "why" of the narrative. What happens? Why? Then what happens? Why? These are questions of the plot. Biblical critic Norman Petersen presents a very fruitful distinction between Mark's narrative world and Mark's plotted time. The "narrative world is comprised of all events described or referred to in the narrative, but in their causal and logical sequence." The "plotting of this world is to be seen in the ways its components have been selected and arranged in a sequence of narrated incidents."[18] Events are not always plotted in the narrative in the order in which they would occur in the narrative world. The changes from narrative world to the plotted time of the narrative are part of the implied author's discourse with the implied reader.

Gérard Genette, a literary theorist, has worked out an intricate system for discussing the order, duration, and frequency of events in the plotted narrative. An event may be narrated *after* its logical order in the narrative world (analepsis). An event may be narrated *before* its logical order in the narrative world (prolepsis). And, of course, events may occur in the same order in both. An event may be narrated with a longer, shorter, or equal duration in comparison with its duration in the narrative world. An event that occurs once in the narrative

17. On the larger issues of apocalyptic and temporality in relation to Mark's plot, see Dan O. Via, Jr., *The Ethics of Mark's Gospel: In the Middle of Time* (Philadelphia: Fortress Press, 1985), esp. 27–66.

18. Norman R. Petersen, *Literary Criticism for New Testament Critics* (Guides to Biblical Scholarship; Philadelphia: Fortress Press, 1978), 49–50.

world may be narrated once or more than once. Changes in order, duration, and frequency are ways the implied author has of leading the implied reader through the story-as-discoursed to an interpretation.

Markan examples will clarify these distinctions. The three passion predictions that the Markan Jesus makes to his disciples (8:31; 9:31; 10:33) point proleptically to what will occur later—but still within the narrative. The Markan Jesus' prediction, echoed by the young man at the empty tomb (14:28; 16:7), that he will go before his disciples to Galilee, points proleptically to an event that is not narrated within the story-as-discoursed. The implied reader, however, has been cued to presume its occurrence in the narrative world (see, e.g., 13:9-13). This narrative technique contributes to the often noted open ending of Mark's Gospel. A short but surprising and significant analepsis is narrated at 15:40-41. The Markan Jesus' twelve disciples have fled; he is crucified, bereft of their presence. But at the cross "there were also women looking on from a distance." Three are named, but "many other women" are mentioned. At this crucial point the narrator tells the narratee that these women used to follow Jesus and minister to him in Galilee. *Follow* and *minister to* are discipleship words in Mark. So the implied reader learns at the last hour that Jesus had other followers, women followers, from the first. Moreover, these surprising followers stay to the last—although at a distance. Three of them are there at the empty tomb as well.

Conflict is the key to the Markan plot. As Markan characterization does not depend on psychological development within the characters, so the plot does not turn on high suspense and complicated intrigue among the characters. The plot moves by conflicts between groups of characters or, rather, between God or Jesus and groups of characters. There are multiple conflicts, along several dimensions. The kingdom of God is in conflict with all other claims to power and authority. Jesus is in conflict with demons and unclean spirits. Jesus and the Jewish authorities are in continuing conflict over issues of authority and interpretation of the Law (Torah). Jesus and the disciples are in conflict over what it means to be the Messiah and thus what it means to follow him. All the conflicts have to do with power and authority. Where do ultimate power and authority lie? How should human power and authority be exercised? But all the conflicts are not the same. The disciples, for example, are not portrayed and evaluated by the implied author in the same way as the Jewish leaders are. And, of course, the Markan Jesus responds to the disciples very differently from how he reacts to the other groups with whom he comes into conflict.

Thus the elements of narrative include the five Ws one might expect in the first paragraph of a news story: who (characters), where and when (settings), what and why (plot). To the extent that story and discourse can be separated analytically, these three are elements of story. A fourth narrative element is rhetoric, the how of the story-as-discoursed. Rhetoric refers to how the implied author persuades the implied reader to follow the story. Because narrative criticism (like literary criticism in general) asks, "*How* does the text mean?" narrative criticism takes a keen interest in rhetoric.

Rhetoric

Rhetoric is the art of persuasion. Persuasion, of course, works differently in varying contexts. Markan rhetoric is narrative rhetoric. By the way the story is told, the implied author persuades the implied reader first to understand and then to share and extend the story's levels of meaning. Mark's rhetoric is one of juxtaposition—placing scene over against scene in order to elicit comparison, contrast, insight. This juxtaposition includes repetition, not only of scenes but also of words and phrases; duality is widespread. Juxtaposition also includes intercalation—splicing one story into another—and framing—placing similar stories as the beginning and the end of a series. In addition, juxtaposition includes foreshadowing and echoing of words, phrases, and whole events. Echoing and foreshadowing may be intratextual (within the text) or intertextual (between texts). The intertextual echoes heard in Mark's Gospel reverberate with the Septuagint. Symbolism involves the juxtaposition of a literal meaning and a metaphorical one. Irony involves the juxtaposition of an apparent or expected meaning and a deeper or surprising one. Repetition, intercalation, framing, foreshadowing and echoing, symbolism, and irony are favorite Markan rhetorical devices. They are part of the discourse of the narrative. Without the implied author's discourse, the implied reader could not receive the story. The story is never received directly but only as discoursed, only rhetorically.

The interwoven scenes of Jesus' trial before the high priest and Peter's denial (14:53-72) illustrate a number of these rhetorical techniques. The two stories are intercalated. The narrator first tells that Jesus was taken to the high priest (v. 53) and then that Peter followed "at a distance" into the courtyard of the high priest (v. 54). The scene between Jesus and the high priest and other chief priests is played out (vv. 55-65), and then the scene between Peter and the high priest's servant girl and other bystanders is played out (vv. 66-72). The implied reader cannot forget the presence of Peter "warming himself at the fire" (v. 54) all the while Jesus endures the fiery rage of the high priest. Jesus' scene concludes with the guards taunting him to "Prophesy!" (v. 65). Peter's scene concludes with his remembrance of Jesus' prophecy of his denial (v. 72), an ominous echo of the earlier foreshadowing. It is sadly ironic that Peter's noisy denial of his discipleship in order to save his life is narrated almost simultaneously with Jesus' quiet affirmation of his messiahship, although it will lead to his death. The rhetorical juxtaposition of these scenes—characters, words, actions, settings—in the unfolding plot pushes the implied reader not only to judge the two contrasting characters but also to judge himself or herself.

The order of stories or scenes in Mark 8:22—10:52 illustrates the rhetorical devices of repetition, framing, and symbolism. In this section of the narrative, the Markan Jesus three times predicts his passion and resurrection (8:31; 9:31; 10:33). After each prediction, the disciples manifest their limited understanding of serving and suffering as aspects of Messiahship and discipleship (8:32-33; 9:32-34, 38; 10:35-41). After each misunderstanding, Jesus renews his teaching on this topic (8:34-38; 9:35-37, 39-50; 10:42-45). Of course, each time Jesus teaches the disciples, the implied author teaches the implied reader. Repetition adds clarity and force.

Around these three three-part scenes (passion prediction units), other scenes (of teaching and healing) are set. Then all these scenes are framed by the only two Markan stories of the healing of blindness. At the beginning of the series, the two-stage healing of blindness at Bethsaida is narrated (8:22-26). At the close, the healing of blind Bartimaeus, who follows Jesus "on the way," is recounted (10:46-52). Blindness and sight are symbolic of misunderstanding and insight. As Jesus healed the blind man of Bethsaida in two stages, so he must teach the disciples in two stages about his messiahship. At Caesarea Philippi, Peter tells that he "sees" Jesus' power and shows that he is "blind" to Jesus' suffering service (8:27-33). As the mighty deeds of chapters 1–8 were the first stage of Jesus' teaching, so the passion prediction units of chapters 8–10 are the second stage. The goal of the journey is for all—disciples and implied readers—to "see" as Bartimaeus does and to follow "on the way."

Understanding the narrative rhetoric is central to the work of the narrative critic because rhetoric is the how of the story's telling and "*How* does the text mean?" is the literary question. Earlier source, form, and redaction critics found Mark's rhetorical style rough and primitive. This judgment may be true at the level of the sentence. (English translations always smooth out Mark's Greek a bit.) But Mark's narrative rhetoric must be appreciated at the level of the scene. In the intriguing juxtaposition of scenes—with their characters, settings, and plot developments—the rhetoric of the Markan Gospel works its persuasive ways with the implied reader.

Narrative criticism compensates for the fragmentation of the text into smaller and smaller units by form and redaction criticism. Even redaction criticism—with its potential to be concerned for the Gospel as a whole—frequently bogs down in ever more meticulous divisions between "tradition" and "redaction"—what Mark received and what he added. Nevertheless, perhaps narrative criticism—in its holistic passion—overcompensates. Deconstructive criticism (see chap. 4) compensates for the totalizing effect of narrative criticism—creating a self-consistent unity of the text. Deconstructive criticism may overcompensate as well. But it is good for narrative criticism to be reminded of what it also knows—and often proclaims—of the tensions, gaps, and mysteries of the text itself—and even the text against itself.

Narrative criticism seeks to avoid the "intentional fallacy" of redaction criticism. The narrative critic does not pursue the quest for the real author's intention. Instead, the narrative critic seeks to analyze and appreciate the implied author's effect—that is, the text itself. But what is "the text itself"? Narrative critics affirm that it is the center of a communication process involving author, text, and reader. They (we) focus on the text, partly in reaction to redaction critics' focus on the author, but mostly because we find the text so intriguing.

Reader-response criticism (see chap. 3) seeks to avoid the objectivism of narrative criticism—viewing the text as an autonomous object. Reader-response criticism may overcompensate as well. Perhaps narrative criticism's appreciation for the role of the implied reader guards it from the extreme of objectivism. No doubt biblical criticism would benefit greatly from an approach that could—if

not simultaneously at least sequentially—keep in view all parts of the communication process: author, text, and reader. Then, *"What did* the text mean?"
and *"How does* the text mean?" might contribute more fairly and more fully to
the older and enduring question, "What does the text mean—to me—to us?"

Narrative Examples

We turn now to an extended example of narrative criticism at work in chapters
4–8 of the Gospel of Mark. Such an example should help to clarify and integrate
the narrative elements. Chapters 4–8 have been chosen because of their rhetorical richness, because they hold together as a subunit within the entire Gospel,
and because what Mark does here with these smaller stories is quite distinctive
from what Matthew and Luke do with many of the same stories in their Gospels.
We could study each narrative element in turn; first characters, then settings,
and so on. This type of analysis is often done by narrative critics. But here we
will look at the interrelated narrative elements as the story unfolds from 4:1
through 8:26, a pattern increasingly frequent within narrative criticism. (Let
the reader understand: my implied reader is reading Mark 4–8 along with this
chapter.)

Parables on the Sea (4:1-34)

At the beginning of chapter 4, the Markan narrator takes considerable trouble
to make sure the narratee locates Jesus at the sea. Within one verse the word
sea occurs three times and the word *boat* once. The narratee knows from 1:16
that the Sea of Galilee is intended. The setting places Jesus opposite the crowd.
Jesus is in the boat on the sea. (The Greek is even more dramatic: "he got into
a boat and sat on the sea.") The crowd is beside the sea on the land. Spatial
location underlines the differences between characters.

This setting represents a change from the previous scene. The action also
changes. Jesus had been healing and exorcising demons; now he is teaching.
The Markan Jesus is often said to be teaching or preaching, but few examples
are given. Chapter 4, the parable chapter, is an important exception. The narrator's introductory comment, "he began to teach them many things in parables," is followed by Jesus' telling of one parable, that of the sower.

Verse 10 presents a change of characters and thus a new scene. It has proven
very difficult for real readers to agree on which characters are now assumed
by the narrator to be present. It becomes immediately clear that when Jesus
was "alone" means when the large crowd had left, not when he was solitary.
What does not become immediately clear is who are "those who were around
him along with the twelve." If there are two groups (the Twelve, the others),
they speak as one and Jesus so responds. It seems likely (although this observation is clear only from further analysis throughout the Gospel) that the implied
author creates ambiguity about who is hearing Jesus in order to encourage the
implied reader to read himself or herself into the story. The implied author, the

narrator, and the Markan Jesus have a shared point of view, and they simultaneously address the characters, the narratee, and the implied reader. The would-be two groups who are really one (the Twelve plus the others) are one over against "those outside."

To those inside has been given (the passive voice suggests "given by God") "the secret [or, better, 'mystery'] of the kingdom of God." For those outside, everything "comes in parables." Parables are comparisons or riddles. In understanding parables, those outside are no better off than those to whom the prophet Isaiah spoke: they may hear, but they do not understand. This ironic allusion to Isaiah 6:9-10, which is itself ironic, is an intertextual echo of the Septuagint.

This mysterious little scene about the mystery of the kingdom is followed by the Markan Jesus' allegorical explanation of the parable of the sower. Each element of the parable is taken to represent some element in the larger story of the growth of "the word." "The word" (logos) is an early Christian synonym for the Gospel, the good news, the message by and about Jesus as the Christ. According to this explanation, the parable of the sower is about improper and proper ways of hearing the word. In its Markan narrative context (parable/insiders and outsiders/explanation), the story of the sower is symbolic of hearing parables as outsiders and as insiders. Insiders receive not only "the mystery" but also an additional explanation.

This twofold pattern, parable plus explanation, seems to be repeated. Verse 21 is a little parable about a lamp; verse 22 is a brief explanation. Verse 24 is a little parable about a measure; verse 25 is a brief explanation. Verse 23, right in the middle, is the echoing refrain: "Let anyone with ears to hear listen!" (cf. 4:9). Next the narrator presents Jesus presenting two slightly longer parables, both about seeds. Neither one is followed by an explanation, but verses 33-34 restate this pattern. To "them" (the outsiders) Jesus spoke the word in parables, "as they were able to hear it." To "his disciples" (and other insiders?) he explained everything privately. As other features in the Markan narrative make even more clear, who is inside and who is outside is not a matter of social status or role but of response to Jesus. "Let anyone with ears to hear listen!"

The final two seed parables offer explicit comparisons to "the kingdom of God." The kingdom of God comes *from God*, not from human effort. It comes in God's time and thus, from a human point of view, it always comes as a surprise. All three seed parables suggest that the best predictor of the kingdom's fulfillment is not its beginning but God's power. But all of these implications are rhetorically shown, not told. Like the characters within the story, the implied readers of the narrative must have ears to hear and eyes to see. One becomes an insider by perceiving and understanding. The Markan Jesus and the Markan implied author recognize all such insight as a mysterious gift.

Mighty Deeds on and by the Sea (4:35—5:43)

The sea continues to be the dominant setting for Markan narrative events from 4:1 through 8:21. When the dominant setting switches to "the way" at 8:27, the plot also takes a turn. Narrative elements frequently echo each other in

Mark's narrative. At 4:35 the narrator reports a dramatic event that occurs on the sea. Jesus is already in the boat; the disciples join him, as well as other people in other boats. A windstorm comes up, threatening to fill the boat with water from the waves. Yet Jesus is asleep in the stern. The desperate disciples wake him, saying, "Teacher, do you not care that we are perishing?" Apparently they assume Jesus *could* do something to help—if he just *would*. He does. He "rebukes" the wind, as he had earlier rebuked unclean spirits; and he tells the sea to become still. It does. Jesus also questions the disciples: "Why are you afraid? Have you still no faith?" The disciples—not too surprisingly, "filled with great awe"—question themselves: "Who then is this, that even the wind and the sea obey him?"

The sea scene ends there. No character answers this question. It is forwarded to the implied reader, who shares with the implied author knowledge of the Hebrew Bible in the form of the Septuagint. Psalm 107:23-32 is especially relevant.

> Some went down to the sea in ships,
>   doing business on the mighty waters;
> they saw the deeds of the LORD,
>   his wondrous works in the deep.
> For he commanded and raised the stormy wind,
>   which lifted up the waves of the sea.
> ....
> Then they cried to the LORD in their trouble,
>   and he brought them out from their distress;
> he made the storm be still,
>   and the waves of the sea were hushed.
>   PSALM 107:23-25, 28-29

Who then is this, that even the wind and the sea obey him? The Lord God. The Lord Jesus Christ. The power of Jesus the Christ is the power of God. All these affirmations are shown, not told. The fact that the disciples do not explicitly answer their own rhetorical question has more to do with the discourse than with the story. The implied author has the disciples leave the question open for the implied reader. The implied author seems to know that a conclusion the implied reader must work to arrive at will be held more strongly. The narrative rhetoric is persuasive.

Despite the storm, Jesus and the disciples arrive on "the other side of the sea" at "the country of the Gerasenes." Historical interpreters, perhaps beginning with Matthew, who substitutes the name Gadarenes (Matt 8:28), have had difficulty locating such a place. From a narrative critical point of view, the country of the Gerasenes is gentile territory opposite Jewish Galilee. If the implied reader does not know that narrative fact from the name, he or she will surely know it from the great herd of swine found there. Because Jewish law classifies the pig as an unclean animal, one unfit for humans or God, primarily Jewish areas do not support large herds of swine. The casting out of a legion of demons from the Gerasene man, who had lived as a wild man among the tombs, is the Markan Jesus' first healing of a Gentile. When the exorcised demons enter the swine, as they had requested, and the swine rush to their deaths in the sea, the gentile region seems to be purged of evil and made ready for Jesus' preaching of the good news. Jesus tells the healed Gerasene to go home and tell how much "the Lord" has done for him. Instead, the man goes throughout the "ten (Greek) cities" of the region, the Decapolis, proclaiming "how much Jesus had done for him." Who then is the Lord? The scene ends with all marveling.

The sea, however, still orients the scenes and the movements of the plot. At 5:21 the narrator tells that Jesus crossed "again in the boat to the other side," where a great crowd gathered about him "by the sea." For any implied reader who might be confused about which side of the sea is now "the other side," the implied author again gives a second indication: Jairus, one of the rulers of the synagogue, appears. No synagogues are needed where herds of swine are kept. Back in Jewish Galilee, Jesus heals his own people again. Two healing stories are intercalated: the raising of Jairus's daughter and the healing of the hemorrhaging woman. A third indication of the Jewishness of the setting is the repeated number twelve: a twelve-year flow of blood, a twelve-year old girl. As was mentioned above, twelve is symbolic of the twelve tribes and thus of Israel.

The intercalation is done very naturally. At times it has even been taken literally and historically rather than narratively and rhetorically. Because the woman interrupted Jesus on his way to Jairus's house, Jairus's daughter died. Here intercalation, the inserting of one story into another, is an integral part of the plot. But Markan intercalation is always for interpretive purposes. The framing story is to be interpreted in light of the inside story, and vice versa. Both suppliants have extreme needs. Jairus's daughter is "at the point of death" and then dead; the woman has spent everything she had on medical treatment, only to grow worse. In addition, both suppliants have extreme faith. The woman believes that Jesus' power is so great that merely touching the hem of his garment can heal her; Jairus, with Jesus' encouragement, believes that even if his daughter is dead Jesus' power can enable her to live again. According to Jewish law, the continual uncleanness of the hemorrhaging woman made her a social and religious outcaste, as dead socially as Jairus's daughter was physically. The child becomes again a daughter to her father, and the woman becomes again a "daughter" (5:34) of Israel.

At the close of the raising of Jairus' daughter, and thus of the two intercalated healing stories, the narrator adds—not too surprisingly—"at this they were overcome with amazement." But the next addition is surprising: "[And] he strictly ordered them that no one should know this. . . ." Impossible! The commotion, weeping, and wailing mentioned in verse 38 were, in effect, the first phase of the girl's funeral. It would be more than a little difficult not to say something to the mourners. As is frequently the case, what cannot be taken literally can be meaningful at another level. Redaction critics labeled Jesus' command to secrecy here and elsewhere "the messianic secret" and interpreted it in terms of Mark's editing of tradition to meet the needs of his community. Narrative critics see it as a plot device that calls attention to the complexity of the image of messiahship in the Markan Gospel. If Jairus told all that he knew about Jesus, he would tell *only* that Jesus was powerful beyond imagining. For the implied author of Mark that statement would be a half-truth; the other half, developed in the other half of Mark's Gospel and equally beyond imagining, is that Jesus is committed to using that power only for service, even in the face of suffering and death. At 5:43 the implied reader knows more than Jairus knows, but not yet the whole truth. Jesus' charge to keep quiet his powerful deed is another way for the implied author to raise the question of his identity. If Lord, if Messiah, what kind of Lord? what kind of Messiah?

Preaching/Rejection/Death (6:1-30)

The event that follows the raising of Jairus's daughter in the plotted narrative suggests another reason for the Markan Jesus' hesitancy in making his mighty deeds known: even a half-truth about his power can be misunderstood. Jesus is rejected in the synagogue in his hometown. His teaching results not only in the astonishment of the people, as it had done earlier, but also in their anger and offense at him. Who does he think he is, anyway? He's just Mary's son (probably a slur, because a male child was normally identified as his father's son). His brothers and sisters are not anything special. Jesus says, "A prophet is not without honor, except in his own country [hometown], and among his own kin, and in his own house" (6:4, RSV). The implied reader says, "Jesus is a prophet."

The Markan Jesus' response to this rejection is threefold: (1) to heal whomever he can, limited, it would seem, by the people's unbelief, (2) to move on to other villages and teach; and (3) to send out the Twelve on a mission of their own. Jesus commissions the Twelve, two by two, to go out to preach and exorcise unclean spirits, just as he had been doing. He charges them not to rely on their own provisions ("no bread, no bag, no money") but on the hospitality of others. He warns them that they will be rejected, just as he has been. They go and carry out their double mission of preaching and healing.

While the Twelve are gone, as it were, the narrator tells another story, one about John the Baptizer. This is an intercalation, and it is arranged for interpretive purposes, not just for the convenience of the plot. The link is King Herod's learning about how Jesus' name had become known. What does Herod think about this famous Jesus? Others may think he is Elijah or a prophet, but Herod, apparently feeling the pangs of guilt, thinks Jesus is John the Baptizer raised to life again. For Herod, Jesus raises again the trauma of John's beheading.

In 1:14, passing reference is made by the narrator to the "handing over" (Greek, *paradidonai*) of John the Baptizer: "Now after John was arrested, Jesus came to Galilee, proclaiming the good news of God, . . ." John preached and was rejected. Jesus is preaching. Nothing more is said about John's arrest until 6:14-29, at which point Jesus has been rejected and the Twelve are preaching. John's imprisonment and beheading at the command of Herod is told in a lively and detailed narrative flashback or analepsis. As this story within a story closes with John's death, Jesus' disciples return from a successful preaching tour. (They are sent out as "the twelve" [6:7], but they return as "the apostles"

[6:30]. *Apostles* means the "ones sent out.") The Markan narrative rhetoric discloses a parallelism between the preaching, being rejected, being "handed over," and death of John, Jesus, and the disciples. At chapter 6 John is dead, Jesus is rejected, and the disciples are preaching. What will happen to Jesus next? What will happen to the disciples?

Mighty Deeds by and on the Sea (6:31-56)

Jesus is concerned for his "apostles"; he takes them away from the crowd by boat to a wilderness place. But Jesus' attempt to find the leisure to eat with his disciples leads, ironically, to the work of teaching and feeding the crowd. Jesus teaches the great multitude that awaits him in the hoped-for deserted place because "they were like sheep without a shepherd." This echo of a common image of aimlessness from the Hebrew Bible (e.g., Num 27:17; 1 Kgs 22:17; Ezek 34:5) alerts the implied reader to the Jewishness of the setting.

The story of the multiplication of the loaves and the fishes and the feeding of the five thousand is filled with dialogue between Jesus and the disciples. "Send the crowd away to get food." "No, you feed them." "How can we feed them?" "Start with what you've got." The miraculous meal in the wilderness echoes God's provision of manna in the wilderness, but it also foreshadows for the implied reader the eucharistic meal. The four verbs *took, blessed, broke,* and *gave* (6:41) are repeated in the narration of the last supper (14:22), which models (actually is modeled after) the Eucharist. As is appropriate for meals that God hosts, everyone eats and is satisfied, *and* twelve baskets full of leftovers are collected. The number twelve reminds the implied reader (symbolically) that the recipients are Jews. The surplus of bread outshines the miracle of the manna, in which nothing extra could remain, except for use on the Sabbath (Exod 16:13-30).

"Immediately" Jesus sends the disciples off by boat again, not to some nearby deserted place this time, but to Bethsaida, a city on the other (gentile) side of the sea. Jesus dismisses the crowd and goes "up on the mountain" to pray. Which mountain? A mountain by the lakeshore in Galilee? No, the mountain where all of God's prophets communicate with God. The narrator's use of the contrast between land and sea to contrast characters at 6:47 is reminiscent of 4:1: "[And] when evening came, the boat was out on the sea, and he was alone on the land." The disciples are unable to complete their mission to "go on ahead" of Jesus to gentile Bethsaida. The wind is against them. Then they think they see a ghost passing by them, walking on the water. The implied reader knows it is Jesus yet is able to understand their terror. Jesus' words are another intertextual echo from Exodus: "I am" (usually translated "It is I"). God said "I am" to Moses from the burning bush (Exod 3:14). Who then is this? It does not surprise the implied reader that the wind ceases.

The narrator's next comment, the conclusion to this scene, does surprise. "And they [the disciples] were utterly astounded, for they did not understand about the loaves, but their hearts were hardened" (6:51b-52). Why doesn't the narrator say, "They did not understand about the wind or the walking on water"? What do the loaves have to do with the sea? And why are so many images from Exodus being stacked up here? Bread in the wilderness, walking on (through) the sea, "I am"—and now hardened hearts. The passive voice ("their hearts were hardened") suggests that the disciples' hearts, like Pharaoh's, were hardened by God so that God's overall purpose for the people of God could be worked out. The implied reader must keep reading!

Surprising closings and openings of scenes are becoming the norm. From the cryptic reference to hardened hearts, the implied reader moves not to an anticipated arrival at Bethsaida on the east but to a surprising landing at Gennesaret, still on the west. In the midst of so many other amazing narrative events, one would not have been shocked to read of a successful, even miraculous, crossing to Bethsaida once Jesus entered the boat. But Jewish Gennesaret it is, where a narrative summary of Jesus' ministry of healing is presented. People bring the sick to him from everywhere; as many as touch even the fringe of his cloak are made well. The faith and healing of the hemorrhaging woman echoes for the implied reader. By the sea Jesus feeds five thousand; on the sea Jesus walks; by the sea Jesus heals many. Jesus has authority over the sea—and quite a bit more.

Conflict over Jewish Law (7:1-23)

Authority is the issue in the next series of scenes. Jesus' antagonists are "the Pharisees and some of the scribes who had come from Jerusalem" (7:1). Pharisees and scribes were the chief antagonists of the Markan Jesus in a series of five controversy stories narrated earlier (2:1—3:6). The "scribes who came down from Jerusalem" appeared earlier as the ones accusing Jesus of being possessed by Beelzebul, the prince of demons (3:22-30). Jerusalem itself, which has a high positive connotation in traditional Judaism, has a negative connotation in the Gospel of Mark. So, when Pharisees and Jerusalem scribes gather together to see Jesus, the implied reader anticipates conflict. And conflict there surely is.

The conflict is triggered by the failure of Jesus' disciples to observe the Jewish (and particularly Pharisaic) regulations about ritual handwashing before meals. The implied author finds it necessary in a parenthetical aside to explain this "tradition of the elders" for any implied reader who may be unfamiliar with it. Because at other times the implied author assumes the implied reader is quite familiar with the Hebrew Bible (in Greek translation), a mixed group of Jewish and gentile implied readers may be indicated, or implied readers who are familiar with Jewish *Scripture* but not Jewish *tradition* may be assumed. In the explanatory aside, the Pharisees and all the Jews are "they."

The conflict is expressed more in monologue than in dialogue. The Markan narrator's telling is one-sided from the start. The Pharisees and scribes get one question, "Why do your disciples not live according to the tradition of the elders, but eat with defiled hands?" Even that question has been elaborately anticipated by the narrator (7:2-4). Jesus gets two paragraphs of direct defense and counterattack. Jesus turns a statement from the prophet Isaiah against his antagonists. The Isaiah passage underlines what is at stake here for the Markan Jesus: divine commandment versus human tradition. As an example of this opposition, Jesus suggests the disparity between one of the Ten Commandments, "Honor your father and your mother," and the traditional use (and abuse) of Corban. *Corban* refers to money or property that was verbally "offered" or "dedicated" to God, that is, withdrawn from ordinary use. Although the money was not handed over directly to the Temple treasury, it was not required to be used for care of one's parents. The "tradition of the elders" that may momentarily sound honorable on the lips of the Pharisees and scribes is clearly condemned when it is reclassified by Jesus as "human tradition" in opposition to "divine commandment." Jesus appeals to a higher authority—Scripture—and one that his antagonists themselves profess to honor. His antagonists are silenced.

A change of scene occurs with the entrance of a new group of characters. Jesus calls the crowd to himself again and opens with these words: "Listen to me, all of you, and understand." The words echo similar uses of "listen" and "understand" in chapter 4, the parable chapter, and, indeed, these words introduce a parable here. It is a very brief parable (comparison or riddle) about defilement being caused by what comes out of people, not by what goes into them. Because the previous scene concerned the "defiled hands" of the disciples, the topic continues despite the change of scene.

This pattern occurs again immediately (7:17): a change of scene without a change of topic, a third scene concerned with defilement. There is a spatial change: Jesus enters a house. The narrator had not commented on his location earlier; it was presumably out-of-doors. There is a shift in characters: Jesus leaves the crowd. Then his disciples ask him about the parable. The presence of the disciples was not mentioned at the narration of the parable. The implied author does not make everything explicit; thus what is made explicit becomes all the more important.

The shift from Jesus' public teaching of the crowd to his private teaching of the disciples occurs throughout the Markan narrative. It occurs in chapter 4: parable to the crowd, explanation of the parable to the disciples (and "those who were around him"). Frequently, as in chapter 7, this character shift is paralled by a spatial shift: from out-of-doors or an unspecified location to in "the house."

Chapter 7 also echoes chapter 4 in the introduction of Jesus' explanation of the parable by questioning the disciples' lack of understanding (7:18; 4:13). Only when characters to whom the Markan Jesus is willing to give additional teaching misunderstand does the Markan implied author have an opportunity to give additional teaching to the implied reader. And here the narrator goes beyond Jesus! Jesus says that persons are not defiled by anything that enters their stomachs and passes through their digestive systems. The immediate implication is that persons are not defiled by dirt from unwashed hands. But the narrator notes, parenthetically: "(Thus he declared all foods clean)." (As the implied reader is aware, observing clean and unclean foods was one of the more obvious ways Jews were distinct from Gentiles.) Then Jesus says that persons are defiled by evil thoughts that come out of their hearts. The riddle is solved. The implicit is explicit.

Contact with Gentiles (7:24—8:10)

"[And] from there he set out and went away to. . . ." From where? Where have we been? the implied reader might well ask. The topic was defilement, and the antagonists were Pharisees and scribes, so the territory must have been Jewish; there is where they would be. In fact, the last landfall was Gennesaret. "[And] from there he set out and went away to the region of Tyre [and Sidon]"(7:24). These place-names indicate quite a change. Tyre and Sidon are in the ancient land of Phoenicia, the Roman province of Syria, as far north as the Markan narrative reaches and definitely gentile territory. But the Markan narrator likes to make sure the narratee follows. The second indication of the gentile setting of the scene is the double description of the woman who seeks Jesus' help: "a Gentile [a Greek], of Syrophoenician origin."

The narrator tells that Jesus' intention in going north was not to seek out more crowds to heal. "[And] he entered a house and did not want anyone to know he was there. Yet he could not escape notice" (7:24b). The fact that the Syrophoenician woman seeks out the secluded Jesus is just the first indication of her persistence on behalf of her demon-possessed daughter. The Markan Jesus rebuffs her initial request, and he does so with a powerful and degrading metaphor. "Let the children be fed first, for it is not fair to take the children's food [bread] and throw it to the dogs." The children are Israel. She is the dog, and she yaps right back! Two can play at metaphors. "Sir, even the dogs under the table eat the children's crumbs." She has him. She has risked a second rebuke and won her daughter's health. "For this saying [word, logos]" (7:29, RSV), Jesus says, you may go home to a healed child, a healed gentile child. (Jesus, too, seems to have experienced healing.)

The story of the Syrophoenician demoniac is not the first story in Mark of a Gentile healed by Jesus. (This fact interests form critics and bothers redaction critics, who say that it would make more sense if it were the first gentile healing.) Even as the story echoes the healing of the Gerasene demoniac, it has a certain freshness. It explains more fully the outreach of Jesus' healing power. The Markan Jesus is not opposed to giving additional explanations—even in actions.

The next spatial shift is perhaps the most confusing one in the entire Markan narrative. "Then he returned from the region of Tyre, and went by way of Sidon towards the Sea of Galilee, in the region of the Decapolis" (7:31). Sidon is north of Tyre, and the region of the Decapolis is east of the Sea of Galilee. So Jesus went north to return south, through the east. The implied author seems less concerned with the logic of the travel route and more concerned with the nature of the destinations: Tyre, Sidon, the Decapolis. Gentile place-names are accumulated for emphasis. The deaf-mute who is healed is also a Gentile.

The healing is, for Mark's Gospel, a particularly physical one (touching, spitting), but the techniques are common to healers in the Greco-Roman world. The man is healed privately, away from the multitude, and Jesus charges those who know of it to tell no one. But the charge backfires: "the more he ordered them, the more zealously they proclaimed it" (7:36). Astonishment beyond measure is the end result of this encounter with one who "makes the deaf to hear and the mute to speak."

Two stories of gentile healings have followed the three-scene discussion of defilement. Maybe it is not just all *foods* that the Markan implied author thinks Jesus has declared clean. That possibility is strengthened by the next story: the feeding of the four thousand. The feeding stories resound with the loudest and clearest intratextual echoes of the Markan narrative. Their overall similarities set off their significant differences. The five thousand are fed somewhere on the west (Jewish) side of the sea; the four thousand are fed somewhere on the east (gentile) side of the sea. (There have been no place references since the mention of the Decapolis.) In the former case, the Markan Jesus' compassion is linked to the people being like sheep without a shepherd, an image from the Hebrew Bible. In the latter case, Jesus' compassion is linked to their hunger, a universal human problem. In the former case, twelve baskets of leftovers are collected; in the latter case, seven. As twelve is a number symbolic of the Jews, so seven is a number symbolic of "the nations," the Gentiles. (In Acts 6, at the instigation of the "Hellenists," seven deacons are chosen to assist the twelve apostles.)

The allusions—backward to the manna of the exodus and forward to the bread of the last supper and the Eucharist—remain constant between the two feeding stories. What is added is that such bread is for Gentiles as well as for Jews. Jesus heals and feeds his own; that would be story enough. But Jesus also heals and feeds outsiders. That action takes some explaining; it is harder to understand.

Signs and Seeing (8:11-26)

After dismissing the four thousand, Jesus "immediately" gets into a boat with his disciples and goes to the district of Dalmanutha. The location of such a place is no longer known, although it is generally thought to be in Galilee on the sea. Will the Markan narrator give a second clue about the setting? Yes! "The Pharisees came and began to argue with him . . ." (8:11). The implied reader knows the journey has returned to Galilee. Just before his departure from Galilee to gentile Tyre and Sidon, Jesus was arguing with the Pharisees. Now on his return from the gentile Decapolis, Jesus and the Pharisees pick up where they left off. If Jesus has so much authority, surely he can produce a sign from heaven, that is, from God, for the Pharisees. Something clear and explicit would be nice. Jesus sighs. No such sign will be given—to them or to "this generation." In Mark's Gospel Jesus performs mighty deeds (*dynameis*) but not signs (*sēmeia*). (Contrast John's Gospel.) To ask for a sign is to demand that divine power be present on one's own terms rather than to perceive it wherever it manifests itself. So Jesus leaves the Pharisees. He gets into the boat again and departs "to the other side."

Yet the next scene is not on "the other side" but on the sea itself. It is the third scene carried out on the sea in Mark's narrative: first, calming the sea; second, walking on the sea; third, a conversation in the boat on the sea. This dialogue is not just another conversation between Jesus and the disciples. It is a careful, symbolic drawing together of themes that have been developed since 4:1. The implied reader's ears ring with echoes: the sea, the boat, loaves of bread, hardened hearts, eyes that do not see, ears that do not hear, five thousand, twelve baskets, four thousand, seven baskets, understand? So many things have happened, and then happened again in a different setting. Jesus tells a parable to all, and then explains it to some. Jesus heals and feeds at home and then far beyond. There is much to hear and see, to perceive and understand.

As the disciples did not answer their own rhetorical question at 4:41 ("Who then is this, that even the wind and the sea obey him?"), so they do not answer Jesus' rhetorical question at 8:21 ("Do you not yet understand?"). The beneficiary of both silences is the implied reader, the one for whom the story is being told. To hear only the silence of the disciples and not also the rhetoric of the implied author is to try to read the story without the discourse. Narrative is always story-as-discoursed. Markan rhetorical discourse relies on juxtaposition: item, item, item; comparison, contrast, insight. The implied reader must make the connections—and *may*—because neither the characters nor the narrator make them explicit. Sea, boat, bread, twelve, seven. Do *you* not yet understand?

The conclusion of a large section of Mark (4:1-8:21) with Jesus' questioning of the disciples (8:14-21) suggests that Jesus' disciples are distinguished from his opponents not by possessing the right answers but by being possessed by the right question: not "Why does he not perform a sign from heaven?" (see 8:11), but "Who then is this . . . ?" (4:41). Jesus responds to opponents and followers with both questions and answers: "Why does this generation ask for a sign?" (8:12). "Truly I tell you, no sign will be given to this generation" (8:12). "Do you not yet understand?" (8:21). "I am" (6:50). "I will go before you to Galilee" (14:28; cf. 16:7). Some interpreters—including redaction, narrative, and reader-response critics—see the misunderstanding (or incomprehension) of the disciples as central to Mark 4–8. Others, including the present author, see as a central thrust of these chapters the search for understanding—understanding of who Jesus is and thus of what following him entails. The disciples embody that search, that ongoing process. Like Mark's Gospel itself (its opening line is "The beginning of the good news . . . "), the search for understanding does not come to a decisive end in the Markan narrative. But neither the Markan narrator nor the Markan Jesus (nor his messenger at the empty tomb) gives up on the disciples. In this action, too, the implied reader is asked to follow.

"[And] they came to Bethsaida" (8:22). Bethsaida! Because of the significance of the sea conversation, a real reader, at least, and perhaps the implied reader as well, could almost forget about crossing the sea and surely about Bethsaida. Many scenes back—after feeding the five thousand and before walking on the sea—Jesus had tried to send the disciples across the sea before him to gentile Bethsaida. They never made it on their own. And now Jesus has led them there, led them to the Gentiles by an elaborate detour, through an additional explanation, as a second chance to see and hear the given mystery. The detour involved starting from the familiar (healings at Gennesaret, 6:53-56), arguing against the conventional (the tradition of the elders, 7:1-23), responding to the "other" (Syrophoenician woman and deaf mute in the Decapolis, 7:24-37), feeding all who are hungry (feeding the four thousand, 8:1-10), departing from those who demand divine presence on their own terms

(Pharisees requesting a sign, 8:11-13), and questioning those who travel alongside (conversation with the disciples on the sea, 8:14-21). So they came at last to Bethsaida, and at Bethsaida the blind see, even if by stages.

Several echoes of the healing of the deaf mute in the Decapolis are heard in the story of the healing of the blind man of Bethsaida. Both suppliants are Gentiles and suffer from communicative disorders. Both persons are healed away from the crowd. Jesus even leads the blind man out of the village. Both stories involve physical healing techniques: applying spittle or saliva to the affected body part and touching with the fingers or hands. Both accounts conclude with Jesus' admonition not to make the healing known. Jesus tells the once-blind man not even to go into the village. The distinctive aspect of the healing of the blind man of Bethsaida—not only in Mark but in all the Gospels—is a healing process of two stages. Blindness and sight are frequently used symbolically in the ancient (and modern!) world. The two-stage transition from one to the other increases the symbolic possibilities.

The two-stage healing of the blind man outside Bethsaida is almost universally recognized as a pivotal scene in the Markan Gospel. It is generally linked symbolically with the two scenes that follow it: the "confession" of Peter (8:27-30) and Jesus' first passion prediction (8:31-33). Peter "sees" that Jesus is the Messiah, the Christ. But he fails to "see" that, as the Christ, Jesus must suffer. To heal Peter (and perhaps the implied reader) of that blindness will require a second stage, the second half of Mark's Gospel. The narrative clearly supports this reading.

But the two-stage healing of blindness is a transitional scene, and it also has symbolic links with the scenes that precede it. Jesus has been working in two stages all along: parables and explanations, Jewish healings and gentile healings, Jewish feeding and gentile feeding. The duality of the Markan Jesus' technique reflects the twofoldness of the Markan implied author's convictions: Jesus is Messiah for both Jews and Gentiles; Jesus is Messiah of power and suffering service. To see that is to see everything clearly.

Conclusion

The implied author of Mark is a storyteller—and a masterful one. For this reason, narrative criticism seems an especially appropriate approach to reading and interpreting the Gospel of Mark. Narrative critics seek to learn more about *how* the story means, that is, how the implied author uses characters, settings, plot, and rhetoric to communicate meaning. If such study can help us align ourselves with the implied reader, our own roles as real readers—and re-readers—of Mark will surely be enriched. We will look intently—and see.

FURTHER READING
General

CHATMAN, Seymour. *Story and Discourse: Narrative Structure in Fiction and Film*. Ithaca, N.Y.: Cornell University Press, 1978. A classic presentation of the elements of "story" and "discourse" that has been widely influential in biblical narrative criticism; includes thorough discussions of plot, setting, characters, implied author, types of narrators (covert versus overt), and point of view, with examples drawn from secular literature and film.

GENETTE, Gérard. *Narrative Discourse: An Essay in Method.* Translated by Jane E. Lewin. Ithaca, N.Y.: Cornell University Press, 1980. An attempt at a comprehensive, systematic theory of narrative and simultaneously a study of Proust's *A la recherche du temps perdu,* which focuses on careful delineations of the order, duration, and frequency of narrated events and the mood and voice of narratives.

RIMMON-KENAN, Shlomith. *Narrative Fiction: Contemporary Poetics.* London and New York: Metheun, 1983. A clear, concise, and very helpful overview of narrative aspects: events, characters, time, characterization, focalization, levels and voices, speech representation, the text and its reading, with examples drawn from various periods and various national literatures.

Biblical

BERLIN, Adele. *Poetics and Interpretation of Biblical Narrative.* Sheffield, Eng.: The Almond Press, 1983. A thoughtful and accessible discussion of aspects of (theoretical) poetics and (practical) interpretation of Hebrew Bible narratives, focusing on character and characterization in the stories of David's wives and on point of view; includes also an extended analysis of the book of Ruth and a reflection of the interrelations of literary and historical methods.

CULPEPPER, R. Alan. *Anatomy of the Fourth Gospel: A Study in Literary Design.* Philadelphia: Fortress Press, 1983. A thorough and rich reading of the narrative of John's Gospel, exploring, in turn, the narrator and point of view, narrative time, plot, characters, implicit commentary, and the implied reader.

FUNK, Robert W. *The Poetics of Biblical Narrative.* Sonoma,Calif.: Polebridge Press, 1988. An extensive presentation of narrative grammar, how narratives work; especially strong in analyzing smaller segments within narratives.

KELBER, Werner H. *Mark's Story of Jesus.* Philadelphia: Fortress Press, 1979. A brief, dramatic retelling of the Markan narrative focused on the negative portrayal of the disciples.

KINGSBURY, Jack Dean. *Matthew as Story.* 2d ed. Philadelphia: Fortress Press, 1988. A literary critical reading of Matthew with emphasis on the plot or story line of Jesus and the story line of the disciples.

MALBON, Elizabeth Struthers. *Narrative Space and Mythic Meaning in Mark.* New Voices in Biblical Studies. San Francisco: Harper & Row, 1986. The Biblical Seminar 13. Sheffield, Eng.: Sheffield Academic Press, 1991. A detailed analysis of the spatial settings of Mark based on a (literary) structuralist methodology and a suggestion of their significance to the Gospel as a whole.

MOORE, Stephen D. *Literary Criticism and the Gospels: The Theoretical Challenge.* New Haven and London: Yale University Press, 1989. A lively, scholarly critique of narrative criticism and reader-response criticism from the point of view of deconstruction and postmodernism; includes an extensive bibliography.

PETERSEN, Norman R. *Literary Criticism for New Testament Critics.* Guides to Biblical Scholarship. Philadelphia: Fortress Press, 1978. A rich, yet accessible introduction to literary criticism of the New Testament; includes helpful discussions of the differing approaches of historical and literary criticism, contributions of structuralism, story time and plotted time in Mark, and narrative world and real world in Luke-Acts.

POLAND, Lynn M. *Literary Criticism and Biblical Hermeneutics: A Critique of Formalist Approaches*. American Academy of Religion Academy Series 48. Chico, Calif.: Scholars Press, 1985. A critique of the New Critical influence on biblical studies, focusing on examinations of the work of John Dominic Crossan, Dan Otto Via, Jr., and Hans W. Frei.

POWELL, Mark Allan. *What is Narrative Criticism?* Guides to Biblical Scholarship. Minneapolis: Fortress Press, 1990. A clear and inclusive introduction to narrative criticism of the Gospels, moving from a sketch of the relationship of narrative criticism to other critical approaches (biblical and secular) to an overview of narrative elements (story and discourse, events, characters, settings).

RHOADS, David, and Michie, Donald. *Mark as Story: An Introduction to the Narrative of a Gospel*. Philadelphia: Fortress Press, 1982. An indispensable and inviting introduction to narrative criticism of Mark, focusing on the rhetoric, settings, plot, and characters; includes a fresh translation of Mark.

TANNEHILL, Robert C. *The Narrative Unity of Luke-Acts: A Literary Interpretation*. Vol. 1, *The Gospel according to Luke*. Philadelphia: Fortress Press, 1986. An exploration of the narrative and theological unity of Luke, with emphasis on the shifting and developing relationships between Jesus and other individual characters and groups of characters.

3

Reader-Response Criticism:

Figuring Mark's Reader

ROBERT M. FOWLER

What or Who Determines
the Meaning of Mark?

What is the meaning of the Gospel of Mark? In what direction do we look to
find it? What kind of meaning are we looking for? Is the meaning of the Gospel
the author's conscious intention in writing the text? Is the meaning of the
Gospel whatever it tells us about the historical circumstances in which it was
produced? Can the meaning of the Gospel be as simple as a basic understanding
of the language in which it was written? Or is the meaning a more sophisticated
understanding of the way in which the story was constructed, its plot, characters,
and settings?

Take, for example, the two extraordinarily similar episodes of the feeding
of the five thousand, in Mark 6:30-44, and the feeding of the four thousand,
in Mark 8:1-10. What is the meaning of these two stories? Even if we agree

that their meaning is historical in nature, there are still several ways to understand them. Perhaps they serve to report the fact that Jesus fed two different crowds, on two different occasions, with just a few loaves and fishes. Perhaps Jesus fed only one crowd on one occasion, but the story was told so often that different versions developed, two of which Mark (accidentally?) includes in his Gospel. Maybe the real significance of the two feeding stories is the historical insight that ancient people generally believed in the powers of holy men and women to manipulate the forces of nature, that Jesus was regarded as such a holy man, and consequently that stories such as these would inevitably be told about him. If the meaning of the stories is taken to be theological instead of historical, other possibilities appear. Could the feeding stories be symbolic allusions to the Lord's Supper? Still further down that same path, is Mark's Gospel suggesting what John's Gospel clearly does, that Jesus himself is the "bread of life," "the bread that came down from heaven" (John 6:25-59)? Instead of historical or theological meaning, could the meaning of the feeding stories be literary in nature? Do the feeding stories in Mark contribute to the advancement of the plot of the narrative? Do they reveal the character of Jesus or the Twelve? Could the setting of both feeding stories (in the desert, like Moses and the Israelite tribes in Exodus[1]) be the most significant thing about the stories?

Whether we take the meaning of Mark to be historical, theological, or literary, all of these approaches focus on the written text. They presume that some kind of meaning is bound to the text and waiting there to be discovered. These approaches take the text of the Gospel of Mark either as a window through which to look out on historical events, theological ideas, or cultural attitudes, or as a house of mirrors, reflecting internally the grammar, syntax, plot, characters, and settings of the narrative.

All of these perspectives assume that meaning is available in or through the text, independent of the reader. What if we take seriously the role of the reader in determining the meaning of the text? Regardless of whether the text is considered a window or a mirror, does it matter who is doing the looking, and when, where, why, and how they are looking? What if we consider meaning not as a property of the text itself, but rather as a function of the experience of the reader in the act of reading the text? What if, instead of considering meaning as something static, unchanging, and preceding the reading experience, we consider it the dynamic, ever-changing creation of the reader in the act of reading?

A text does not come to us wearing its meaning, like a campaign button, on its lapel. The reader-response critic argues that whatever meaning is and wherever it is found the reader is ultimately responsible for determining meaning. In reader-response criticism, meaning is no longer considered a given. It is not something ready-made, buried in the text, and just waiting to be uncovered. Rather, it is something produced in the act of reading through the

---

1. John 6:25-59 explicitly compares Jesus' feeding of the multitude with Moses' providing manna for the Israelites during their wilderness wanderings. Many interpreters of Mark have suggested that a similar allusion, however vague, is present also in Mark.

unique interaction of the text and the particular reader doing the reading, at a particular moment, from a particular slant. Instead of *What* determines the meaning of a text? reader-response critics prefer the question, *Who* determines the meaning? The immediate answer is "the reader," which in turn leads to further questions. When, where, why, and how does the reader read?

Reader-response criticism is only one among many forms of criticism today that advocate a change in our understanding of meaning. A shift is taking place, away from a static, objective meaning bound to the text to a more subjective meaning experienced by the reader in the temporal flow of the reading experience. Some of the other approaches to the Gospel of Mark introduced in this book advocate, to a greater or lesser degree, a similar shift in focus to the reader and the reading experience. Approaches such as feminist and deconstructive criticism have explicitly focused attention on the reader and the reading experience. They could be described as first cousins of reader-response criticism. Even approaches that claim to be text-centered—narrative criticism, for example—nevertheless talk a great deal about the reader and the experience of reading. Many kinds of biblical and literary criticism today are closely related to reader-response criticism.

Who Is the Reader and
What Happens in the Reading Experience?

Reader-response critics talk a lot about the reader and the experience of reading, but who is this reader, and what happens when this reader reads? One way to understand the reader of Mark's Gospel is to think of him or her as the average, everyday reader on the street or in the church pew, anyone who picks up the Gospel and reads it for personal enrichment or pleasure. Some reader-response critics like to study the responses of such average readers. Then again, we can think of the reader of Mark as the informed, expert reader. An expert reader is someone who has received specialized training in order to be able to probe the Gospel more deeply than the average reader. Many reader-response critics are concerned about how informed, expert readers read.

A similar distinction made by the literary critic George Steiner between "the reader" and "the critic" is helpful. What Steiner means by "the reader" is someone who honors, reveres, and "serves" the text she or he is reading. What he means by "the critic" is someone who probes, questions, challenges, and "masters" the text.[2] Both roles are common in the church (laypersons are usually readers and clergy are often critics). They are definitely acted out in the college or seminary classroom (students in introductory Bible courses tend to be readers, and their professors tend to be critics). This book is written by critics in the hope that it will help our readers to read and to talk about their reading experience more thoughtfully. The critic aims to deepen and enrich the experience of the reader. Some of our readers may even become critics themselves.

2. George Steiner, "'Critic'/'Reader,'" *New Literary History* 10 (1979): 423–52.

However, both readers and critics read the Gospel of Mark, so what difference, if any, is there between their reading experiences?

Both the reader and the critic of the Bible have their reading experience shaped by the communities of which they are members. Many average readers of the Bible are members of churches or synagogues that have given them some explicit and much implicit instruction in how to read the Bible "correctly." Depending on the beliefs, presuppositions, and style of the religious community, its members may approach the Bible with a fairly clear idea of what they should find there. People tend to find in the Bible what they have been taught to find there.

Critics also are members of communities that tell them how they ought to read the Bible, but often today these are academic instead of religious communities. Once upon a time, the most rigorous training in how to read the Bible was to be had only in religious communities. In the United States of the late twentieth century, however, most expert readers of the Bible receive their training in academic institutions that may or may not have an affiliation with a religious denomination. Such expert readers are typically taught to ask historical and literary questions about the Bible. They may or may not ask the old familiar religious or theological questions. Let us be clear: an expert reader can be a member both of a religious community and an academic community. Such a reader has to wear a different hat and behave in a different way when participating in the life of one community or the other. The situation is awkward, but it is a fact of life in American culture today. Many of us regularly get our costumes and behaviors mixed up because we belong to so many communities at once.

What is the difference between the kind of Bible reading taught in religious and academic communities? Generalizations here are risky, but perhaps a fair statement is that academic communities are generally more committed to open, public dialogue about the Bible than many religious communities. Why? Religious communities are obligated to remain faithful to their founding vision or to their dream of the future. Being religious does not necessarily mean being closed-minded, but religious people do have definite ideas about how life is or how it ought to be. In their common life they attempt to live out of that understanding. If they are Jews or Christians, they will read the Bible in the light of their particular experience of God in their life together. To belong to a religious community is to have a tradition to uphold.

The tradition in the academic world, however, is to question and challenge traditions. In contrast to the duty of a religious community to preserve a precious legacy, the business of an academic community is to challenge old ideas and to create new ones. Furthermore, these ideas are usually of a different sort than the ones cherished in a religious community. Today the reading experience of the expert reader of the Bible is typically more intellectual than religious.[3]

3. That is, it is more a matter of mind than heart, more cognitive than emotive. However, we must not draw too sharply the distinction between religious and academic communities or between matters of the mind and the heart. Presumably, using one's intellect does not preclude being religious, and vice versa.

Although average readers are deeply influenced by the community that has taught them how to read the Bible, nevertheless their reading experiences are frequently personal and private. Such personal experiences can be very powerful to them. Indeed, almost everyone who has learned how to read has had such personally meaningful experiences. However, even the most powerful of private reading experiences is limited, in several ways. For one thing, it often hinges upon personal history or psychology. In such cases, others in the same community may not be able to share the experience, to say nothing of outsiders. Also, everyone's knowledge of the world is limited. Everyone has biases and personal opinions. But average readers are often not aware of their own limitations and biases. Many of the average reader's experiences are based on presuppositions and opinions that have never been questioned or even acknowledged. The average reader may also be limited by having read only a narrow range of literature, perhaps a mere handful of favorite texts. For example, some Christian churches teach their members that the Bible is the only literature a Christian should read, a restriction that most of the authors of the biblical books themselves would probably find unnecessarily severe.

The expert reader, by contrast, believes that to read well one must first read widely and deeply. The more literature and more kinds of literature one has read, the better equipped one is to read with skill and insight. In order to read the Bible well, reading widely outside the Bible helps. Moreover, expert readers try to be constantly aware of the limitations and biases of all readers, most especially their own. One of the best ways to learn about one's limitations and biases in reading is to submit one's reading experience to the scrutiny and criticism of other readers. The community of readers to which one belongs can render great service here. Average readers may challenge each other, but expert readers must do so. They probe, question, and challenge, not only the text they are reading, but other critics as well, thereby gaining greater insight into one another and into the text being read.

The average reader often does not talk about reading at all. To him, reading is such a personal matter that he may feel uncomfortable talking about it. The expert reader, however, talks passionately about reading. Whether we realize it or not, whenever we open ourselves up and talk with other people about our reading experience, we are acting as a critic or expert reader. "The reader" and "the critic" are actually roles that we have all acted out from time to time. When an average reader chooses to talk about his reading experience, he is slipping for a moment into the role of critic. When a critic grows weary of talking about reading, she may relax and just savor reading for a while.

Other characteristics further distinguish the expert reader or critic. Unlike the average reader, who may or may not know about others' reading experiences, the expert reader makes it her business to know what other people have experienced as they have read. The expert reader of Mark, for example, is familiar with the history of the reading of Mark's Gospel, sometimes called its *reception history*, some of which was discussed in chapter 1. Consequently, the expert reader is familiar with the problems, questions, and puzzles that generations of readers have encountered. Expert readers are acutely aware that they are participating in an age-old conversation—often an argument!—about what happens when we read a particular text. One of the major goals of an introductory course in the Gospels is to introduce beginning students to the Gospels' reception history, so that they, too, may participate in the ongoing conversation.

Critics also talk about imaginary, ideal readers of the texts they discuss. Because expert readers are conscious of participating in a centuries-long history of reading, when they talk about the reader they are often thinking about an imaginary, ideal reader who is familiar with this entire reading history. Critics often write as if they themselves were all-knowing ideal readers, but this pose is always a fiction; no flesh-and-blood reader ever really becomes this imaginary superreader.

Another kind of ideal reader is the reader or hearer of the story that we can imagine the Gospel of Mark itself suggests. The most common labels for the imaginary reader or listener in the text of Mark are *implied reader* and *narratee*, terms that were already introduced in chapter 2. Much reader-response criticism of biblical texts has concentrated on discerning the features of the implied reader or the narratee of each text. Some biblical scholars have argued that this approach might be a fresh, new way to gain historical insights into early Christian readers. In this direction lie all the usual pitfalls of historical research, chief among them the temptation to assume that the ancients were just like us. In chapter 6 David Rhoads discusses the growing body of knowledge about how different people in first-century Mediterranean cultures were from ourselves. Therefore, we should be cautious in making claims about how first-century readers read Mark's Gospel. Admitting that ultimately the reader whose reading experience one is talking about is really one's own self is probably wiser.

Even if we admit that the implied reader and narratee are our own imaginative constructions, we can still imagine them in a multitude of ways. For example, we can imagine the implied reader or the narratee either as entities suspended in the amber of the ancient text or as lively and dynamic roles recreated and performed anew every time a real reader reads. Some kinds of literary criticism of the Bible discuss the reader in the former, static style, in which meaning is still regarded as something frozen in the text. The reader-response critic, however, emphasizes the reading experience through time. When the reader-response critic discusses the implied reader or narratee, she will return constantly to the question of what happens in the temporal flow of language in the act of reading. There are many illuminating ways of talking about the temporal experience of reading, as we shall now see.

Figuring Out the Experience of Reading Mark

All language is based on figures of speech. Words never communicate perfectly to reveal exactly how things *are*. The best we can ever do is to use figures of speech that hint at what things are *like*. It follows that the experience of reading can never be captured fully in words. As we talk about our experience of reading, we can use a variety of metaphors or other figures of speech. In the rest of this chapter I shall apply several of these metaphors to the experience of reading Mark's Gospel.

These metaphors are tools in the reader-response critic's tool kit. In the sections that follow, I shall introduce a handful of these tools and demonstrate how to use them on interesting passages in Mark. I need to stress that only a handful of tools are introduced and demonstrated. As the critic gains experience, she will want to collect a more complete set than I shall discuss here. In addition, I need to stress that I shall not discuss any section of Mark at length, for several reasons. For one thing, verse-by-verse discussions of the entire Gospel are readily available in commentaries on Mark, and there is little need to produce more of that kind of discussion here. Moreover, extended discussions can be dull because the critic has to pretend that every verse is as weighty as every other verse, and we all know that is not true. To the contrary, we all like to talk about the high points or challenging moments of the reading experience. Reader-response critics like to focus their attention on the pivotal moments in reading that have provoked the most arguments through the years. So, these few tools are introduced to you, and their use only briefly illustrated, to entice you to use them yourself to talk about your experience of reading Mark's Gospel. Add your own tools to the kit and use them on the many passages not discussed in this chapter.

The Temporal Experience of Reading

To talk about the temporal experience of reading requires using images about time. In fact, reader-response critics use a variety of time or movement figures of speech to talk about the "temporal," "kinetic," "dynamic," "flow" of reading. As already suggested, reader-response critics are trying to lay aside images of static, fixed meaning embedded in texts. They favor instead images of dynamic processes that focus on the reader in the act of reading. The "response" in reader-response criticism is always a fluid, shifting response, mutating throughout the time of the reading experience.[4]

Assume that we are reading a sequence of words (or sentences, or episodes, etc.), A, B, C, D, E, and so forth. Our understanding of and attitude toward what we are reading changes at each step along the way.[5] For example, at point A we may have a vague idea of what lies ahead at point C. At point C our suspicions about C may be confirmed, denied, or revised. By the time we reach point E, our attitude toward C may be changed yet again, in retrospect. Or again, point A may appear one way at point A, another way from the vantage point of B, another way at point C, another way at point D, and so forth. In brief, the reading experience, if we stop to think about it, is full of twists and turns, surprises and developments. Our minds change constantly as we read. As our minds change, meaning changes.

4. Stanley Fish, *Is There a Text in This Class? The Authority of Interpretive Communities* (Cambridge and London: Harvard University Press, 1980), 26.
5. Ibid., 27.

Many traditional approaches to interpretation unconsciously hurry past the reading experience in order to get to its conclusion. Discussions of narratives often look back upon the story from the vantage point of the end of the reading experience. The end of reading—moment Z, let us call it—may be a very important moment, but it is just one moment among many. We have all read stories that were so enjoyable that we were sad to finish them. Endings are often anticlimactic, in contrast to the intriguing journey that led up to the ending. Like many things in life, the trip itself is often more interesting than the arrival. This approach does not minimize the importance of the final moment in the reading experience, which may be a moment of illumination or power. However, one of the virtues of reader-response criticism is that it encourages us to take seriously every moment of the reading experience, not just the final moment. Accordingly, all of the metaphors that will be introduced here are "temporal experience of reading" metaphors. They try to do some justice to our journey through the text.

Because reader-response criticism is not primarily interested in historical meaning, the fact that the emphasis on the temporal experience of reading can help us to understand better the experience of first-century audiences of the Gospel may come as a surprise. In antiquity all reading was done out loud, even when a person read in solitude. A piece of religious literature such as Mark's Gospel would typically have been read to an assembly of interested listeners. The Gospel would not have been read silently, the way average readers are taught to read today. It would not have been scrutinized with a critical eye, the way critics analyze texts today, patiently flipping printed pages back and forth. Rather, the typical first-century experience of the Gospel would have been to hear it performed orally, probably in a continuous recitation and probably from beginning to end. The first encounters with the Gospel were thus temporal experiences of oral performance. Nineteen centuries later, people can still hear portions of Mark read in public worship, but the portions are usually so small that the cumulative effects that are possible in an extended reading are lost. A wide gulf separates first-century hearing of the Gospel from twentieth-century silent reading of it, but reader-response criticism's exploration of the temporal experience of reading is a valuable resource that can deepen our appreciation of the temporal experience of the first-century oral performance of Mark.[6]

Looking Forward, Looking Back

We have already used one metaphor for the reading experience that is virtually universal: as we read we constantly "look forward" and "look back." That is,

6. A good way to gain insight into first-century oral performance of the Gospel is to perform it orally today. For a performance of Mark's Gospel using a contemporary American English translation, see the videotaped performance by David Rhoads (available from SELECT, 2199 E. Main St., Columbus, OH 43209). Rhoads performs the entire Gospel of Mark from memory, an astonishing feat today, but commonplace in antiquity.

as we read we try to anticipate what lies ahead, and we constantly review and reevaluate what we have already read. In order to make maximum sense of what we are reading, the reader must ponder not just the present moment of reading, but how the present moment relates to moments remembered from the past and anticipated in the future.

Writing is hard work, and so is reading. Wolfgang Iser suggests that the reader's toil in constantly reviewing the past and previewing the future is like the original creative struggle of the author in writing the text: "We look forward, we look back, we decide, we change our decisions, we form expectations, we are shocked by their nonfulfillment, we question, we muse, we accept, we reject; this is the dynamic process of recreation."[7]

Consider the senses that are evoked by our metaphors. Looking forward and looking back are visual metaphors, playing on the sense of sight. One could just as easily substitute an acoustic metaphor, playing on the sense of hearing: a reader "hears" whispers, faint sounds, or maybe trumpet fanfares of what lies ahead, and echoes, loud or soft, clear or indistinct, of what has preceded.

What are some good examples of moments in reading the Gospel of Mark where the reader looks forward or back? When considering the temporal experience of reading, we can talk about both small-scale, micromoments in reading or large-scale macromoments. We shall look at some micromoments first, the frequent occurrence of "immediately" (*euthys*) and "again" (*palin*) in the discourse of the narrative.

Everyone who has read Mark's Gospel carefully has observed that the author seems to make everything in the story happen "immediately" (the Greek word is *euthys*). Sometimes this word occurs in one sentence after another.

> 1:18 And *immediately* they left their nets and followed him. . . .
>
> 1:20 And *immediately* he called them. . . .
>
> 1:21 And *immediately* on the Sabbath he entered the synagogue and taught. . . .
>
> 1:23 And *immediately* there was in their synagogue a man with an unclean spirit. . . .[8]

The author so overworks this word that embarrassed translators scramble to introduce as much variety as possible in their English translations. They may translate *euthys* as "immediately," "at once," "just as," "just then," or "as soon as," or sometimes in frustration they just leave the word out of the translation altogether.

In current literary discussions of Mark, this quirk in the author's writing style is credited with setting a mood of urgency for the actions of the characters in the story being told. Rather than addressing the mood it sets for the action in the story, however, the reader-response critic prefers to ask how the frequent

---

7. Wolfgang Iser, "The Reading Process: A Phenomenological Approach," *New Literary History* 3 (1972): 293.

8. The translation used here is the Revised Standard Version (RSV).

*euthys*es affect the reader. What kind of storytelling strategy is at work here? What does having to negotiate this steady flow of *immediately*s do to the reader?

To do full justice to this question, we would have to examine each individual instance of *immediately*. We would have to ask ourselves how to relate each instance to moments before and after in the reading experience. The reader-response critic will not automatically assume that each *immediately* works the same way. Nevertheless, we might hazard the generalization that the cumulative effect of all the *euthys*es is to drill into the reader that this narrative has relentless forward thrust. Readers who want to read this narrative must jump on the narrative bandwagon, hold on tight, and be attentive to what lies ahead. *Euthys* never says much about *what* to look forward to; it just reminds us to keep looking forward.

Somewhat like *euthys*, but pointing in the opposite direction, the Greek word *palin* stops us dead in our tracks and demands that we look backward momentarily. In Mark *palin* is usually best translated as "again." Unlike *euthys*, which points forward but vaguely, *palin* usually points us backward to a fairly certain moment earlier in the reading of the narrative. If we stop to think, usually we can recall the previous moment to which the *palin* is pointing us.[9]

To cite just one example, in Mark 8:1 the narrator introduces a scene that should easily remind the reader of the setting for the earlier episode of the feeding of the five thousand in Mark 6:30-44:

> In those days when there was *again* a great crowd without anything to eat, he called his disciples and said to them, "I have compassion for the crowd, because they have been with me now for three days and have nothing to eat. If I send them away hungry to their homes, they will faint on the way—and some of them have come from a great distance" (8:1-3).[10]

Countless readers have puzzled over why the disciples in Mark seem so dense. When Jesus first invites the disciples to feed a hungry crowd in Mark 6:37, they do not know what to do. They have no understanding of what Jesus is capable of doing to satisfy the needs of the crowd. Any reader, however, is bound to understand better than the disciples, especially after Jesus proceeds to feed five thousand men with just a few loaves and fishes. Mark 8:1-3 reminds the reader of this earlier episode. These verses alert the reader to anticipate a second feeding incident in the episode about to unfold. In contrast to the reader's recollection of the past feeding incident and anticipation of another, in Mark

---

9. Frans Neirynck, with Theo Hansen and Frans Van Segbroeck, has counted twenty-eight instances of *palin* in Mark, nearly all of which point back clearly to an antecedent moment in the reading experience; see *The Minor Agreements of Matthew and Luke against Mark with a Cumulative List*, Bibliotheca ephemeridum theologicarum lovaniensium 37 (Leuven: Leuven University Press, 1974), 276–77.

10. The translation used here is the New Revised Standard Version (NRSV), with emphasis added.

8:4 the disciples reveal to the reader that they learned nothing from the earlier feeding incident and therefore are oblivious to the possibility that Jesus might do it all over again: "His disciples replied, 'How can one feed these people with bread here in the desert?' " (Mark 8:4). How could they *not* know, the reader may say to herself, given their experience back in Mark 6:30-44? The reader-response critic recognizes here and elsewhere that Mark's Gospel is narrated in such a way that the reader perceives and understands what characters in the story do not.

The two feeding stories in Mark 6 and 8 are a classic example of the widespread repetition or duality in Mark. What is the meaning of such repetition? Some possible historical solutions to the problem were listed previously. But what if we are not content with any of these possible historical meanings of the dual stories? What if we suspect that the meaning of these stories lies less in ancient history and more in how they strike the reader who must encounter them now in the act of reading? As you might anticipate, the reader-response critic will ask, "What happens when the reader reads seemingly repetitious material?" And again, the reader-response critic will want to consider every instance on its own terms because the rhetorical possibilities of repetition (as with any storytelling strategy) are endless. By repetition, the reader's insight into the narrative can be built up or solidified; repetition can also weary us, confuse us, or make us suspicious. Repetition giveth and repetition taketh away. It is always wise to consider each moment of reading on its own merits.

Operating at a slightly wider scope than *euthys* and *palin*, the reader looks forward whenever Jesus predicts something and looks back whenever one of his predictions is fulfilled. In Mark's story Jesus can accurately predict the future. This characteristic of Jesus is so prominent in the story that only with difficulty can we shift our attention away from the *story* to the *discourse*—the way the story is told by the storyteller and received by the reader, as explained in the previous chapter.

Perhaps the boldest predictions uttered in the story are Jesus' three predictions of his impending passion, or suffering and death. These three passion predictions (Mark 8:31; 9:31; 10:32-34) provide the framework around which the central chapters 8–10 are constructed. The three predictions are offered so boldly, so clearly, and above all so frequently that no reader can fail to have his expectations for the rest of the narrative shaped by them. As we read on to the end of the Gospel, the reader can have little doubt about what lies ahead. Once again, the reader experiences an ironic tension between what he understands about the story and what the characters in the story do not understand. No one in the story seems to learn anything from these predictions (see Mark 8:32-33; 9:31-34, 38-39; 10:32, 35-45). The reader, by contrast, cannot help but be educated by these signposts to future moments in the narrative.

Although Jesus issues his predictions boldly, their fulfillment is seldom observed by characters in the story (by contrast, see Luke 24:6-8, 44). Rather, the reader, at the level of the discourse, is left to connect the fulfillment back to the prediction. A good example may be found in Jesus' trial before the Sanhedrin, the council of chief priests and elders in Jerusalem (Mark 14:53-72). The entire scene fulfills Jesus' passion predictions, especially the third and most detailed prediction in 10:32-34. Jesus' tormenters spit upon him, strike him, and taunt him to "prophesy" (14:65), not realizing that Jesus had "prophesied" their actions. However, the reader understands. Still further along in the same passage, Peter saves his own life by denying Jesus three times, just as Jesus had said he would (14:29-31; see also 8:35-38). Apparently Peter's denial is taking place at the same time that Jesus is being taunted by his tormenters, thus the irony that several different predictions by Jesus are being fulfilled simultaneously. Peter eventually remembers that Jesus had predicted his triple betrayal (14:72), a rare instance of a character in the story making a connection between present and past. Only the reader habitually makes the connections between past, present, and future in this narrative. The characters in the story, with the exception of Jesus, generally do not make these connections. Only the reader *can* make them, thanks to the resources provided to the reader alone by the discourse of the narrative.

To sum up, "prediction and fulfillment" has typically been treated as a function of the character Jesus within the story of Mark's Gospel. The reader-response critic would rather take prediction and fulfillment as a function of the experience of reading Mark's Gospel. Prediction and fulfillment is almost never observed in Mark's story; it is observed frequently in the experience of reading Mark's story.

Filling Gaps

Another metaphor for the reading experience has been popularized by Wolfgang Iser: as we read, we encounter "gaps" in the narrative that must be "filled."[11] Any narrative always has holes, places where something is missing. Reading is not only a matter of making sense of what is there in the narrative but also what is not there. Filling is not the only way to handle a gap. Sometimes we can rig a simple bridge across the gap, we might be able to jump across it, or we might exercise prudence by walking around it. The gaps that appear in the path we walk through the reading experience must be negotiated somehow, but readers often have considerable freedom to handle them as they see fit. Many of the arguments between readers are over how best to deal with gaps in the texts we read. As long as there are gaps (which is forever), readers will argue about how to handle them.

Once again, we can look at some small-scale examples and work our way up. At the level of grammar and syntax, in Mark's Gospel the subjects and objects of sentences are unspecified in many places.[12] In such cases the reader is left to figure out who is who in the sentence. A Greek composition instructor would probably assign Mark a poor grade in style and grammar for such a performance. In Mark's defense, however, his unspecified subjects and objects usually present little difficulty to the reader, and sometimes the reader is caught

11. Wolfgang, Iser, *The Act of Reading: A Theory of Aesthetic Response* (Baltimore and London: Johns Hopkins University Press, 1978), 167–72.
12. Neirynck, *Minor Agreements*, 261–72.

for a moment in a most intriguing ambiguity. Whether the grammatical gap is intriguing or merely awkward, it represents a challenge to the reader that, however minor, must be negotiated before the reading experience can continue. It guarantees the involvement of the reader in the ongoing business of making sense of the text. This kind of gap may not be stylish, nevertheless it is often engaging, effective rhetoric.

Although many comments by reader-response critics focus on ideal, hypothetical readers, we know a great deal about how actual readers have negotiated Mark's gaps. Two ancient readers who have left us evidence of their gap filling in Mark are the authors of the Gospels of Matthew and Luke. Most scholars believe that Matthew and Luke produced their Gospels by rewriting Mark's, so their Gospels may be understood as implicit reports of their experiences of reading Mark. Just like us, Matthew and Luke had to steer their way through the discourse of Mark's narrative. We are lucky that they left a record of their response to their experience of reading Mark. If we read Mark's Gospel side by side with Matthew and Luke, we can easily find "gaps" in Mark that have been "filled" by Matthew, Luke, or both.

- Mark 1:14 reads: "Now after John was arrested, Jesus came into Galilee, proclaiming the good news of God." A gap lies here between the arrest of John and the beginning of Jesus' preaching ministry. What connection, if any, is there between these two events? The storyteller gives us no indication, so the reader is free to imagine all sorts of connections. Without doubt, Matthew felt there had to be a connection, for in Matthew 4:12 we read: "Now when Jesus heard that John had been arrested, he withdrew to Galilee." Exactly *why* Jesus went to Galilee remains unclear, but that he went *because* of John's arrest is clear. Such minimal gap filling is often sufficient to allow us to continue reading.

- In Mark 3:6 we are told that the Pharisees and the Herodians plotted Jesus' death. Then, in 3:7 we are told that Jesus withdrew to the Sea of Galilee. Should we construct a bridge between these two comments? Matthew does bridge the gap by stating that Jesus "knew" about the plot and consequently "withdrew" (Matt 12:15).

- In Mark 3:31-35 Jesus is teaching inside a house. Next thing we know he is teaching alongside the sea (Mark 4:1). How did he suddenly get from one place to the other? Matthew fills the gap, if only slightly: "That same day Jesus went out of the house and sat beside the sea" (Matt 13:1).

- Another equally wrenching gap in Mark's narrative occurs between Mark 6:14-29, the story of the death of John the Baptist, and Mark 6:30-44, the story of the feeding of the five thousand. Mark juxtaposes these two episodes with no transition from one to the other. How the reader is to connect them, if at all, is not indicated. Matthew reworks Mark 6:30 into an explicit transition from one episode to another. In Matthew 14:12 Jesus' disciples go to tell him of John's death, which they do not in Mark, and in Matthew 14:13 Jesus hears their report, which of course he cannot in

Mark. As a result, in Matthew's Gospel, Jesus and the Twelve's withdrawal to the wilderness, where the multitude will be fed, is in direct response to the report of John's death. No such connection between the two episodes is suggested by Mark. Nevertheless, Mark does give us the gap between Mark 6:29 and 6:30, and Matthew's bridge is one reader's reasonable attempt to negotiate the gap. If we do not like Matthew's bridge, we are free to build our own.

The gap filling by Matthew and Luke is exactly what any reader must do when reading Mark's Gospel. The service provided by the reader-response critic is to alert us to what we have always done while reading but seldom stopped to think about.

Other gaps in Mark's narrative are of still larger scope. These gaps occur either in the story or in the discourse of the narrative. To spot such gaps requires recognition that story and discourse need not always go together hand in hand. If he wants to, the storyteller can leave something out of the story; if he wants to, he can leave something out of the discourse. The analogy is imperfect, but imagine yourself watching a movie in which occasionally the picture continues while the sound is turned off, and at other times the picture is blanked out while the sound continues. Some examples may help us appreciate how Mark's Gospel can function occasionally with either story or discourse turned off.

An example of a gap in the discourse may be found in Mark 4, the parable chapter. Historically, the parables of Jesus of Nazareth were surely designed to provoke and intrigue his audiences, for they still provoke and intrigue us today. The challenge of Mark 4 to the reader-response critic is to be sensitive not only to the provocation of Jesus' audience within the story, but at the same time to be attentive to how the parables strike us, the readers, who hear them thanks to the narrator's discourse. Furthermore, if we are open to the possibility that something can happen in the story that is missing from the discourse (and vice versa), then we will be in position to discover how we handle this kind of gap in Mark 4.

Mark 4 begins with the famous parable of the Sower (Mark 4:1-9). Immediately afterward, disciples approach Jesus, asking for help in understanding his parables. His response is perhaps more perplexing than the parables themselves: "And he said to them, 'To you has been given the secret of the kingdom of God, but for those outside, everything comes in parables; in order that "they may indeed look, but not perceive, and may indeed listen, but not understand; so that they may not turn again and be forgiven"'" (Mark 4:11-12). Verse 12, in which Jesus seems to say he uses parables with the purpose of preventing people from understanding him, has been a source of arguments for generations of readers. I shall deal with it further later, in considering another metaphor for the reading experience. For now I want to concentrate on Jesus' comment that his listeners have "been given the secret of the kingdom of God."

The reader has a major problem here. If we review the first four chapters of the Gospel, we cannot find the place in the story where the "secret of the kingdom of God" was given to Jesus' followers. Countless expert readers have offered countless suggestions as to when this event happened in the story, but there is no consensus solution. Average and expert readers alike want to believe that if a Gospel refers to a scene or an episode in the story, then surely the storyteller meant to narrate that scene or episode in the discourse of the narrative. In other words, is not the storyteller obliged to make all the action of the story take place on the stage, in front of our eyes? Surely Mark would not make something happen offstage, where the audience can neither see nor hear it?

As soon as the question is put this way, most readers will realize that nothing prevents the storyteller from referring to portions of the story that, for whatever reasons, he does not tell us. An analogy between Mark and a play performed on a stage may be helpful. Perhaps you have seen a play by Shakespeare in which a murder or a battle is announced on the stage after it has supposedly happened offstage, out of our sight and hearing. Similarly in storytelling, omitting from the discourse a portion of the story is a standard technique among skilled storytellers. The "giving of the secret of the Kingdom of God" is just such a gap in the discourse of Mark's Gospel. It is an allusion to an episode in the story that the storyteller declines to narrate.

Besides gaps in the discourse, Mark's story also has gaps. The stage analogy would be the scene that takes place on the stage, seemingly in full view of the characters and the audience, but the characters on stage are utterly oblivious to it; only the audience sees and hears. In such a case, as far as the characters are concerned, what happens on stage has no bearing on them. For all practical purposes it happens only for the sake of the audience. That is, in narrative terms, the only thing that is moving forward is the discourse; the story has momentarily halted.

An example of such a gap in the story is Jesus' cry from the cross in Mark 15:34-35: "At three o'clock Jesus cried out with a loud voice, 'Eloi, Eloi, lema sabachthani?' which means, 'My God, my God, why have you forsaken me?' When some of the bystanders heard it, they said, 'Listen, he is calling for Elijah'" (15:34-35). Jesus cries out to God, using the opening words of Psalm 22. But these words are not in Greek, like the rest of Mark's Gospel—they are in Aramaic! Fortunately for the Greek-speaking implied reader of the Gospel, the storyteller slips in a translation, which tells us exactly what the otherwise exotic words say: in his forsakenness, Jesus is crying out to God. The characters standing around the cross, however, do not understand what he is saying. They hear Jesus' cry as an appeal to the prophet Elijah.

So where is the gap? The gap is opened by the storyteller's parenthetical comment to the reader, which translates Jesus' words for our benefit alone. Without the translation, the Greek-speaking reader might be just as lost as those characters on the stage around the cross, who mistakenly hear Jesus cry to Elijah. They hear the same cry that we do, but whereas we are made to understand it by the storyteller's parenthetical comment, they utterly misunderstand. We have been drawn into a charmed, inner circle of understanding. The characters in the story, however, are excluded from understanding the story. As far as they are concerned, the story has halted, but without their knowledge. In Mark 15:34-35 no one in the story (except maybe Jesus) understands the story, which is to say that for them Mark 15:34-35 is a gap in the story. Only the reader outside the story understands, not so much the story as the discourse of Mark 15:34-35.

Other figures of speech may be helpful in our quest to appreciate gaps in story and discourse. Aside from the metaphor of gaps, in Mark an opaque veil often seems to have been dropped between the audience receiving the story-teller's discourse and the characters in the story. In Mark 4:11, for instance, the opaque veil seems to favor the disciples while shutting the reader of the Gospel out of the secret of the Kingdom of God. In Mark 15:34-35, on the contrary, the reader is the privileged insider while the characters in the story are excluded by a veil that prevents them from understanding what they are seeing and hearing.

Whether we use the metaphor of the gap or of the veil of exclusion, fundamental here is the distinction between the story and the discourse of a narrative. Distinguishing between story and discourse allows us to recognize the occasional possibility of having story without discourse or discourse without story. (Later we shall see that sometimes story and discourse can work simultaneously but at cross-purposes, for instances in dramatic irony.) In such cases, the reader does not so much fill gaps in the story or the discourse as endure them, or, if the veil metaphor is used, the reader must live and learn through the dropping and lifting of veils. Like so many of our reading experiences, we are so accustomed to negotiating the gaps or enduring the veil that we seldom stop to think about it.

Reconstruction

In recent years finding irony galore in the Gospels has become fashionable among biblical critics. The Gospel writers, they commonly argue, constructed their narratives with a strong ironic twist in order to intrigue their readers. Many of these discussions have been inspired by the literary critic Wayne Booth, whose insights into the rhetorical uses of irony have proven to be a rich resource for biblical critics.[13]

Booth is fascinated by the process readers go through, first to decide whether an author is being ironic, and second to figure out what the author really means to say if indeed she is using irony. Booth suggests that the process of discerning and deciphering irony can be best described by using the metaphor of "reconstruction."[14] At its most basic, an ironic utterance is one that cannot be taken at face value. The true, intended meaning of the words lies hidden somewhere behind the surface meaning. An ironic utterance is like a wobbly building standing on a shaky foundation—we cannot take it the way it stands, so the reader must dismantle and reconstruct the ironic edifice on a more solid footing. Booth proposes a four-step process for reconstructing the meaning of an irony.

13. Wayne C. Booth, *A Rhetoric of Irony* (Chicago: University of Chicago Press, 1974).
14. Ibid., 10–14, 33–44.

"*Step one*. The reader is required to reject the literal meaning."[15] An ironic utterance is incongruous or inconsistent, either within itself or with something else. This incongruity or inconsistency makes accepting it at face value impossible. So the first step is for the reader to decide that the author does not mean exactly what she says.

"*Step two*. Alternative interpretations or explanations are tried out."[16] If the author does not mean what she says, what could she possibly mean? Did she misspeak? Was she careless? Has she forgotten what she has said or done elsewhere in the narrative? Has she gone mad? What could she possibly be up to?

"*Step three*. A decision must therefore be made about the author's knowledge or beliefs."[17] This step is pivotal. The reader must step back and make a judgment about the author. What does the author really think? Where does she really stand? What are her true convictions and motives? Only with such a judgment in hand can the reader hope to reconstruct what really lies behind the irony.

"*Step four*. Having made a decision about the knowledge or beliefs of the speaker, we can finally choose a new meaning or cluster of meanings with which we can rest secure."[18] This step is the reconstruction proper. Having decided where the author really stands, the reader can dismantle the ironic utterance and reconstruct it. The result is, Booth says, a "stable" new construction of meaning.

Turning to examples, Booth himself discusses a much-discussed instance of irony in Mark, the ironic mockery hurled at Jesus as he hangs dying on the cross:[19]

> Those who passed by derided him, shaking their heads and saying, "Aha! You who would destroy the temple and build it in three days, save yourself, and come down from the cross!" In the same way the chief priests, along with the scribes, were also mocking him among themselves and saying, "He saved others; he cannot save himself. Let the Messiah, the King of Israel, come down from cross now, so that we many see and believe." Those who were crucified with him also taunted him (Mark 15:29-32).

Exploring Booth's four-step process in detail should not be necessary here. Clearly, when Jesus' detractors call him "Messiah" and "King of Israel," they do not mean what they say. These characters do not for a second believe that Jesus is Messiah or King (step one). Indeed, the storyteller himself signals that all those surrounding Jesus are "deriding," "mocking," and "taunting" him (step three). The conclusion is easy to draw: everyone is heaping verbal abuse on a dying man (step four).

Thus far we have identified and reconstructed *verbal irony* in the crucifixion scene. At the same time, however, *dramatic irony* is at work here. As the name

15. Ibid., 10.
16. Ibid., 11.
17. Ibid.
18. Ibid., 12.
19. Ibid., 28–29.

suggests, verbal irony is an ironic utterance, such as the words said in mockery at the cross. Dramatic irony is ironic incongruity in situations or events in a narrative. It is a classic technique used by playwrights in dramas written for the stage. In the theater, dramatic irony occurs when the audience recognizes and comprehends an ironic incongruity between what the characters on the stage know or understand and what the audience in the seats knows or understands. In a narrative such as the Gospel of Mark, dramatic irony typically involves an incongruity between what is known or understood by characters at the level of the story and what is known or understood by the reader at the level of discourse.

Although the process of perceiving and fathoming dramatic irony is similar to that for verbal irony, Booth's reconstruction metaphor works better for verbal irony. With verbal irony, we can often reconstruct "what the person really meant to say," and thus arrive at a stable, reconstructed meaning. With dramatic irony, however, the ironic incongruity is one of circumstances and events, not necessarily of words, and once the reader has understood the dramatic irony of circumstances or events, it does not go away. Indeed, once the dramatic irony is grasped by the reader, its ironic tension may grow in magnitude. Dramatic irony, like verbal irony, needs to be figured out, if not entirely reconstructed, but dramatic irony continues to reverberate even after it has been comprehended.

The dramatic irony in Mark 15:29-32 is that, unknown to the mockers at the foot of the cross, Jesus *really is* the Christ, the King of Israel. Ironically, the words they use to insult him are the truest and best possible description of him (step four). They do not realize this fact, however. Only the reader of the Gospel is in position to understand what the characters in the story do not understand. The entire experience of reading Mark's Gospel up to this point has prepared the reader to see the deeper truth: for the author of this Gospel, Jesus is exactly who the mockers think he is not (step three). Whereas the verbal irony in the crucifixion scene is openly signaled as such by the storyteller, the accompanying dramatic irony is unannounced. The reader has to recognize and come to terms with it entirely on her own. This irony represents a great challenge to the reader, but it is at the same time a tremendous expression of trust by the author in the reader's ability to figure things out for herself.

Other verbal ironies are found on the lips of characters in the story. In the passion narrative especially, many words spoken by characters are ironic:

- Judas calls Jesus "rabbi" (my teacher), kisses him, thereby betraying him (14:45).

- Peter, confronted with being a follower of Jesus, says of Jesus: "I do not know this man you are talking about" (14:71).

- Pilate, speaking to the crowd, asks, "Do you want me to release for you the King of the Jews?" (15:9).

- The execution squad conducts a mock coronation, complete with pretend royal garb and a crown of plaited thorns, and calls out to Jesus, "Hail, King of the Jews!" (15:18).

Earlier in the Gospel, on occasion Jesus himself speaks ironically. In Mark 7:9, for example, Jesus "congratulates" the Pharisees and scribes for setting aside one of God's commandments: "You have a fine way of rejecting the commandment of God in order to keep your tradition!" Given everything that surrounds this comment by Jesus in Mark 7, there is little danger of any reader taking Jesus at face value; he does not intend to congratulate, but rather to condemn the Pharisees and scribes for substituting their own traditions for the commandments of God. The verbal irony in Mark 7:9 is easily recognized and reconstructed.

Other examples of dramatic irony in the Gospel are numerous. A favorite technique of the storyteller to create ironic tension between the story and the discourse is to narrate two almost identical incidents in which the disciples of Jesus seem to learn absolutely nothing. Wonderful examples of these matched pairs of stories are the stilling of the storm in Mark 4:35-41 and the walking on the water in Mark 6:45-52, the feeding of the five thousand in Mark 6:30-44 and the feeding of the four thousand in 8:1-10, and the two incidents in which Jesus welcomes and embraces children in Mark 9:35-37 and 10:13-16. Let us examine this last pair of episodes.

> He sat down, called the twelve, and said to them, "Whoever wants to be first must be last of all and servant of all." Then he took a little child and put it among them; and taking it in his arms, he said to them, "Whoever welcomes one such child in my name welcomes me, and whoever welcomes me welcomes not me but the one who sent me" (9:35-37).

> People were bringing little children to him in order that he might touch them; and the disciples spoke sternly to them. But when Jesus saw this, he was indignant and said to them, "Let the little children come to me; do not stop them; for it is to such as these that the kingdom of God belongs. Truly I tell you, whoever does not receive the kingdom of God as a little child will never enter it." And he took them up in his arms, laid his hands on them, and blessed them (10:13-16).

The story content of these two episodes is so similar that the temptation is to concentrate on that. The reader-response critic will resist that temptation, however, by concentrating on the reader's encounter with the storyteller's discourse.

Unlike the verbal ironies we examined in the passion narrative, no explicit signals here indicate that anyone is saying something that he does not really mean. Dramatic irony is typically more subtle than that, and consequently the business of reconstruction is less straightforward. At the level of the story, the reader easily grasps Jesus' consistent attitude toward children. Just as clear to the reader is the disciples' persistent and stubborn rejection of Jesus' example. Here we begin to detect an ironic tension between what is happening in the story and what we understand about the story thanks to the narrator's discourse.

The introduction to the first of the two episodes is already unflattering to the Twelve: they had been discussing among themselves "who was the greatest"

(9:34). Such egotism is unlikely to impress the reader favorably, especially in that the reader realizes that the disciples were debating their own greatness at the same time that Jesus was trying to instruct them about his own impending death (9:31). Jesus has death on his mind; the disciples, their own glory. In that setting Jesus embraces the child as a lesson to the self-centered disciples that instead of seeking to be great, they should seek to be "last of all and servant of all" (9:35). Accepting someone as insignificant as a child is like accepting God himself (9:37). Still, in this first of the two episodes, we may be willing to give the disciples the benefit of the doubt—perhaps they will learn their lesson. However, the reader has been instructed that the disciples stand apart from Jesus in their attitude toward children. Will they do better when a second opportunity arises?

They do not. The second episode jumps immediately into the issue of receiving or not receiving children. The disciples want to turn children away. This makes Jesus angry (10:13-14). He insists, again, that children must be embraced—the Kingdom of God belongs to them (10:14)!

The obtuseness of the disciples is quite remarkable. If we were so inclined, we could forever offer psychological explanations for the disciples' insensitivity in the story. More important to the reader-response critic, however, is observation of how our response to the two episodes is shaped by the way the storyteller narrates them to us. What allows us to recognize and reconstruct dramatic irony here? Two observations are key. First, the disciples' obtuseness and self-centeredness is already firmly established for the reader even before the first child-embracing scene unfolds. The alert reader may already be prepared to encounter insensitivity on the part of the Twelve in the first of the two scenes, to say nothing of the second. The second key is that when Jesus repeats his warm embrace of children and the disciples are, if anything, more insensitive than before, the reader is struck by the insight that the Twelve have learned nothing from their previous encounter. The reader experiences an ironic incongruity between the logical expectation that the Twelve would learn from their past mistakes and the reader's observation that they do not in fact learn a thing. The reconstruction metaphor does not work well here; although the reader may perceive and comprehend this ironic incongruity, the incongruity is not resolved or "reconstructed." Rather, the ironic tension continues to haunt the reader. That the disciples have learned nothing from their experience is solidly established. But, the average reader may ask, Why have they learned nothing? And what is it that they have not learned? The expert reader may go a step further and ask, If the disciples have learned nothing, what has allowed *us* to learn a great deal? And have we learned all that we should? A reader-response critic goes still further and observes that average and expert readers alike are dealing with a narrative whose fabric is woven with powerful ironic tensions. All readers of this narrative must work their way through ironic tensions between the story and the discourse. All readers of this narrative are regularly challenged to reconstruct irony, to the extent possible.

Besides describing the reader's encounter with irony, the reconstruction metaphor also helpfully describes many other reading experiences. Whenever the reader has to deal with incongruity or with aspects of the story or the discourse that cannot be accepted at face value, the reconstruction metaphor may help us to describe the experience of dismantling a portion of the narrative in order to reconstruct it on a firmer footing.

The Self-Consuming Artifact

Our next metaphor for the reading experience comes from one of the classic works of reader-response criticism, Stanley Fish's *Self-Consuming Artifacts*.[20] The title of the book is self-explanatory. Fish is concerned with pieces of literature that seem to say something but then take it back, or that do something to us and then undo it, in the course of the reading experience. In fact, Fish does not limit himself to a single metaphor—the text that consumes itself as we read it—but instead he includes a whole family of similar metaphors. The "self-consuming artifact," he says, is a text that "self-destructs," "self-subverts," "inverts," "undermines," "unbuilds," "reverses," "disappoints," "frustrates," "unsettles," "breaks down," "self-cannibalizes," and so forth.[21] To add my own figures to the collection, some texts operate like a knitting machine that knits but at the same time unravels what it has knitted. When you get to the end of the reading experience, although a lot of knitting has taken place, you may not have a sweater, just loose piles of yarn. Or, the self-consuming literary artifact is like a railroad locomotive and crew who tear up the track behind the locomotive in order to relay the track in front so that the locomotive can continue to roll forward. As we read, we often cover ground that can never be revisited because continuing to read requires that we leave those places behind us, sometimes forever.

Mark's narrative seldom unravels itself to the degree that Fish likes to find in seventeenth-century European literature, but at times it comes close. The examples from Mark that I wish to examine all involve surprising revelations to the reader about aspects of story or discourse that the reader could not have anticipated. The first, Mark 10:17-22, is an episode often called "the rich man"— an unfortunate label, as we shall see. At the beginning of this episode a man approaches Jesus and asks what he must do "to inherit eternal life." We know nothing about the man, so most readers will be inclined to hear him out. The question he asks is significant, and we have no reason to suppose that he is not a sincere seeker. Besides, would we not like to hear Jesus' answer to this weighty question ourselves? Jesus responds by quizzing the man about his observance of several of the Ten Commandments. The man replies that he has faithfully kept them all. The episode hurries toward its resolution, as Jesus replies: "You lack one thing; go, sell what you own, and give the money to the poor, and you will have treasure in heaven; then come, follow me." Presumably Jesus' demanding prescription strikes at the heart of the man's question.

20. Stanley E. Fish, *Self-Consuming Artifacts: The Experience of Seventeenth-Century Literature* (Berkeley, Los Angeles, and London: University of California Press, 1972).
21. This list has remarkable affinities with what Stephen Moore will have to say in chapter 4 about a "deconstructive" interpretation of the Gospel of Mark.

We cannot imagine how Jesus' words are relevant, however, until we hear the final comment by the storyteller: "When he heard this, he was shocked and went away grieving, *for he had many possessions.*" Only now do we grasp what stands between the man and eternal life: his many possessions. He is a rich man, something we had not known until the last two words of the episode. The story sets us up, encouraging us to think favorably of the man, only to pull the rug out from under us at the end. The traditional title given to the episode is unfortunate because it tips off readers to the punch line, thereby robbing it of its punch. This self-consuming narrative artifact has lost much of its power for generations of readers because everyone knows, or thinks he knows, what the lesson of the story is before ever reading it.

Let us turn to another moment of surprise and reversal in reading, one that stills packs considerable punch after all these years. In Mark 14:32-42 Jesus and his disciples visit Gethsemane, where Jesus prays an anguished prayer in anticipation of his death. In 14:34 Jesus tells the disciples how deeply grieved he is by the prospect of death, and he charges them to keep watch while he prays. Next, in 14:35-36 he moves on a little farther, where he prays this prayer: "Abba, Father, for you all things are possible; remove this cup from me; yet, not what I want, but what you want." He returns to the disciples and finds them sleeping (14:37)! Then he issues his famous rebuke of the slumbering disciples ("the spirit is willing, but the flesh is weak"). If the story were not so horrific, it would be slapstick comedy that Jesus pours out his soul to God three times, and then comes and finds the disciples sleeping every time.

The moment of surprise and reversal in the reading of this passage is the moment when Jesus first returns to find the disciples sleeping (14:37). When Jesus goes on just "a little farther" and prays his prayer, the reader has no reason to suppose that the disciples are not watching and hearing his prayer from a short distance away. Certainly, the reader "watches" Jesus and "hears" his prayer. So should not we assume that the disciples are watching and hearing the same things that we are? However, when we return with Jesus to find the disciples sleeping, we are shocked, just as he is shocked. He assumed they were watching and hearing him. We assumed they were watching and hearing him along with us. Both he and we are surprised and disappointed. The disciples have failed Jesus, but they have also failed us. No one in the story stayed awake and heard the prayer. The only faithful, wide-awake witness to Jesus' prayer was the reader. Only the reader of the storyteller's discourse has fulfilled the role of the faithful follower. The master storyteller knits us into the fabric of his narrative at the same time that he unravels the disciples' role inside the story. Further, he successfully keeps us from learning of it until after the fact, much to our surprise.

The last example we shall examine not only is a good example of a self-consuming artifact—it, too, offers surprise by means of reversal—but also demonstrates other interesting reading experiences, including an encounter with a gap and a challenge to reconstruct irony.

Mark 4:10-13 was already mentioned in our discussion of gaps. We observed that 4:11 reveals a gap in the discourse of the Gospel. There Jesus says that his followers have "been given the secret of the kingdom of God," but the giving of that secret was never narrated. Presumably the giving of this secret happened in the story, but nevertheless it was omitted from the discourse. However, that is just the beginning of the dance steps this passage puts the reader through. Let us see what happens when we continue to read.

To add further insult to the exclusion of the reader from the secret of the kingdom, 4:11 goes on to state that "for those outside everything is in parables." Apparently the secret of the kingdom is reserved for insiders only; to outsiders, such as the reader, it is a mysterious puzzle or riddle.[22] A curtain seems to separate the reader from Jesus and his disciples: they are on the privileged side, while we stand on the other side, wondering what we are missing. Lest we despair, however, we need to read on.

Just a few steps down the road, a double reversal springs forth. In 4:13 Jesus turns to the "insiders" of 4:11 and asks them: "Do *you* not understand this parable? How then will you understand all the parables?"[23] The tables are turned; roles are reversed. The disciples, the insiders of 4:11, are now revealed to be outsiders, those for whom the parables are riddles. The reader of the Gospel, the outsider of 4:11, now understands that the disciples do not understand. This insight is not much, but it is enough to make the reader a modest insider. No longer do we stand on one side of the curtain, wondering what is happening on the other side. Now we realize that those on the privileged side did not understand what was being given to them, and they have no advantage over us. Indeed, that we understand at least this much gives us an advantage over them. The insiders of 4:11 are revealed in 4:13 to be outsiders; the outsiders of 4:11 discover themselves in 4:13 to be insiders.

This double reversal in 4:13 encourages us to look back over the preceding verses to reconsider and reevaluate what we have just read. Once we hear Jesus' sharp rebuke of the disciples in 4:13, we may want to reevaluate his comment to them back in 4:11 that they are the recipients of the secret of the kingdom of God. In retrospect, in 4:11 could Jesus have been speaking with tongue in cheek? Could he have been speaking a verbal irony? His words might not have sounded ironic when we were at 4:11, but viewed in hindsight from 4:13, they may have changed in tone.

Our suspicion that 4:11 is ironic may be strengthened as we grapple with a verse we have avoided so far, the notoriously difficult verse in 4:12. This verse says that Jesus teaches in parables "*so that* in seeing, they may see and not perceive, and in hearing, they may hear and not understand, lest they should turn and be forgiven."[24] In other words, Jesus uses parables with the express purpose of keeping people from understanding them. Otherwise they would turn their lives around and receive forgiveness, and we would not want that, would we? Of course we would! If taken literally, however, this is the logic of 4:12, and it strikes us as absurd. (Thus step 1 in the process of reconstructing irony is invoked: the literal meaning of 4:12 is nonsense.) But maybe

22. The word *parable* in 4:11 and elsewhere in Mark seems to have the sense of "puzzle" or "riddle."
23. RSV, with emphasis added.
24. My own translation.

we should not take it literally (step 3—surely both Mark and his protagonist Jesus want to have an impact on their respective audiences, so that they will turn their lives around; see Mark 1:1 and 1:15). Could Jesus be speaking with tongue in cheek throughout 4:11-12, teasing his disciples (step 2)? Then in 4:13 he gets serious and levels a severe rebuke at the supposed insiders of 4:11. The result is an experience of dramatic irony in 4:13, when the reader realizes that the apparent roles of 4:11 have been reversed (step 4—Mark loves to construct powerful moments of dramatic irony, and this is one of them).

Altogether in 4:10-13 we experience a gap in the discourse in 4:11, a strong possibility of verbal irony in 4:11-12, and an experience of a self-consuming artifact in 4:13. Becoming aware of the double reversal in 4:13 requires looking back to reconstruct what was happening in 4:11-12, and the result is a powerful moment of dramatic irony. All of the figures for reading that we have discussed thus far—looking forward, looking back; gaps; reconstruction; the self-consuming artifact—can be used to help us to understand what happens when we read Mark 4:10-13.

The Resisting Reader

Our last metaphor for the reading experience is "the resisting reader." This metaphor comes from Judith Fetterley's book by this title, a classic work of feminist reader-response criticism.[25]

Fetterley's specialty is the study of American fiction, which she claims is thoroughly androcentric (male oriented and dominated). The masculine perspective is so pervasive in American literature, and among the teachers of American literature, that women as well as men are indoctrinated "to identify as male" as they read:

> The cultural reality is not the emasculation of men by women but the *immasculation* of women by men. As readers and teachers and scholars, women are taught to think as men, to identify with a male point of view, and to accept as normal and legitimate a male system of values, one of whose central principles is misogyny.[26]

Fetterley exposes the sexism and misogyny in standard works of American fiction by male authors such as Nathaniel Hawthorne, Henry James, William

25. Judith Fetterley, *The Resisting Reader: A Feminist Approach to American Fiction* (Bloomington and London: Indiana University Press, 1978); idem, "Reading about Reading: 'A Jury of Her Peers,' 'The Murders on the Rue Morgue,' and 'The Yellow Wallpaper,' " in *Gender and Reading: Essays on Readers, Texts, and Contexts,* ed. Elizabeth A. Flynn and Patrocinio P. Schweickart (Baltimore and London: Johns Hopkins University Press, 1986), 147–64. For a discussion of the basics of feminist criticism and for an application of feminist reader-response criticism, see chapter 5 by Janice Capel Anderson.
26. Fetterley, *The Resisting Reader*, xii, xx.

Faulkner, Ernest Hemingway, F. Scott Fitzgerald, and Norman Mailer. The female characters in these novels and short stories are routinely victimized by men, often without raising the eyebrows of the male characters in the story. Presumably the reader is also expected not to raise his (or her?) eyebrows. Such is woman's inevitable (and deserved?) fate, the stories seem to imply. In several stories a female character dies, requiring a male character to suffer nobly *his* loss. If a female reader is not careful, she can easily absorb from these texts and perpetuate the very misogynist attitudes that would rob her of "nothing less than sanity and survival."[27]

Accordingly, Fetterley conceives of her book "as a self-defense survival manual for the woman reader lost in 'the masculine wilderness of the American novel.'"[28] Once the sexism and misogyny of American literature and the American educational system are recognized, the woman reader can learn to read without giving automatic assent to the sexist indignities of these texts, which the educational system insists she must read. Rather than granting unthinking assent to the text, the woman reader can become a resisting reader:

> The first act of the feminist critic must be to become a resisting rather than assenting reader and, by this refusal to assent, to begin the process of exorcising the male mind that has been implanted in us. The consequence of this exorcism is the capacity for what Adrienne Rich describes as re-vision—"the act of looking back, of seeing with fresh eyes, of entering an old text from a new critical direction."[29]

Notice how the metaphor of "resisting reading" mutates into the metaphor of "re-vision," which returns us to "looking back," the first metaphor for reading discussed in this chapter. Resisting reading is practiced not only by feminist readers as a defensive strategy in the face of misogyny. It can also be practiced by any reader who finds that resistance, rather than assent, is the responsible, conscientious course of action in a threatening situation.

That the Bible itself is full of examples of resisting or re-visionary reading is immensely important. The Israelites would be still be in Egypt and the Exodus would never have happened if they had not resisted the enslaving words of Pharaoh rather than giving them assent. Christianity would never have been born if the Jewish followers of the Jewish Jesus had not found in him good reason to re-vision their Jewish legacy in the light of the Gospel. Today, both Jews and Christians, both women and men, are awakening to the age-old history of sexism and misogyny, which permeates the Bible and the religions that revere the Bible. Jews and Christians, women and men, are only now learning to read the Bible resistantly with regard to what it has to say about gender roles. At the same time, however, they are also learning to read resistantly what it seems to say regarding a number of contemporary life-and-death issues, such as war, racism, ethnic and religious strife, the environment, and economic justice.

27. Fetterley, "Reading about Reading," 164.
28. Fetterley, *The Resisting Reader,* viii.
29. Ibid., xxii.

Persons professing biblical faith need not be fearful that resisting reading of the Bible is somehow unfaithful reading. To the contrary, one could argue that the most faithful reading of all is resisting reading. Some of the noblest moments in Jewish and Christian history are moments of resistance to officially approved oppression, injustice, or traditions gone sterile. Therefore, resisting reading is practiced not only by feminist literary critics. It has been and will always be practiced by all kinds of people struggling for dignity, justice, or new relevance for their old traditions.

I want to turn to one passage in Mark where resisting reading can be practiced at several levels. What follows is not a feminist reading, but I shall point out some possibilities for a feminist reading of this passage. Also, my example will not address directly the issues of justice and dignity, but it could easily be led in that direction, if a reader were so inclined. Again, I shall only illustrate briefly the exercise of the metaphor. It is up to you to put it to further good use.

The passage I want to consider is Mark 16:1-8, the last episode of Mark's Gospel, the discovery of Jesus' empty tomb.[30] Actually, Mark 16:1-8 was already read resistantly long ago by the author of the Gospel of Matthew, and I would like to make the focus of our own reading Matthew's resisting reading of the ending of Mark (Matt 27:62—28:20).

The majority of biblical scholars believe that Matthew composed his Gospel by editing the Gospel of Mark. I share that presumption, but with a crucial difference in language. Rather than talking about Matthew as an editor of Mark, I like to describe him as one of the first known readers of Mark. Matthew's Gospel is a record of Matthew's response to his experience of reading Mark's Gospel. Although Matthew often reads Mark with assent to what Mark is trying to do, frequently Matthew is a resisting reader of Mark.

Resisting reading is adversarial reading. It is reading against the grain of the text. It is reading in conflict with other possible readings of the text. Matthew and Mark are in competition with each other, each of them striving to control how you and I read the story of the empty tomb. Matthew's resisting reading of Mark's empty tomb story has been so successful that we tend to read Matthew's version of the story back into Mark's version. That is, in order to read Mark's empty tomb story, we have to resist the urge to read Matthew's story instead. *We have to read resistantly Matthew's resisting reading of Mark.* Unless we read against the grain of Matthew's Gospel, we cannot really read Mark's Gospel at all, either with or against the grain.

Let us consider some of the features of Matthew's resisting reading of Mark 16:1-8:

- *The guard at the tomb.* In Matthew, a guard is set at the tomb, supposedly to prevent Jesus' disciples from stealing his corpse and dishonestly proclaiming him resurrected from the dead. In Mark, there is no guard. Nothing

30. Although some ancient manuscripts of the Gospel of Mark include additional verses at the end of the Gospel, the oldest and most accurate manuscripts end at Mark 16:8. The manuscript copies of Mark that tack on extra verses beyond 16:8 themselves represent resisting readings of Mark's ending. Certain copyists did not want Mark to end at 16:8, so they took it upon themselves to supplement the ending.

in Mark's story safeguards against someone telling a rival story about the corpse being stolen.

Matthew expertly deploys his Guard story, placing one piece before Mark's empty tomb story (Matt 27:62-66), one piece in the middle (Matt 28:4), and one piece afterward (Matt 28:11-15). Matthew's *story* of the guard surrounds Mark's empty tomb *story* to resist the illegitimate *story* of the disciples' theft of the dead body to which Mark's story is vulnerable.

● *The women who come to the tomb.* In Matthew, two women, Mary Magdalene and "the other Mary," come to the tomb merely to see it. They succeed. In Mark, three women, Mary Magdalene, Salome, and "Mary the mother of James," come with spices to anoint the body. They gain entrance to the tomb, but they fail to anoint the body.

In Matthew, the identity of "the other Mary" is unclear. By contrast, "Mary the mother of James" in Mark 16:1 is well known. She is also described as "Mary, the mother of Joses" in Mark 15:47 and as "Mary, the mother of James the younger and of Joses" in Mark 15:40. Because the Gospel has already introduced to us a woman named Mary who has sons named James and Joses (Mark 6:3), it makes sense to conclude that these are all references to the same woman.[31] This conclusion, however, yields some surprises. The Mary introduced in Mark 6:3, along with her sons James and Joses, is none other than Jesus' own mother. Why does Mark refuse to call her "Mary, the mother of Jesus"?[32] Rather than clarifying who she is, why does Matthew hide her identity completely? Is Matthew posting another guard, this time around the reputation of Jesus' mother and his brothers?

Not only does Matthew mask Mary's identity but also he erases any mention of the women's intention of anointing the body. In Mark, the mention of an anointing may strike us as a dramatic irony. The reader has already heard that an anonymous woman anointed Jesus for his burial (Mark 14:8). When three named (prominent? important?) women come to the tomb to anoint the body, the thoughtful reader may suspect that they are doomed to failure because what they intend to do has already been done. By hiding Mary's identity and by changing the women's purpose from anointing to merely viewing the tomb, Matthew resists several innuendos about the women in Mark 16:1-8.

31. In making this identification, I am in agreement with Werner H. Kelber, John Dominic Crossan, and Thomas Boomershine; see Kelber's discussion in *The Oral and the Written Gospel: The Hermeneutics of Speaking and Writing in the Synoptic Tradition, Mark, Paul and Q* (Philadelphia: Fortress Press, 1983), 103–4.

32. Some clues: in Mark 3:21, Jesus' family come to take him home because they think he "has gone out of his mind." When his mother and brothers arrive to take him away, Jesus acknowledges that he is estranged from his family (Mark 3:33-35). This estrangement is alluded to again in 6:4. Altogether this suggests that Mark avoids calling Mary "the mother of Jesus" in 15:40, 47; 16:1 in order to imply to the reader that Jesus is still alienated from his mother and his brothers.

• *Rolling the stone away from the tomb.* In Matthew, because the women have no need to go inside the tomb, they do not need to have the stone rolled away for them. Nevertheless, the stone is rolled away, before their very eyes (and before the reader's eyes) by an angel from heaven. In Mark, although the women need to gain entry to the tomb, and although they have the foresight to buy spices (before sunrise!), they talk to themselves (and to the reader) about their lack of foresight in recruiting someone to roll the large stone away from the tomb. In spite of their incomplete preparations, they go to the tomb anyway and find the stone already rolled away (Mark 16:3-4).

Preserving the rolled-away stone is Matthew's one nod of assent to Mark 16:2-5 (Matt 28:2). Otherwise, Matthew so freely adds and subtracts that Mark is completely re-visioned. Among the material Matthew subtracts is the question posed by the women in Mark: "Who will roll away the stone for us from the door of the tomb?" (Mark 16:3). This question is an ironic reminder to the reader that Jesus had four brothers (Mark 6:3) who could have helped their mother with funeral observances for their dead brother. He also had twelve disciples who all said they would never forsake him (Mark 14:31). In Mark everyone seems to abandon Jesus, even God (15:34), but the question by the women in 16:3 points out especially the absence of men who might have accompanied the women in paying their last respects. Are we to contrast the faithlessness of the men with the faithfulness of these three women? Is this a place where a feminist reading of Mark can produce interesting results? We will return to this question later.

In Mark, the women find the stone already removed. Who removed it, when, how, and why is a mystery. Matthew adds to Mark's material and explodes Mark's mysteries by describing an earthquake and an angel descending from heaven (Matt 28:2-4). Matthew resists Mark's ambiguity and replaces it with a blindingly clear revelation of divine power.

• *The angel.* In Matthew, because "an angel of the Lord" rolls away the stone before our eyes, we have no doubt who, when, and how the stone was removed. (However, the answer to the why question remains unclear.) After flexing its heavenly muscles, the angel sits on the stone, outside the tomb (Matt 28:2). In Mark, there is no "angel." Rather, a mysterious "young man" (*neaniskos* in Greek) is discovered by the women sitting inside the tomb (Mark 16:5).

In the long history of reading Mark's Gospel, the puzzle of the young man in the empty tomb has been much debated. Frequently this puzzle is linked to the even more bizarre puzzle of the young man running naked through Gethsemane (14:51-52). Because the word *neaniskos* is used in Mark only in 14:51 and 16:5, and because both young men seem to be distinguished primarily by what they wear or do not wear, one option is to conclude that both are the same young man. Even with this much decided, many questions remain. Who is he and what is he all about?

What could it mean that he is unclothed in 14:52 and resplendently clothed in 16:5?[33] Both *neaniskos* puzzles in Mark remain a mystery.

And both puzzles are neatly solved by Matthew. The young man of Mark 16:5 is turned into an angel, and the young man of Mark 14:51-52 is erased from Matthew's narrative. The ambiguity and mystery associated with both young men in Mark are resisted and resolved in Matthew.

• *The women's report.* In Matthew, the angel instructs the women to go tell the disciples that Jesus has been raised from the dead. "With fear and great joy" (Matt 28:8), they run to fulfill this charge. In Matthew, joy overcomes fear. In Mark, the young man gives similar instructions, but the women run away in "terror and amazement" and say "nothing to anyone, for they were afraid" (16:8). In Mark, fear paralyzes the women into silence. Matthew resists the fear and the silence with which Mark's Gospel ends and re-visions it as joy that must be proclaimed (Matt 28:7, 10, 19-20).

• *Encounters with the risen Jesus.* In Matthew, as the women run to report to the disciples, they encounter the resurrected Jesus himself (Matt 28:9-10). He greets them and repeats the instructions of the angel to tell the disciples. Matthew's Gospel then ends with the famous Great Commission to "make disciples of all nations," a mountaintop encounter between the resurrected Jesus and his rehabilitated disciples (Matt 28:16-20). In Mark, no one encounters the risen Jesus. The mysterious young man says that Jesus has been raised up, but no one in the story experiences it personally. Mark's Gospel ends with no one in the story either witnessing the resurrection of Jesus or reporting it.

Matthew must have been extraordinarily dissatisfied with the way Mark's Gospel ends. In Matthew's resisting reading of the ending of Mark, ironies that cast a doubtful light on the mother, the brothers, and the disciples of Jesus are erased. Puzzles are either resolved or eliminated. Fear is swallowed up by joy, and silence is overcome by proclamation. The absence of Jesus, as well as that of the disciples, is replaced by the glorious appearance of Jesus and a fantastic mountaintop reunion with the disciples. Finally, the mystery of the empty tomb and the ambiguity of the young man are thoroughly clarified with bright beams of heavenly glory.

We could go on and on discussing Matthew's resisting reading of Mark 16:1-8, but this much must suffice. Mark's Gospel is comfortable with offering its reader an abundance of irony, ambiguity, and mystery. Matthew's Gospel is not. Therefore, Matthew's reading of Mark is typically a resisting reading, a

33. A common historical solution for the puzzle of Mark 14:51-52 is that the young man is the author himself, which would make Mark an eyewitness of the scene in the garden. A common literary-theological solution to the puzzle of Mark 16:5 is that the young man is really an angel (as in Matthew). Both of these solutions are ingenious, but neither is explicitly authorized by the Gospel of Mark. Mark likes to give us puzzles without obvious solutions.

reading against the grain of Mark's Gospel. Mark's narrative seems designed to intrigue and perplex the reader. Matthew wants to instruct us, openly and clearly. Matthew likes to tell us what to think; Mark wants us to learn to think for ourselves. Mark can live with the possibility that his narrative might be misunderstood and misappropriated—witness his unguarded and ambiguous empty tomb story, vulnerable to many conflicting interpretations. By contrast, Matthew wants to guard against misunderstanding and misappropriation— witness his carefully guarded tomb story. Given Mark's Gospel, one can easily imagine someone like Matthew coming along to clarify and to straighten out Mark's mysteries; given Matthew's Gospel, it is hard to imagine how someone like Mark could hope to interest anyone in giving up Matthew's clarity in favor of Mark's mysteries. Matthew's Gospel is well designed to outshine Mark's Gospel, which it has done throughout the history of the reading of both Gospels.

Matthew and Mark are not merely different narratives; they are narratives in conflict with each other. Mark 16:1-8 and Matt 27:62—28:20 are competing versions of the same story, all tangled up in each other like a bad knot in a pair of shoelaces. If we wish to read either Gospel apart from the other, first we must untangle them. Most readers unconsciously read the Gospels of Matthew and Mark (along with Luke and John) in their native tangled state, and, the clarity and directness of Matthew are typically more appreciated by the average reader than the mystery and ambiguity of Mark. If you want to read *Mark*, however, you have to resist Matthew's resisting reading of Mark.

If we can read Matthew resistantly, then we can decide whether to read Mark with assent or with resistance. I am not going to attempt a resisting reading of Mark 16:1-8 here, but one way it might be done is through a feminist reading. I shall point out how this might be done and leave my reader to explore further the possibilities.

A common feminist reading of Mark 16:1-8 argues that the three women are worthy models of Christian discipleship. By witnessing the crucifixion and burial of Jesus and then by visiting the empty tomb, they have succeeded where the male disciples in the story have all failed.[34] From a feminist perspective, this reading has several attractions. First, it resists and shatters the dominant assumption throughout two thousand years of Christian experience that the chief witnesses to the resurrection of Jesus were men. Second, it uncovers a crucial, prestigious role for women in the early church. Third, it thereby provides encouragement to women today to assume significant roles in the Christian church.

However, as I indicated before, there are severe problems with this reading of Mark 16:1-8.[35] To read Mark 16:1-8 as a story of the success of the three

34. Elisabeth Schüssler Fiorenza, *In Memory of Her: A Feminist Theological Recon-struction of Christian Origins* (New York: Crossroad, 1983), 138–39, 321–23; Elizabeth Struthers Malbon, "Fallible Followers: Women and Men in the Gospel of Mark," *Semeia* 28 (1983): 29–48.

35. A feminist critic who also has problems with this reading is Mary Ann Tolbert, *Sowing the Gospel: Mark's World in Literary-Historical Perspective* (Minneapolis: Fortress Press, 1989), 291–99.

women is an unconscious reading of the ending of Matthew back into Mark. Therefore, it is not a resisting reading at all, but an assenting reading of Matthew masquerading as a reading of Mark. Matthew grants the women a positive role in witnessing the resurrection and reporting to the disciples, but it is a minor role, entirely subservient to the major role of the male disciples, who are the only ones to appear in the Great Commission (Matt 28:16-20). Because the brothers of Jesus and the twelve disciples are utterly absent at the end of Mark, the minor success of the women in Matthew can appear a major success when it is imported into Mark. However, this success is only an illusion, the result of reading Mark the way Matthew would have us read it.

If we can resist Matthew's resisting reading of Mark, we can recognize that the three women in Mark 16:1-8 fail, just as so many others in the story have failed before them. All is not doom and gloom at the end of Mark, however. Many biblical critics are now recognizing that the ending of Mark, just like the rest of the Gospel, is mostly concerned to make an impact on the reader.[36] Mark's Gospel may end without insight and faith among the characters in the story, but that does not mean that the audience of the Gospel has not been well instructed and deeply moved by the experience of reading the Gospel. The key to understanding the ending of Mark is not to understand the women or men in the story, but to understand what is happening in the women or men reading the story.

Maybe a resisting, feminist reading of Mark 16:1-8 could be constructed, but it would have to take another shape. Readers recognize today that Mark's Gospel contains some remarkably positive images of women, such as the woman with a flow of blood in Mark 5:25-34, the Syrophoenician woman in Mark 7:24-30, and the woman who anointed Jesus in Mark 14:3-9. Mary Ann Tolbert takes care to observe that the women just mentioned are all anonymous. By contrast, the three women who come to the tomb are all named, as if they were prominent and well-known persons, as indeed Jesus' mother surely was. Tolbert suggests that the conspicuous naming of the women at the tomb may be an attempt to criticize the "the human desire for fame, glory, status, and authority."[37] Speaking of names, the brothers and disciples of Jesus, whose absence is underlined by the women's question in Mark 16:3, are all prominently named in the course of Mark's narration (Mark 3:16-19; 6:3). What might Mark be suggesting to the reader by leaving unnamed most of the minor but successful women and men characters in the story, while prominently naming major women and men characters who fail?[38] Gender roles may indeed be

36. Regarding the impact of the ending of Mark on the reader, see Tolbert, *Sowing the Gospel*; regarding the entire Gospel's orientation toward the reader, see Robert M. Fowler, *Let the Reader Understand: Reader-Response Criticism and the Gospel of Mark* (Minneapolis: Fortress Press, 1991).

37. Tolbert, *Sowing the Gospel*, 292–93.

38. Mary Ann Tolbert also seems to be asking this question, but does not go far in pursuing an answer *(Sowing the Gospel*, 274, 292–93). On the minor characters or "little people" in Mark, see David Rhoads and Donald Michie, *Mark as Story: An Introduction to the Narrative of a Gospel* (Philadelphia: Fortress Press, 1982), 129–35.

significant in Mark, but gender in Mark (or anywhere) is always tangled with other weighty issues, such as psychology, race, class, ethics, and politics. Any and all of these issues may need to be considered in a feminist reading of Mark. Furthermore, even the brief introduction to reader-response criticism provided by this chapter is enough to teach us that a feminist reading of Mark 16:1-8 might have to look back and re-vision preceding episodes involving (or not involving) other women (or men) characters, negotiate the gaps in 16:1-8, reconstruct the ironies there, and be open to the possibility that in the end the Gospel of Mark may unravel itself, just as it has so many times before. Reading the ending of Mark resistantly may mean resisting our own desire for neat and simple solutions to the puzzles it presents to us or that we present to it.

The tangled endings of Mark and Matthew illustrate the lesson that the Bible itself is full of adversarial, against-the-grain, resisting reading. Printed side by side in our Bibles, the Gospels appear to be cozy bedfellows, comfortably snoozing in the same bed. Appearances, however, can be deceiving. The Gospels are far more in competition with each other than is commonly suspected. They may share the same bed, but like rambunctious siblings, they tussle over who gets the covers. Self-conscious, self-critical, and honest reading of the Gospels requires us to recognize this conflict and to be willing to jump into the fray ourselves. Moreover, what is true of reading the Gospels is true of the Bible generally: To read the Bible is to participate in a rich, long legacy of resisting reading.

Conclusion

Reader-response criticism is a critical practice that helps readers read with greater awareness and self-consciousness. As we become more aware of what we are doing as we read (looking forward, looking back, filling gaps, and so on), we become more aware of our response to our reading experience. Our reading and our response to reading become more thoughtful, more considered, which can lead us to take greater personal responsibility for our reading and our response. Particularly if we practice resisting reading, we can become more self-conscious about our acts of assent and our acts of resistance. Our commitments may deepen and be strengthened. Then again, our commitments may change altogether, if we are wise enough to practice resisting reading on ourselves or if we are lucky enough to have friends who challenge us to change.

Reading and responding to our reading is not optional. The question is, Do we read with more or less self-consciousness? Do we respond with more or less awareness and sensitivity? Assenting and resisting are not optional. The question is, To what shall we give our assent? What shall we resist? Reader-response criticism can help us to answer these important questions.

FURTHER READING

BOOTH, Wayne C. *A Rhetoric of Irony*. Chicago: University of Chicago Press, 1974. Classic work on the reader's encounter with irony.

———. *The Rhetoric of Fiction*. 2d ed. Chicago: University of Chicago Press, 1983. Booth's brand of rhetorical criticism is closely related to reader-response criticism and has greatly influenced biblical literary criticism.

DETWEILER, Robert, ed. *Reader Response Approaches to Biblical and Secular Texts*. Semeia 31. Decatur, Ga.: Scholars Press, 1985. Diverse collection of essays; addresses more biblical than secular texts.

FETTERLEY, Judith. *The Resisting Reader: A Feminist Approach to American Fiction*. Bloomington and London: Indiana University Press, 1978. Influential work of feminist reader-response criticism; popularized the image of "resisting reading."

———. "Reading about Reading: 'A Jury of Her Peers,' 'The Murders on the Rue Morgue,' and 'The Yellow Wallpaper.'" In *Gender and Reading: Essays on Readers, Texts, and Contexts*. Edited by Elizabeth A. Flynn and Patrocinio P. Schweickart, 147–64. Baltimore and London: John Hopkins Unversity Press, 1986. Illuminating discussion of the differences between reading as a man and reading as a woman.

FISH, Stanley E. "Literature in the Reader: Affective Stylistics." *New Literary History* 2 (1970): 123–62. Important discussion of the temporal experience of reading.

———. *Self-Consuming Artifacts: The Experience of Seventeenth-Century Literature*. Berkeley, Los Angeles, and London: University of California Press, 1972. Essays exploring the reading experience alluded to in the title.

———. *Is There a Text in This Class? The Authority of Interpretive Communities*. Cambridge and London: Harvard University Press, 1980. Fish here shifts his focus of attention away from the interaction of text and reader to the influence of "interpretive communities" on how readers read.

FLYNN, Elizabeth A., and Patrocinio P. Schweickart, eds. *Gender and Reading: Essays on Readers, Texts, and Contexts*. Baltimore and London: Johns Hopkins University Press, 1986. Important collection of essays from a feminist reader-response perspective.

FOWLER, Robert M. *Loaves and Fishes: The Function of the Feeding Stories in the Gospel of Mark*. Society of Biblical Literature Dissertation Series 54. Chico, Calif.: Scholars Press, 1981. Discusses the irony of the two feeding stories and other matched pairs of stories in Mark. The first application of reader-response criticism to a biblical text.

———. *Let the Reader Understand: Reader-Response Criticism and the Gospel of Mark*. Minneapolis: Fortress Press, 1991. Describes the major features of reader-response criticism and applies it to the experience of reading the Gospel of Mark.

ISER, Wolfgang. "The Reading Process: A Phenomenological Approach." *New Literary History* 3 (1972): 279–99. Classic discussion of the temporal experience of reading.

———. *The Implied Reader*. Baltimore and London: Johns Hopkins University Press, 1974. Popularized the term "implied reader" in literary criticism.

———. *The Act of Reading: A Theory of Aesthetic Response*. Baltimore and London: Johns Hopkins University Press, 1978. Theoretical discussion of the reading experience.

MCKNIGHT, Edgar V., ed. *Reader Perspectives on the New Testament*. Semeia 48. Atlanta: Scholars Press, 1989. Essays on biblical texts emphasizing "the reader in the text."

MOORE, Stephen D. "Stories of Reading: Doing Gospel Criticism as/with a Reader." Chapter 6 of *Literary Criticism and the Gospels: The Theoretical Challenge*. New

Haven and London: Yale University Press, 1989. Excellent survey of the use of reader-response criticism in biblical criticism.

RESSEGUIE, James L. "Reader-Response Criticism and the Synoptic Gospels." *Journal of the American Academy of Religion* 52 (1984): 307–24. Brief discussion of reader-response criticism and a consideration of several Gospel texts.

SULEIMAN, Susan, and Inge Crosman, eds. *The Reader in the Text: Essays on Audience and Interpretation.* Princeton: Princeton University Press, 1980. Along with the Tompkins volume, one of the two best anthologies available of essays on reader-response criticism. Good bibliography.

TOMPKINS, Jane P., ed. *Reader-Response Criticism: From Formalism to Post-Structuralism.* London and Baltimore: Johns Hopkins University Press, 1980. Important anthology of reader-response essays. The concluding essay by Tompkins helpfully situates reader-response criticism in the history of criticism. Good bibliography.

4

Deconstructive Criticism:

The Gospel of the ~~Mark~~

STEPHEN D. MOORE

What is deconstruction?[1] Article- or book-length answers to this question now run in their thousands across an astonishing array of fields—modern languages and comparative literature, mainly, but also philosophy, psychology, cultural studies, linguistics, anthropology, political theory, history, legal studies, art theory, architectural theory, film theory, even theology and biblical studies— a colossal body of introductions and applications perched precariously atop the shoulders of a slight but slippery body of "exemplary" deconstructive texts, those of Jacques Derrida in particular. Derrida, a French philosopher revered, sometimes feared, more in the United States than in France, and better known to students of literature than to students of philosophy, continues to occupy a

---

1. This chapter contains reworked excerpts from Stephen D. Moore, *Mark and Luke in Poststructuralist Perspectives: Jesus Begins to Write* (New Haven: Yale University Press, 1992). Reprinted by permission of the publisher.

role of central importance in Anglo-American literary studies, from a position on its margins.

Why this success? Derrida is most often associated with a particular interpretation of the intellectual history of the West, which at first glance hardly explains his influence on literary criticism. According to Derrida, Western thought has always been built on binary oppositions: soul/body, nature/culture, male/female, white/nonwhite, inside/outside, conscious/unconscious, object/representation, history/fiction, literal/metaphorical, content/form, primary/secondary, text/interpretation, speech/writing, presence/absence, and so on. In each pair, as Derrida notes, the first term is assumed to be superior to the second and has been forcibly elevated over it. All such oppositions are founded on suppression; therefore, the relationship between the two elements is one of subordination rather than equality.

We shall return to Derrida's interpretation of Western thought in due course, summaries of which can be misleading—for deconstruction is much less an exercise in abstract speculation or in historical reconstruction than a highly flexible strategy of reading. Derrida always writes best curled up inside some text or other, and the same can be said of Paul de Man, whose influence on American deconstruction has been second only to that of Derrida. Hence their interest for literary criticism, and for us.

Let us climb into our text, Mark, and begin to read. Mark will carry us deep into deconstructive territory. I shall point out some of the better-known landmarks of deconstructive criticism as we go along. These landmarks, or monuments, have inscriptions carved into them. Here are some that we shall encounter:

● "The paradigm for all texts consists of a figure (or a system of figures) and its deconstruction" (de Man).

● "A deconstruction always has for its target to reveal the existence of hidden . . . fragmentations within assumedly monadic totalities" (de Man).

● "The text . . . tells the story, the allegory of its misunderstanding" (de Man).

● "It has been necessary to . . . set to work, within the text . . . , certain marks . . . that . . . I have called undecidables, . . . that can no longer be included within philosophical (binary) opposition, but which, however, inhabit philosophical opposition, resisting and disorganizing it" (Derrida).

● "I do not 'concentrate,' in my reading . . . , either exclusively or primarily on those points that appear to be the most 'important,' 'central,' 'crucial.' Rather, I de-concentrate, and it is the secondary, eccentric, lateral, marginal, parasitic, borderline cases which are 'important' to me and are a source of many things, such as pleasure, but also insight into the general functioning of a textual system" (Derrida).

● "Deconstruction is inventive or it is nothing at all; it does not settle for methodical procedures, it opens up a passageway, it marches ahead and marks a trail; . . . it produces rules—other conventions" (Derrida).

Our readings of Mark will shed some light on these inscriptions, even as the inscriptions shed light on Mark—although deconstruction is not all light reading, as we are already discovering.

Deconstruction reads with an eye and ear extended for the excluded, the marginal, the blind spot, the blank. To what features of Mark, then, might deconstruction be drawn as to a magnet? To features that have been repressed or subordinated throughout Mark's long interpretive history. And no element in Mark has been the object of more resolute cover-ups than 16:8, the verse most Markan scholars now believe formed the Gospel's original ending.

Demanic Reading:
The Self-Deconstructing Text

Traditionally, Mark's symbol has been the lion. Mark's belly is bottomless, as we shall see. It devours the readings that we throw to it, ripping their pages to shreds. But Mark is a lion with at least four tails. Consider the Markan endings. First, there is 16:9-20, which scholars have dubbed "the longer ending of Mark." It is composed of three resurrection appearances of Jesus, followed by his ascension. Second, there is "the shorter ending of Mark," which amounts to a thumbnail version of the longer ending. On manuscript evidence, combined with other criteria such as vocabulary, style, and content, most Markan scholars now believe both these endings to be later additions. Was Mark's real ending lost in transmission, then (it would be the third ending)? Or did Mark actually intend his Gospel to end with 16:8: "And they [the women disciples] went out and fled from the tomb; for trembling and astonishment had come upon them; and they said nothing to any one, for they were afraid"?

Deconstruction is scrupulously attentive to difficulties in the texts that it reads. Recent scholarship on the Markan ending has taken a similar line, dismissing 16:9-20 and the other variant endings as attempts to blunt the bite of 16:8. To seize on 16:8 as Mark's original ending is to risk being savaged by the lion. Mark 16:8 seems to be saying that the discovery of the empty tomb was never reported. But if it was never reported, how can *Mark* know that Jesus has risen?

Mark trails off before narrating "circumstances in which one could imagine something like the Gospel of Mark being narrated. The story *in* Mark's Gospel seems to preclude the telling *of* Mark's Gospel."[2] Mark's ending undercuts its beginning; it saws through the branch on which the book is perched. Outside the tomb, as the women flee and say nothing, Mark rips up its own birth record. In contrast to Matthew and Luke, each of which *begins* with a virginal conception (Matt 1:18; Luke 1:34-35), Mark *ends* with a virginal conception— its own. Its tomb becomes a miraculous womb.

2. Robert M. Fowler, "Reading Matthew Reading Mark: Observing the First Steps toward Meaning-as-Reference in the Synoptic Gospels," in *Society of Biblical Literature 1986 Seminar Papers,* ed. Kent Harold Richards (Atlanta: Scholars Press, 1986), 14.

To adopt the terminology of Paul de Man, Mark by its ending "simultaneously asserts and denies the authority of its own rhetorical mode," its strategies of argumentation and persuasion.[3] For de Man, every literary text turns on such moments of self-division, one hand stealthily withdrawing what the other had straightforwardly extended. This process yields the following formula: "The paradigm for all texts consists of a figure (or a system of figures) and its deconstruction."[4] In short, texts deconstruct themselves. The text will always have anticipated any deconstructive operation that the critic might perform on it. For de Man, this self-deconstructing drive in texts is to be explained with reference to language. Because language is a bottomless quicksand of rhetorical figures (such as metaphor), it is fatally unstable. This assumption of instability dictates the task of deconstruction: "A deconstruction always has for its target to reveal the existence of hidden . . . fragmentations within assumedly monadic [i.e., unified] totalities"—such as texts.[5]

Introducing *Allegories of Reading*, his most important work, de Man explains that his inclusion of Proust and Rilke among the writers he will deal with is dictated in part by their stubborn resistance to his way of reading: "One could argue that if *their* work yields to such [readings], the same would necessarily be true for writers whose rhetorical strategies are less hidden"[6]—Mark, for example? In large letters across its chest Mark flaunts that admission of self-division that only the most skilled reading can coax from so much modern literature. Thus we can say that, given the unusual degree of openness with which Mark at once asserts and subverts its own rhetorical stance, it is exemplary of the self-deconstructive text, and to that extent of literature in general.

On the inside Looking in

If the Markan lion has at least four tails, it also has more than one set of teeth. Scarcely less daunting than its ending is its baffling use of the term *parable*. Here is a second set of jaws into which we can feed a deconstructive reading.

Between the parable of the Sower (4:3-9) and its interpretation (14-20) is Mark's so-called parable theory. Jesus' listeners question him concerning the parables, to which he responds: "To you has been given the secret of the kingdom of God, but for those outside everything is in parables; so that they may indeed see but not perceive, and may indeed hear but not understand; lest they should turn again, and be forgiven" (4:11-12). Now, the expression, "so that they may indeed *see* but not perceive," coupled with the expression, "for those outside *everything is in parables*," suggests that "parable" in Mark (*parabolē* in Greek) may mean more than just a traditional teaching device taken over by the historical Jesus. The term may encompass Jesus' enigmatic

3. Paul de Man, *Allegories of Reading: Figural Language in Rousseau, Nietzsche, Rilke, and Proust* (New Haven: Yale University Press, 1979), 17.
4. Ibid., 205.
5. Ibid., 249.
6. Ibid., ix.

ministry as such, a fusion of word and deed. Indeed, some scholars have gone on to suggest that given Mark's many startling features, not least its paradoxical ending, the Gospel as a whole can be said to function parabolically, parable being a type of paradox.

Contrasted as they are with "those outside" (4:11), Jesus' disciples must be insiders (cf. 3:31-35). And whereas outsiders are expected to see but not perceive, hear but not understand, insiders are, by implication, expected both to see and to perceive, to hear and to understand. But do they?

Mark's parables discourse ends on a reassuring note: "privately to his own disciples he explained everything" (4:34). Yet Mark's next episode, the calming of the storm, has Jesus rebuking his followers for their lack of faith (4:40). Later, following the first feeding miracle, we read that the disciples "did not understand about the loaves, but their hearts were hardened" (6:52; cf. 3:5). More damaging still is the third boat episode, which elicits the following outburst from Jesus: "Why do you discuss the fact that you have no bread? Do you not yet *perceive* or *understand*? Are your hearts hardened? *Having eyes do you not see and having ears do you not hear?*"—like the outsiders of 4:11-12. He ends: "Do you not yet understand?" (8:17-18, 21; cf. 7:18).

Corresponding to these three boat scenes are the three misunderstandings that follow Jesus' three predictions of his suffering and death. In response to the first prediction, Peter reproves Jesus and is sharply rebuked in turn: "Get behind me, Satan! For you are not on the side of God, but of men" (8:32-33). Following the second prediction, we learn that the disciples "did not understand the saying, and they were afraid to ask him" (9:32). Afterward they argue among themselves about which of them is the greatest (9:34). Following the third prediction, two of the disciples request seats of honor from Jesus, to which he replies: "You do not know what you are asking" (10:35 ff.). To all this must, of course, be added Judas' betrayal of Jesus (14:10-11), the other (male) disciples' desertion of him at his arrest (14:50; cf. 15:40-41), Peter's threefold denial of him (14:66-72), and the women disciples' confused flight from the tomb (16:8).

Right to the end of the Gospel, then, the insiders are on the inside looking in, as though they were in fact outside.[7] The secret of the kingdom has indeed been presented to them (4:11), but although they are poised before it they cannot penetrate it. Between seeing and perceiving, hearing and understanding, something intervenes, something that also keeps those whom the Gospel *explicitly* designates outsiders outside, something it calls *parable*: "for those outside everything is in parables." What distinguishes disciples from outsiders is that disciples long to be inside, to *be* the insiders they are said to be.

The obscurity of Jesus' parabolic words and deeds does not suffice to explain the depth of the disciples' ignorance. When Jesus begins "to teach them that the Son of Man must suffer many things, and be rejected . . . and be killed, and after three days rise again," thereby administering the fatal blow to their faltering understanding, the narrator adds: "And he said this plainly [*parrēsia*]"

---

7. See Frank Kermode, *The Genesis of Secrecy: On the Interpretation of Narrative* (Cambridge: Harvard University Press, 1979), 27, 46–47.

(8:31-32). It seems that the mystery of the kingdom can meet only with mis-understanding (at least for now), whether parabolic or plain speech be used to express it.

Indeed, all of Jesus' speech and all of his actions in Mark quickly reduce to "parable" once they become vehicles of this mystery. "For those outside ev-erything is in parables"—but for those "inside" also, who in consequence are neither fully inside nor yet fully outside. Like the seed scattered by the sower, Jesus' parabolic speech falls ineffectually on rocky ground, unable to take root in the "hardened" hearts of the disciples. Precisely at this point, however, it begins to take root in the texts of Jacques Derrida.

The Written V(o)ice

Earlier we noted Derrida's contention that Western culture is established upon a series of hierarchical oppositions. One opposition in particular has been of special interest to Derrida. In the West, the spoken word has almost always been privileged over the written. But what could be more *natural* than to privilege speech? As I speak, my words appear to be one with my thoughts. My meaning appears to be fully present both to me and to my hearer. At such moments, the voice appears to be consciousness itself, presence itself: voice, presence, truth. In the West, speech has always been the model not only for every form of presence but also for every form of truth. All the names used to express theological or philosophical fundamentals have always been inseparable from the idea of presence: God, being, essence, existence, and so on—the list is very long.

Writing, in contrast, cut off at its source from the authorizing presence of a speaker, has often been thought to threaten truth with distortion and mischief. As lifeless written marks in place of present living speech, writing has seemed to be an inferior, if necessary, substitute for speech. An orphan, no sooner born than set adrift, cut loose from the author who gives birth to it, writing seems fated endlessly to circulate, if not from foster home to foster home, then from reader to reader. And the reader can never be sure of properly grasping what the author intended to say. Authors have a way of being absent, even dead, and their intended meaning can no longer be directly intuited or double-checked through question and answer, as in the face-to-face situation of speech. Writing defaces speech.

Derrida approaches the speech/writing opposition by asking, What if the alien, the parasite, were already within? What if speech were already the host of writing?[8] Let us extend his question to Mark: What if *Jesus'* speech were inhabited by writing? What if it were haunted, infected, afflicted by it? It is time we returned to *parabolē*.

8. His argument is complex and need not concern us here. I have already sum-marized it in my *Literary Criticism and the Gospels: The Theoretical Challenge* (New Haven: Yale University Press, 1989), 157–59, 132–33.

Jesus as a Man of Letters

Effective speech, as commonly understood, is marked by the presence to the hearer of the speaker's intended meaning, whereas writing, traditionally, is the errant medium, its meaning cut adrift from the consciousness of its producer. Mark's text perverts this "normal" relationship of speech to writing. Take, for example, Jesus' three passion predictions (8:31; 9:31; 10:33-34). They can be regarded as some of Jesus' clearer statements in Mark as far as the reader—and the narrator (see 8:32a)—are concerned, whereas they are impossibly obscure as far as Jesus' immediate listeners are concerned. Between speech and hearing, something intrudes. Like a blade it severs the circle of under-standing, the intimate circle of exchange ("looking around on those who sat about him in a circle. . . ."; 3:34) within whose circumference Jesus' voice *should* circulate, coupling with the ears of his disciples, breath to flesh and nothing between.

Sliced through, Jesus' speech is unable to reach its mark. It falls to the ground and is picked up wrongly. It is as if Jesus were *writing* instead of *speaking*, as if his disciples were *reading* instead of *listening*. The severing blade can only be re(a)d; it makes no sound. Silently it makes its cut, forcing Jesus to write without a pen. And the blade appears to be wielded by Jesus' own Father, who wills that the disciples' ears should not yet be impregnated with understanding (cf. 6:52; 8:17-18).[9]

Should not Jesus himself be a father? Traditionally, the speaker is father to his speech. Unlike the written word, the spoken word is able to reach its target easily because it has a living father, a father who is present to it, who stands behind it, making sure that its aim is straight. Jesus cannot be such a father to his speech. The blade of his own father has cut off that possibility, severing the "natural" bond that should exist between thought and voice, meaning and sound.

Jesus must write upon the dark field of the disciples' understanding, although not in luminous letters. "The alphabet of stars alone does that," as the poet Mallarmé somewhere says. But if the disciples' understanding is dark, it is due to the inky blackness of the letters it must soak up— blue-black letters that release little light.

If John's Jesus is modeled on the *spoken* word ("In the beginning was the word [*logos*]"), Mark's Jesus can be said to be modeled on the *written* word. Not only does Jesus "write" in Mark; he is himself a species of writing—literally, because we know him only through the written letter. Jesus is a man of letters.

Like Jesus who drifts from misunderstanding to misunderstanding across the surface of Mark's page, writing has always been a wandering outcast, drifting from (mis)reading to (mis)reading. At least since the time of Plato, writing has also been read as an orphan or delinquent:

> Once a thing is put into writing, the composition . . . drifts all over the place, getting into the hands not only of those who understand it, but

---

9. Note the passive constructions ("hardened" [*pepōrōmenē*]) in 6:52 and 8:17c (contrast 3:5), which seem, to me at any rate, to imply divine agency, especially in light of such texts as Exod 4:21ff.; Luke 9:45; 18:34; and Rom 11:7-8.

equally of those who have no business with it; it doesn't know how to address the right people, and not to address the wrong. And when it is ill-treated and unfairly abused it always needs its parent to come to its help.[10]

However, "the specificity of writing [is] intimately bound to the absence of the father," as Derrida observes.[11] The present writer is always absent. The orphaned word must circulate without its parent's protective presence, vulnerable to mishandling and misreading. Without its father, it is, in fact, "nothing but . . . writing."[12] As letter, Mark's Jesus is "delivered into human hands" (9:31; cf. 10:33). As writing, he is penned to the cross, cut off from his Father ("My God, my God, why have you forsaken me?"; 15:34), and exposed to the casual violence of any reader who happens by ("Those who passed by derided him, shaking their heads and saying, 'Aha!' "; 15:29 ff.). As writing, Jesus is crucified, stretched out on the wood, the rack, the reading frame. Mark's Jesus does violate the common law of writing by finally uniting with his Father. But even then his status remains more that of an inscription than of a spoken word (or *logos*), marked as it is by absence ("He has risen; he is not here"; 16:6) and exposure to the accidents of (mis)reading ("they said nothing to anyone, for they were afraid"; 16:8).

Mark's Jesus can therefore be read on the model of the written mark (and what is Jesus in Mark but a series of written marks, a marked man?). But Jesus' status in Mark prefigures Mark's own status. Mark's Jesus is a "writer," himself inscribed in a text, but so inscribed as to prefigure the fate of that text. Mark's own destiny as a writing is foreshadowed in the way it writes up the story of Jesus.

Mark is gradually folding back on itself as we read it. Not only is it a writing about Jesus but also it is a writing about writing. In addition, it is a writing about reading, a writing, which, as it retells the story of Jesus, also foretells the history of (mis)reading that the story will generate. As de Man puts it, "the text . . . tells the story, the allegory of its misunderstanding."[13] This itself is a story that deconstructors tell time and again.

Mark's Poisonous Cure for Ignorance

Reading writings *on* writing by Plato, Rousseau, and Mallarmé, Derrida finds that the terms used by each writer to describe writing—*pharmakon* in Plato,

10. Plato, *Phaedrus,* in *The Collected Dialogues of Plato,* ed. Edith Hamilton and Huntington Cairns, trans. R. Hackforth (Princeton, N.J.: Princeton University Press, 1961), 275d–275e.
11. Jacques Derrida, *Dissemination,* trans. Barbara Johnson (Chicago: University of Chicago Press, 1981), 77.
12. Ibid.
13. Paul de Man, *Blindness and Insight: Essays in the Rhetoric of Contemporary Criticism,* 2d ed. (Minneapolis: University of Minnesota Press, 1983), 136. Cf. de Man, *Allegories of Reading,* 205.

supplement in Rousseau, *hymen* in Mallarmé—have a contradictory, double sense. (To take the simplest example, the Greek word *pharmakon* means both *poison* and *cure*.)

What of Mark? Mark is not explicitly about writing, of course, but a speech deeply marked with the traits of writing does figure in it, as we have seen. Interestingly, Mark himself has a term for such speech. He calls it *parabolē* ("parable"), a term whose peculiarities we must now examine more closely.

Parabolai in Mark are a partition, screen, or membrane designed to keep insiders on one side, outsiders on the other. Outsiders are those for whom "everything comes in parables," parables that they find incomprehensible (4:11-12). At the same time, *parabolai* rupture that membrane, make it permeable, infect the opposition with contradiction; those who should be on the inside find themselves repeatedly put out by Jesus' parabolic words and deeds. Appointed to allow insiders in and to keep outsiders out, parables unexpectedly begin to threaten *everyone* with exclusion in Mark, even disciples seeking entry. Deranged doormen, parables threaten to make outsiders of us all.

Derrida remarks of the *pharmakon*, the *supplement*, and the *hymen*:

> It has been necessary to analyze, to set to work, *within* the text of the history of philosophy, as well as *within* the so-called literary text . . . , certain marks . . . that . . . I have called undecidables, . . . that can no longer be included within philosophical (binary) opposition, but which, however, inhabit philosophical opposition, resisting and disorganizing it, *without ever* constituting a third term[14]

—that is to say, without ever neatly resolving the contradiction.

Like *pharmakon* and the other "undecidable marks" that Derrida lifts from the texts he reads, Mark's *parabolē* refuses to be laid to rest within the narrow framework of a classic binary opposition—here, that of inside versus outside. *Parabolē* turns language inside out like a pocket, threatening to empty it of its content(s). *Parabolē* takes a voice that issues from the intimacy of an inside, from the interiority of a speaker, Jesus, a voice that *should* easily be able to leap the gap separating it from the ear of the hearer, and turns it into an unincorporable exteriority. Too blunt to penetrate the ear, it cannot fit inside. "Let anyone with ears to hear listen!" cries Jesus (4:9; cf. 4:23), but nobody has ears big enough.

Parabolē unsettles speech. It inhabits the oppositions of inside and outside, speech and writing, but only that it might disrupt the order of the house, rock the foundation in which these oppositions are embedded, shake the (bed)frames so as to keep the interpreters restlessly turning over. *Parabolē* positions itself between opposing terms, apparently to pull them apart, all the while sowing confusion between them.

14. Jacques Derrida, *Positions*, trans. Alan Bass (Chicago: University of Chicago Press, 1981), 42–43, his emphasis.

Parabolē is prudent. It inflicts a grievous wound on common sense, but takes care to leave it untended. It stays away from the pharmacy, the *pharmakon*. It is wary of the cure that might turn out to be a poison.

Yet it is not as though the outsiders in Mark never get a look in(side). Jesus is identified as Son (of God), not only by God's self (1:11; 9:7) and by the narrator (1:1), but also by the demons (3:11; 5:7; cf. 1:24,34) and by the centurion at the foot of the cross (15:39). But although the demons do have inside information on Jesus, they can hardly be said to be insiders. Among the human characters, only the centurion, a Gentile and hence an outsider, is allowed to look inside ("Truly this man was God's Son!"). The women disciples do advance steadily toward the inside (15:40-41,47; 16:1 ff.)—until *parabolē* leaps out to greet them from the interior of the tomb to drive them back outside: "And they went out and fled from the tomb, for terror and amazement had had seized them . . ." (16:8). But what of the Syrophoenician woman (7:24-30)? Or Bartimaeus (10:46-52)? Assuredly they have faith, but would they accept that Jesus must suffer? And until we know that they would, can they be said to be insiders? In short, there are no insiders in Mark who are not at the same time outsiders.

The contradiction prevails until the end and beyond. Mark 16:7 does seem finally to promise the long-deferred establishment of the insiders *as* insiders: "he is going ahead of you to Galilee; there you will see him." But 16:8, the Markan nonending, parablelike in its demolition of conventional expectations, threatens to leave the disciples stranded yet again in a twilight zone that is neither fully inside nor yet fully outside.

Mark as Stripture

For de Man, as we saw earlier, the literary text unravels itself. But the critic is not a mere passive witness to this self-undoing. *The critic, while appearing to comprehend a literary text from a position outside or above it, is in fact being comprehended, being grasped, by the text.* He or she is unwittingly acting out an interpretive role that the text has scripted, even dramatized, in advance. He or she is being enveloped in the folds of the texts even while attempting to sew it up. For me, this is one of deconstruction's most intriguing propositions and one that biblical scholars have yet to come to grips with.

Take the fleeing young man in Mark 14:51-52, for example, and the ways in which scholars have tackled him. The passage reads: "And a young man followed [Jesus], with nothing on but a linen cloth about his body; and they seized him, but he left the linen cloth and ran away naked." In the 1909 edition of his commentary on Mark, Henry Barclay Swete cited with approval the hypothesis of "many recent commentators" that the fleeing young man of 14:51-52 is none other than the evangelist himself.[15] The episode would then

15. Henry Barclay Swete, *Commentary on Mark: The Greek Text with Introduction, Notes and Indexes*, 3d ed. (Grand Rapids., Kregel Publications, 1977), 354.

be an autobiographical recollection, amounting to the author's personal signature within the text.

Commentators today accord little credence to this hypothesis. What fascinates me, however, is the way a discredited hypothesis such as this one hits
the mark in one sense while missing it in the sense in which it was aimed.
However poor their marksmanship as conventional historians might be, those
who ventured to describe Mark 14:51-52 as an authorial "signature" deserve
excellent marks for their aim. The flight of the naked young man would be an
uncannily apt signature left behind by the author, a glimpse of the author's
vanishing behind.

The scene is one of uncovering, of unveiling. It says that if you attempt to
grasp Mark—and among the "crowd with swords and clubs" that advance on
him, do we not detect a detail of Markan scholars armed with the tools of
critical analysis?—you will be left holding the cloth, the covering, what has
been added to make him seem respectable, while he slips away naked into the
night.

"They seized him, but he left the linen cloth and ran away naked." Is not
criticism itself a form of denuding?[16] Clearly scholars have but one thing on
their minds. They are always eager to undress a work, to expose an original
content concealed beneath secondary revisions, for example, as in their handling
of Mark's (rear)ending. Denuding, undressing, exposing, unveiling: these are
the prurient gestures of scholarship in search of truth. Add the interpenetration
of cloth, textile, and text (text is from the Latin verb texere, "to weave"), and
the disrobing of the young man can be read as having text and critic as its
theme: the text at the moment when the critic, seeking to arrest the movement
of its meanings, lays rough hands on it, exposing the truth of criticism as a
form of denuding, and denuding as a form of violence. Criticism (st)rips the
page.

The undressing is accidental in our scene: those who seize the young man
intend only to arrest him, not to strip him. But an accident is what we are here
to investigate—the accident through which the now discredited hypothesis
identifying the young man as "Mark" lays bare a truth it did not reach for: the
truth that criticism is a fantasy of violent possession instead of the young man's
true identity, the truth of criticism instead of critical truth. Where do we ourselves
lie in relation to this truth? In attempting to pronounce the truth of this scene,
what have we effected? A denuding of criticism as denuding? If so, we ourselves
stand exposed. The text has slipped away, having stripped us on its way out,
and whether it flees naked or clothed we cannot say. The more one appears
to be the master, "the more one presents one's rear."[17]

At issue here are the pretensions of one form of communication (criticism)
to speak authoritatively on behalf of another (literature). What if both these
modes of communication were hopelessly entangled to begin with? Criticism
sets out to subjugate literary language, enlisting language in order to do so.

16. Cf. Jacques Derrida, The Post Card: From Socrates to Freud and Beyond, trans.
    Alan Bass (Chicago: University of Chicago Press, 1987), 415–19.
17. Ibid., 453.

Small wonder if language revolts. In the course of that uncivil war, curious knots, complicities, and contradictions come about. These knots, nets, and traps have been a source of particular fascination for deconstruction.

The Gospel of the ~~Mark~~

"I do not 'concentrate,' in my reading. . . , either exclusively or primarily on those points that appear to be the most 'important,' 'central,' 'crucial,'" Derrida explains. "Rather, I de-concentrate, and *it is the secondary, eccentric, lateral, marginal, parasitic, borderline cases which are 'important' to me* and are a source of many things, such as pleasure, but also insight into the general functioning of a textual system."[18] The "eccentric," "marginal," "borderline" hypothesis identifying the fleeing young man as the evangelist Mark turned out to be an intriguing commentary on the system of Markan criticism itself, no less so for being unintentional. Of course, the episode in question (the flight of the naked young man) has always been a celebrated crux in Markan studies. It is time we strayed farther into the margins.

Mark's theology is commonly said to be a theology of the cross, a theology in which life and death crisscross. Jesus' crucifixation: having cross-examined his dyslexic disciples ("who do people say that I am? . . . who do you say that I am?"), Jesus declares, "If any want to become my followers, let them deny themselves and take up their cross and follow me. For those who want to save their life will lose it, and those who lose their life for my sake, and for the sake of the gospel, will save it" (8:34-35). In Mark, the signature of the disciple can only ever be that of a crisscross or Christcross, which my dictionary defines as "the figure or mark of a cross in general; esp. that made in 'signing' his name by a person who cannot write" (*OED*). But a person unable to write is generally unable to read, and in Mark, the disciples, generally at cross-purposes with Jesus, are singularly unable to read. Jesus must speak cross words to his puzzled disciples (8:33; cf. 8:17-21).

A cross is also a chiasmus, a crosswise fusion in which the order established in the first instance ("whoever would *save* their life will *lose* it") is inverted in the second instance ("and whoever *loses* their life . . . will *save* it"). Central to Mark is the fact of the crucifiction, a fiction structured like a cross or chiasmus.

Chiasmus comes from the Greek verb *chiazein*, "to mark with the letter χ," pronounced *chi*. And *chi* is an anagram of *ich*, which is German for the personal pronoun *I*, and the technical term in Freud (whose appearance here is anything but accidental) that English translators render as *ego*. And Jesus, who identifies himself to his terrified disciples in Mark 6:50 with the words *egō eimi* ("I am," or "it is I"), himself possesses a name that is an echo of the French *Je suis* ("I am"), the single superfluous letter being the *I* (or ego), which is thus marked out for deletion: "Father, . . . not what I [*egō*] want, but what you want" (14:36).

18. Jacques Derrida, *Limited Inc*, ed. Gerald Graff, trans. Samuel Weber and Jeffrey Mehlman (Evanston, Ill.: Northwestern University Press, 1988), 44, emphasis added.

To be marked with the χ, the cross, is painful, for *chiazein* also means "to cut." Another meaning of *chiasma* is "piece of wood." And the *chiasma* on which Jesus writ(h)es is a lectern as well as a writing desk. Dying, he opens the book to Psalm 22 and reads the opening verse: "My God, my God, why have you forsaken me?" *Chi*, the first letter of *Christos* ("Christ"), is also the twenty-second letter of the Greek alphabet.

But *chi*, as *ich*, is also *ichthus*. And *ichthus* ("fish" in Greek) was an early christological acronym: *Iēsous CHristos THeou hUios Sōtēr* ("Jesus Christ Son of God, Savior"). Dragged from the muddy river in Mark 1:10 ("And when he came up out of the water . . ."), Jesus slithers across the surface of the text. Who can ever grasp him? Mark itself comes closest. Mark's plot-lines are fishing lines, as are the lines of its page. And its genre is that of the fishing manual: "I will make you fishers of men" (1:17). Caught and taught by these fishermen, Jesus' followers will be a school of fish.

But first Jesus himself must be caught ("they . . . seized him"; 14:46), and so Mark's book becomes a hook, a clawed fishhook or χ. From the four sharp corners of its page, Jesus-*Ichthus* dangles, gasping for air.[19] At the end of the narrative line, Jesus writhes helplessly. His tale thrashes furiously as its climax approaches. But he is not yet in the net. As fish, Jesus will never be eaten; note that at the last supper (no fish supper) wine replaces the fish of the feeding miracles (6:38,41,43; 8:7; 14:23-25). Jesus can be eaten only as bread. In short, Mark is a standard (ev)ang(e)ler's tale about the one that got away: "he is not here. Look, there is the place they laid him"(16:6).

But the clawed *chi* has cut a deep gash in Mark as well as in Jesus, one that never closes. As we have seen, Mark holds opposites in painful tension: inside/outside, speech/writing, presence/absence. And this takes place within a book whose ending ("they said nothing to anyone"; 16:8) precludes its ever having been able to begin. Now Derrida likes to put concepts "under erasure." He crosses them out, deletes them without erasing them, as in "The Outside ✗ the Inside"[20]—what better epigraph for Mark? These concepts are inadmissible in his text, yet indispensable to it (presence, being, origin, etc.). Does Mark, who speaks with two different voices, who writes with two different hands, who deletes though without erasing, not write his entire Gospel under erasure, under the sign of the cross, the *chi*, the chiasmus, the mark (X)? A writing that "marks and goes back over its mark with an undecidable stroke,"[21] Mark can more aptly be written ~~Mark~~.

Faced with the mystery of Jesus, Mark can only (double) cross itself. Faced with the hit-and-misstery of exegesis, the critic can only repeat the gesture. One thing is certain, however: Mark is a cross-disciplinary text/book ("let them . . . take up their cross and follow me"; 8:34), which demands a cross-disciplinary reading.

19. To die of crucifixion was to die of asphyxia, frequently, the torso slumping forward in exhaustion until the contraction on the lungs gradually cut off respiration.
20. Jacques Derrida, *Of Grammatology,* trans. Gayatri Chakravorty Spivak (Baltimore: Johns Hopkins University Press, 1976), 44.
21. Derrida, *Positions,* 193.

But the real double cross in Mark is the kiss that draws blood, the savage kiss of Judas that initiates Jesus' passion ("And he kissed him"; 14:45), the lewd X near the end of Mark's letter. Mark writes under the sign not of one but of *three* crosses, then: the cross of Jesus, coupled with the colossal double cross of Judas. The latter looms over the story almost from the start (cf. 3:19), driving its action onward and bringing it to an inexorable climax (14:10-11, 18-21, 43-46). This sign of the triple cross is marked by a threefold crucifixion: "And with him they crucified two robbers, one on his right and one on his left" (15:27). Jesus' cross, soon to become a book (Mark), is placed between two cross-shaped bookends.

In short, the author of this Gospel has scattered his autograph, his signature, (his) Mark in the text—a name he does not yet know is his; it will be assigned to him only after his death. This author's real name is lost to us. Originally the Gospel circulated anonymously, "Mark" only later being added to it. This name appears to have been stolen from certain neighboring texts (Acts 12:12, 25; 15:37-39; 2 Tim 4:11; 1 Pet 5:13) that feature a (John) Mark who was a companion of Peter and Paul.

Did (John) Mark write the first Gospel? Most scholars today doubt that he did. However, the hypothesis that he did write it might not be altogether amiss. Like the reading that turns the fleeing young man into the author's signature, it seems to hit (the) Mark a stunning blow while missing it. And it is the striking, "other" logic of that missterious hit that fascinates me—how, flying wide, it nonetheless connects with a truth that conventional historiography would not think to target. Miss-understanding's underestimated striking power has made an accurate miss-ile of an inaccurate reading.

"Silently, laboriously, minutely, obsessionally," like a thief in the night, the author (of) Mark has set his signatures in place. "In the morning . . . you find his name all over the place. . . . He is no longer there, but you live in his mausoleum or his latrines."[22] The cross-stitching in this text is elaborate and delicate: from Mark who signs his name with the sign of the cross, also the sign of erasure, to Jesus who(se name—*Je suis*) is put to death on the cross (thereby erasing the *I* it contains), through an intricate pattern of crosslike marks, crosswise fusions, and irresolvable cruxes, all enacted in the shadow of a colossal double cross. To begin to unravel it is to take hold of a thread that leads not *out* of a labyrinth, but *into* one.

But whose labyrinth is it?

The Objest of the Pun in Exegesis

Midway through "Plato's Pharmacy," his reading of Plato's *Phaedrus*, Derrida stops to ask who the owner of the many meanings coursing through its corridors might be:

> Like any text, the text of "Plato" couldn't not be involved . . . with all the words that composed the system of the Greek language. . . . We do

22. Jacques Derrida, *Glas*, trans. John P. Leavey, Jr., and Richard Rand (Lincoln: University of Nebraska Press, 1986), 41–42.

not believe that there exists, in all rigor, a Platonic text, closed upon itself, complete with its inside and its outside. Not that one must then consider that it is leaking on all sides and can be drowned confusedly in the undifferentiated generality of its element. Rather, provided the articulations are rigorously and prudently recognized, one should simply be able to untangle the hidden forces of attraction linking a present word with an absent word in the text.[23]

What is being called into question here is the power often attributed to authors— and nowhere more insistently than in biblical studies—to bend the language of texts to their will, to use language only and not be used by it, to keep its seething semantic potential at a controlled heat so that a unity of meaning can form in it, to prevent the text from boiling over with scalding force, spoiling the author's recipe. In reponse, Derrida gestures to a "textual unconscious," an unpredictable and hence uncontrollable excess of meaning that simmers within any linguistic production, ever ready to spill over.

The ways into Derrida's own labyrinthine writings are many—doors marked with the names of prominent German philosophers, for example (Heidegger, Husserl, Nietzsche, Hegel). A door no less serviceable, though less often used, is the one that bears the name of the father of psychoanalysis, Sigmund Freud.

As the century that opened with Freud's *The Interpretation of Dreams* draws to a close, Freud's message still sits undigested in our bodies of writing. "It is essential to abandon the overvaluation of the property of being conscious," wrote Freud; "The unconscious is the larger sphere, which includes within it the smaller sphere of the conscious."[24]

Pschoanalytic literary critics who take their lead from Derrida look to psychoanalysis not just for a new way of reading but also for a new way of writing— a reinvigorated academic writing that would take as its point of departure an observation implicit in early Freud, but neglected by Freudian literary critics, Freud himself included. *The unconscious is itself irreducibly "literary" in its workings.*[25] It is a realm of graphic images, startling associations, surrealistic spectacles, and multilingual puns.

In some of his more experimental texts, Derrida would appear to be miming the movements of the unconscious, exploiting chance associations between words across several languages—associations traditional scholarship would disregard as inconsequential—performing interpretations that engage in textual congress with the *letter* of the text being read—its accidents of expression, the minute specifics of its style, the look of its words as well as their sound—as

23. Derrida, *Dissemination,* 129–30; cf. 95–96.
24. Sigmund Freud, *The Interpretation of Dreams,* in the *Standard Edition of the Complete Psychological Works of Sigmund Freud,* ed. and trans. James Strachey (London: Hogarth Press, 1953–74), 5:612–13.
25. Here I am echoing the views of Jacques Lacan, Freud's foremost French disciple. There is a strong family resemblance between the theories of Lacan and Derrida, although Derrida as the younger brother has tried to distance himself as much as possible from Lacan.

opposed to its content. (Needless to say, the firm distinction of form and content is the first casualty of these readings.) Clearly, my own reading of Mark has been increasingly colored by these performances—performances that do not easily reduce to methodological rules and principles. As Derrida himself has remarked: "Deconstruction is inventive or it is nothing at all; it does not settle for methodical procedures, it opens up a passageway, it marches ahead and marks a trail; . . . it produces rules—other conventions. . . ."[26]

Derrida's project in such writings (for example, *Glas, Signsponge, The Post Card, The Truth in Painting*) can be understood in part as an attempt to extend to the domains of philosophical and critical analysis Freud's pioneering explorations of dreams, slips of the tongue and pen, lapses of memory, and all the other "accidents" of conscious life that we ordinarily shove into the margins. At stake in such a project is the deconstruction of a cluster of oppositions that happen—not by chance—to form the foundations of standard academic writing, biblical scholarship included: rational/irrational, intended/unintended, essential/accidental, serious/trivial, central/marginal, content/form, idea/ornament, literal/metaphorical, primary text/secondary text, creative writing/critical writing. . . .

As with all such conceptual pairs (recall our opening discussion), the second term is thought to be inferior to the first. These hierarchies tend to be accepted as natural and self-evident, as though they had not been established at certain moments, as though they had no history. Fixed and frozen, they paralyze thought even as they enable it. But take, for example, the exclusion of homonymns or puns from the Western intellectual tradition. This exclusion can be traced back to such contingencies as Aristotle's strictures against homonyms and Plato's exclusion of poets from his ideal state.

For the serious scholar, puns and anagrams are jest a joke. Language should be heard and not seen. Deconstruction sets up camp precisely at such points and begins to excavate: where what is *written* (for example, "his story") is not identical to what is *heard* ("history), where writing flaunts an excess that is irreducible to speech, and where the history that enslaves writing to the voice begins to flounder before our very eyes (*history, his story, hystery, herstory, mystery, mystory* . . .).[27] Derrida has begun to forge a new academic writing that is no longer fixated on the ear and the voice. (Taste, smell, and touch figure in this new writing along with sight, but that is another story.) Homonymic and other associative clusters, moreover—recall the *chi*-cluster whose inky footprints we tracked through Mark—disrupt binary thinking. A thinking that lives in vertical, two-tiered, oppositional, hierarchical structures is necessarily unsettled by a nomad thinking that picks its steps through horizontal, single-tiered, associative, open-ended word clusters. Outside the city, with Plato's poets, on ground that traditional academe has long deemed a swamp, there is ample room for a

---

26. Jacques Derrida, "Psyche: Inventions of the Other," trans. Catherine Porter, in *Reading de Man Reading*, ed. Lindsay Waters and Wlad Godzich (Minneapolis: University of Minnesota Press, 1989), 42.
27. *Hystery* comes from *hystera*, the Greek word for "womb." *Mystory* is a term concocted by the critical theorist Gregory Ulmer.

different academy that would house alternative approaches to reading and writing.

Mark's Nightmaze: Writ(h)ing on a Bed of Paper

What does Mark, or any other Gospel, have to do with the language of the unconscious, epitomized by the language of dreams? Quite a bit, as a matter of fact. Abstract expression is alien both to the Gospel and to the dream. Clearly, the pictorial language of a Gospel is not the abstract, propositional language of a theological treatise or scholarly commentary. A Gospel is more like a dream than a dissertation. "Abstract expressions offer the same kind of difficulties to representation in dreams as a political leading article in a newspaper would offer to an illustrator," notes Freud,[28] and what is true of the illustrator and the dreamer is also true of the evangelist. Like the cartoon, the dream or Gospel must render in concrete, pictorial terms a subject matter that is generally "colorless and abstract."[29] But biblical scholars and theologians are, for the most part, neither dreamers nor cartoonists, preferring to take a jackhammer to the concrete language of the Gospels, to replace graphic images with abstract categories.

Like dreams, Gospels pose special problems for interpretation. The concrete word-images of which they are composed—seed, water, bread, blood—are far richer in associations than conceptual terms (evangelism, baptism, communion, redemption). When our abstract conceptual language or our commonsense everyday language is displaced by a concrete pictorial language, our understanding falters, because a Gospel or a dream never, or almost never, tells us whether its elements are to be interpreted literally or figuratively—historically, for example (as a recollection of something that actually happened), or symbolically (as having a far looser connection with "reality").

Odd as it may sound, then, Mark is at least as close to the language of the unconscious (that of the dream, for example) as to the theological treatise or scholarly commentary. In consequence, Mark can just as easily be approached through a postcritical writing that would attempt to match its concrete parabolic style by miming it, as through a critical reading that, in getting Mark right (in putting down the riot), would attempt to rewrite it altogether in colorless academese.

The questions remain, How can scholarly writing on the Bible be put into communication with what is said in Genesis about a God who creates the names of the first man and woman through wordplay (2:7, 23; 3:20; cf. 4:1); or what is said in Exodus about a God who, in displaying himself to Moses, plays on his own name (3:14 ff.); or "what is said in Numbers about the parched woman drinking the inky dust of the law [5:23-24]; or what is said in Ezekiel

28. Freud, *The Interpretation of Dreams*, 5:340.
29. Ibid., 5:339.

about the son of man who fills his entrails with the scroll of the law which has become sweet as honey in his mouth [2:8-3:3; cf. Rev 10:8-10]";[30] or what is said in Matthew about a Jesus who founds his church upon a pun (16:18); or what is said in Mark about a Jesus who is both a writer and a writing and who, in a rite, bequeaths himself to his disciples to be (eaten as b)read: "analyze the corpus that I tender to you, that I extend here on this bed of paper"?[31]

FURTHER READING

General

CULLER, Jonathan. *On Deconstruction: Theory and Criticism after Structuralism.* Ithaca, N.Y.: Cornell University Press, 1982. Perhaps the most widely used of the standard introductions to deconstruction.

DERRIDA, Jacques. *Positions.* Translated by Alan Bass. Chicago: University of Chicago Press, 1981. Three interviews with Derrida, often recommended as a useful port of entry to his thought.

KAMUF, Peggy, ed. *A Derrida Reader: Between the Blinds.* New York: Columbia University Press, 1990. Twenty-two selections (essays and book excerpts) from Derrida, each introduced by Kamuf, along with a general introduction.

LEITCH, Vincent B. *Deconstructive Criticism: An Advanced Introduction.* New York: Columbia University Press, 1983. Colorful, exuberant, and a mine of information.

NORRIS, Christopher. *Derrida.* Cambridge: Harvard University Press, 1987. Focuses on Derrida's philosophical underpinnings and on the ethical ramifications of his thought.

NORRIS, Christopher, and Andrew Benjamin. *What Is Deconstruction?* New York: St. Martin's Press, 1988. Two essays, lavishly illustrated: "Deconstruction, Post-Modernism and the Visual Arts" by Norris, and "Deconstruction and Art/The Art of Deconstruction" by Benjamin.

Biblical

BLANK, G. Kim. "Deconstruction: Entering the Bible through Babel." *Neotestamentica* 20 (1986): 61-67. A literary critic explains deconstruction to an audience of biblical scholars.

CROSSAN, John Dominic. *Cliffs of Fall: Paradox and Polyvalence in the Parables of Jesus.* New York: Seabury Press, 1980. Three lively essays in which Derrida makes a number of appearances.

DERRIDA, Jacques. "Edmond Jabès and the Question of the Book." *In Writing and Difference,* 64–78. Translated by Alan Bass. Chicago: University of Chicago Press, 1978. Haunting, lyrical meditations on writing, Judaism, and the Bible.

DETWEILER, Robert, ed. *Derrida and Biblical Studies. Semeia* 23 (1982). Includes an excellent introduction to Derrida by Herbert Schneidau and an essay by Derrida himself that circles the book of Revelation.

JOBLING, David, and Stephen D. Moore, eds. *Poststructuralism as Exegesis. Semeia* 54 (1991). Includes Derrida's "Des Tours de Babel" (in English, despite the title),

---

30. Jacques Derrida, *Writing and Difference,* trans. Alan Bass (Chicago: University of Chicago Press, 1978), 231.
31. Derrida, *The Post Card,* 99.

possibly the most accessible of his biblical forays, along with other deconstructive readings of biblical texts.

KERMODE, Frank. *The Genesis of Secrecy: On the Interpretation of Narrative*. Cambridge: Harvard University Press, 1979. Not deconstruction as such, although it looms in the background. Includes some fine readings of Mark.

MACKEY, Louis. "Slouching toward Bethlehem: Deconstructive Strategies in Theology." *Anglican Theological Review* 65 (1983): 255–72. Highly accessible. It spells out the implications of deconstruction for both Gospel scholarship and systematic theology.

MOORE, Stephen D. *Literary Criticism and the Gospels: The Theoretical Challenge*. New Haven: Yale University Press, 1989. Includes extensive discussion of deconstruction and a deconstructive reading of parts of John's Gospel.

———. *Mark and Luke in Poststructuralist Perspectives: Jesus Begins to Write*. New Haven: Yale University Press, 1992. The parent of the present chapter. More demanding, although also more adventurous.

PHILLIPS, Gary A., ed. *Poststructural Criticism and the Bible: Text/History/Discourse*. *Semeia* 51 (1990). Includes much on Derrida and deconstruction.

5

Feminist Criticism:

The Dancing Daughter

JANICE CAPEL ANDERSON

Scholars often compare a Gospel to a string of pearls. The pearls are small units of tradition such as parables or miracle stories. The string is editorial material that orders, connects, and interprets the pearls. Each evangelist is an editor or redactor. The way the evangelist chooses and shapes his material reflects his theology. It also reflects the rhetorical conventions and historical situation of his community, his intended audience.[1] Are the evangelist and his community Jews or Gentiles? Are they rich or poor? Are they reacting to the fall of Jerusalem in 70 C.E.? Are they familiar with intercalation, the technique of sandwiching one story into another to force the interpreter to read one in the light of the other? Do they view the cross as a humiliating sacrifice or the exaltation of a superhuman being? Each string of pearls is a creation with a unique perspective.

1. Given the environment and the content, the Gospels were probably written by men.

When pressed, scholars admit that their interpretations of the Gospels also reflect their own viewpoints. Their interpretations inevitably reflect their own theological, rhetorical, and historical environment, their own commitments and experiences. Although they acknowledge it theoretically, scholars often forget this point. Interpreters speak and write as if they can reconstruct history, rhetoric, and theology *as it actually was*. They speak as if they can neatly separate what a text meant from what it means to them. Examination of the history of the interpretation of the Gospels, as described in chapter 1, shows that interpretation is always perspectival.

Feminist critics point out that just as theology, historical circumstances, and literary conventions shape the Gospels and interpretations of the Gospels, gender shapes them as well. Indeed, gender is inextricably bound with theology, rhetoric, and history. It is an important category for historical, literary, sociological, and theological analyses of the Gospels.

What is gender? Gender is the social construction of biological sex. Feminists often use the words *women* and *men* to refer to biological sex and *male* and *female* to refer to gender. Women and men are born with different sexual organs. Different social groups assign different meanings to these sexual differences. They define what it means to be male or female and the relationships between genders. In white middle-class American culture, boys play with trucks and girls play with dolls. Males bring home the bacon, females cook it. Multiple, sometimes contradictory meanings are attached to sexual differences. Western culture constructs females as dumb and tricky, virgins and whores, pure and sinful, Mary and Eve. Definitions of gender vary with context and change over time. They do not have a one-to-one correspondence to the behaviors of women and men. The construction of gender also varies with race, class, religion, and other factors. Sojourner Truth, a former slave, pointed this out in 1851. When answering a heckler, she said:

> Dat man ober dar say dat women needs to be helped into carriages, and lifted ober ditches, and to have de best places . . . and ain't I a woman? Look at me! Look at my arm! . . . I have plowed, and planted, and gathered into barns, and no man could head me—and ain't I a woman? I could work as much as any man (when I could get it), and bear de lash as well—and ain't I a woman? I have borne five children and I seen 'em mos all sold off into slavery, and when I cried out with a mother's grief, none but Jesus hear—and ain't I a woman?[2]

Feminist Biblical Scholarship

Who are the feminist biblical scholars who argue that gender is an important analytic category? I am a feminist New Testament critic. I write as a white American middle-class Presbyterian mother trained in academic historical and

2. Quoted in bell hooks, *Ain't I A Woman: Black Women and Feminism* (Boston: South End Press, 1981), 160.

literary biblical criticism. All feminist biblical critics do not look like me. All of them would not describe feminist biblical scholarship the way I do. Each feminist critic is a unique pearl with a unique color and shape formed out of the variables of gender, race, class, sexual orientation, nationality, education, age, religion, and personal experience. Some of us use primarily literary, others historical or sociological methods. Together we form intertwining strands of pearls, pearls of great price.

The most published feminist critics writing in English in the last twenty years have been white middle-class Euramerican or European Christian academic women. These include such mothers of recent feminist biblical criticism as Phyllis Bird, Elisabeth Schüssler Fiorenza, and Phyllis Trible and theologians Rosemary Radford Ruether and Letty Russell. More recently younger scholars of similar backgrounds; African-American womanists[3] like Katie Geneva Cannon, Clarice J. Martin, and Renita Weems; and other women of color like Elsa Tamez, a Mexican Methodist, and Kwok Pui-lan, a Chinese Christian, have published feminist criticism and enriched the strands. Alongside these Christian feminist academics stand Jewish scholars like Esther Fuchs, Amy-Jill Levine, and Judith Plaskow; those who embrace Goddess religion such as Carol Christ and Mary Daly; and those who embrace no particular religion such as Mieke Bal and Julia Kristeva. They are dialogue partners along with the many non-academic women who live and struggle with the Bible, as well as men, academics and not, who will sit at the table with us.

What do feminist biblical critics share in common? All of us witness to different forms and degrees of oppression in patriarchal religious institutions, the academy, and societies. Some of us experience multiple oppressions due to gender, sexual preference, religion, nationality, race, and class. The string that threads us together is a commitment to feminism. We define feminism in many ways. We might agree with bell hooks, who calls it "a common resistance to all the different forms of male domination,"[4] and Linda Alcoff, who says it is "the affirmation . . . of our right and our ability to construct, and take responsibility for, our gendered identity, our politics and our choices."[5] We also share a commitment to the significance of the Bible, whether as possessing positive authority, needing exposure as a tool of oppresssion, or both.

Feminist Biblical Critics at Work

What kinds of biblical scholarship do feminists produce? There is no single model. Our choice of method—historical, literary, or social scientific—influences our work. So do our religious ties. My account will concentrate on

3. The term *womanist* is the self-designation of many black women following Alice Walker in *In Search of Our Mothers' Gardens* (New York: Harcourt Brace Jovanovich, 1974).

4. Quoted in Sandra Harding, "Conclusion: Epistemological Questions" in *Feminism and Methodology*, ed. Sandra Harding (Bloomington: Indiana University Press, 1987), 188.

5. Linda Alcoff, "Cultural Feminism Versus Post-structuralism: The Identity Crisis in Feminist Theory," *Signs* 13 (1988): 432.

Christian feminist criticism, which focuses on the Christian tradition or sees itself as belonging to that tradition. Feminist biblical sholars who study and/or belong to other traditions share in many of the practices of Christian scholars. However, they have their own particular problems and wrestle with different traditions of interpretation. Questions about the nature of the Chrisitian canon and scriptural authority have particularly concerned Christian feminists. Although in practice we often blend them, one way to view our activities is to see them as two-pronged; a feminist critique and a feminist construction.

Varieties of Feminist Critique

1. Critique of the androcentric and patriarchal character of the Hebrew Scriptures and the New Testament

By androcentric I mean male-centered, treating males as the universal human norm. Androcentrism is a male-oriented worldview. The male as model defines the female either as the same, the opposite, or the complement of the male, the universal human. Often the concept of the female as the "Other," the exception, the anomaly, the lack justifies male domination. In order to define themselves as male, men define the female as the Other, often as an opposite. They define male "strengths" in opposition to female "weaknesses." Men also project onto the female what they fear or do not understand in themselves. They define as unimportant, and at the same time fear, women's reproductive and nurturant powers. In Western culture the parallel oppositions male/female, culture/nature, mind/body, reason/passion, good/evil often support dominance. Patriarchy literally means the rule of the father. By patriarchal I mean sanctioning male authority over females and children, especially the authority of males of dominant races and classes. Patriarchy may involve religious, economic, social, and political processes. Even within patriarchy, however, women still have power. Power can mean authority or control. It can also mean the ability to resist, the ability to accomplish goals, disguised power, or power in certain realms of life. In some societies, for example, women control agriculture. Elite women may also have more power than nonelite men and women in patriarchal societies.

Many examples illustrate androcentrism and patriarchy in the Hebrew Scriptures and the New Testament. God is most often presented as male. Male figures and authorities dominate the texts. Patrilineal genealogy and the process that leads to a male heir, including a male messiah, structure many of them. Sometimes the androcentric and patriarchal nature of the texts is obvious. Many passages simply assume that only men are religious or political leaders or that women are property. First Tim 2:11-15 instructs women to keep silent and have no authority over men because women are the authors of original sin. Other passages are more subtle. Barren women such as Sarah (Gen 11–23), Hannah (1 Sam 1), and Elizabeth (Luke 1:5-45) interact with God. However, their barrenness as wives is a reproach, and the stories issue in the birth of sons to ensure the male line. Women like the hemorrhaging woman (Mark 5:25-34) or the Syrophoenician woman (Mark 7:24-30) have faith in Jesus.

However, their faith is an exception and contrasts with weak male faith because they are women. If even a woman, how much more a man.

An experiment can help you to understand the androcentric and patriarchal character of the Gospels and Acts. Read Mark 6:41-44 and Acts 1:15-26—passages that do not deal overtly with male-female relationships—substituting female terms for male terms. How strange and exclusionary the passages now sound.

2. Critique of the androcentric and patriarchal character of biblical scholarship

Biblical scholarship has been androcentric and patriarchal in its failure to explore the construction of male and female gender. Its reconstruction of the histories of Israel and the early church have ignored or denied the roles of women. Its literary analyses have ignored or marginalized women characters. Its interpretations have often been sexist. Its research questions and interests often have been those of primary significance to elite males. Its theological concerns have arisen out of male experiences and needs. Why should we consider war more fundamental to the human experience than birth? Why should we consider sin only in terms of overweening pride rather than lack of self-esteem? Biblical scholarship has sometimes served to help institutions oppress women, especially nonelite women.

Examples of the androcentrism and patriarchy of biblical scholarship are many. Scholars describe the creation of humans last as the crown of creation, the top of a pyramid establishing human superiority over plant and animal creation in Genesis 1. The creation of woman last in Genesis 2 is described not as a climax, but as a mark of her inferiority. Many interpreters and translators treat the reference in Rom 16:7 to Andronicus and Junia as a reference to two men. They consider Junia, although a well-known woman's name, as short for Junianus. They find it improbable that the text calls a woman an apostle even though patristic exegesis thought Junia was a woman.[6] Also in Romans 16 and elsewhere scholars translate references to a woman as *diakonos* as servant or helper, rather than as deacon as for Paul, Apollos, and others.[7]

Biblical archeologists often concentrate on large, urban public sites. They are more likely to excavate city walls, palaces, and religious centers. These sites help to reconstruct the life of urban elite males active in public religious and political activities. They are less likely to aid in reconstructing the life of the average person, male or female, except in relationship to that elite.[8]

That biblical scholarship has been androcentric and patriarchal should not be surprising. For the most part only elite European and American men have

6. Elisabeth Schüssler Fiorenza, *In Memory of Her* (New York: Crossroad, 1983), 47, citing Bernadette Brooten, "Junia . . . Outstanding among the Apostles," in *Women Priests: A Catholic Commentary on the Vatican Declaration*, ed. L. Swidler and A. Swidler (New York: Paulist, 1977), 141–44.
7. Ibid.
8. Carol Meyers, *Discovering Eve: Ancient Israelite Women in Context* (New York: Oxford University Press, 1988), 16–19.

practiced it. Imagine a circle. Cut it in half with a line. One half represents women, the other half men. Divide the male half into thirds. One third represents white males. One small sliver of this third represents elite European and American educated males.[9] It is from this group that most biblical scholars have come.

3. Countering passages that legitimate or have been used to legitimate oppression with counterpassages or liberating interpretations of such passages

Many biblical texts, including Genesis 2–3; 1 Cor 11:3-12; 14:34-36; Eph 5:22-24; 1 Tim 2:9-15; and 1 Pet 3:1-7, have been used to justify the domination of women. There is a long history of women countering these passages with passages they find liberating such as Genesis 1; Judges 4–5; Gal 3:28; John 4; and Acts 2:16-21 (quoting Joel 2:28-32). First Timothy may forbid women to speak in church, but Acts says women will prophesy.

Feminsts have also offered liberating interpretations of passages used to legitimate oppression. Genesis 2 and 3 and 1 Cor 11:3-12 have been frequent sites for such work. They do not read the "curse" against women in Gen 3:16 as God ordaining women's inferior status. Some read it as a description of the results of the Fall violating God's intention for creation, results overcome by Christ (Gal 3:28). Carol Meyers places it in the context of man's toil in Gen 3:17-19 and the harsh environment of ancient Palestine. In order for the group to survive, women had to have many pregnancies. Verse 16 is not about the universal domination of women. Instead, it is about the need to submit to male sexual desire to prevent underpopulation in a very specific historical situation.[10]

Varieties of Feminist Construction

1. Recovering female images of God and concentrating on stories of women in the text in order to recover images of biblical women, images of agency, and images of victimization

One of the first projects of the most recent wave of feminist biblical interpreters was the search for female images of God. They found that the Bible pictures God as a mother (Jer 31:15-22; Isa 66:7-14; Job 38:28-29), a pregnant woman (Isa 42:14), a midwife (Ps 22:9), a mistress (Ps 123:2), a woman who searches for a lost coin (Luke 15:1-10), a woman making bread (Matt 13:31-33 = Luke 13:18-21), and as Sophia (wisdom).[11] Phyllis Trible showed how the Hebrew Scriptures connect the wombs of women and the compassion of God. The root

9. Patricia A. Cain, "Teaching Feminist Legal Theory at Texas: Listening to Difference and Exploring Connections," *Journal of Legal Education* 38 (1988): 168.
10. Carol Meyers, *Discovering Eve*, 95–121.
11. Virginia Ramey Mollenkott, *The Divine Feminine: The Biblical Imagery of God as Female* (New York: Crossroads, 1983); Fiorenza, *In Memory of Her*, 130 ff.

rhm is the source of the noun womb or uterus (*rehem*). The same word in the plural means compassion, mercy, or love (*rahamim*). The womb of God is a metaphor for God's compassion.[12]

Feminists also have written about human women characters. These characters often received short shrift in previous scholarship. The female power and activity of Sarah, Hagar, Ruth, Deborah, Jael, Shiphrah and Puah (the Hebrew midwives in Egypt), Miriam, the woman who anoints Jesus, the Samaritan woman, the Syrophoenician woman, Mary the mother of Jesus, Mary and Martha, the women at the cross and tomb, Lydia, and others have been explored. Although female power and agency remain within an androcentric and patriarchal context and these stories may serve oppressive ends, many women find them empowering. In constructing female gender as "difference" from male gender, as inferiority and loss, paradoxically androcentrism and patriarchy witness to female importance and power. This is especially crucial in biblical texts dealing with birth, nursing, and menstruation, activities showing the lack and dependency of men. Although the text and many interpretations create and reflect a division between a female private domestic sphere and a public male sphere (and nature and culture), feminist exegetes have shown women characters active in the public sphere (Deborah or Prisca), and women characters who bring out the importance of the domestic sphere (Mary) and argued for the social construction and explosion of the polarity.

Feminists have also focused on biblical characters who are victims. One important example is Phyllis Trible's *Texts of Terror*. There she recounts the tales of Hagar, Tamar, the concubine from Bethlehem (Judg 19:1-30), and the daughter of Jephthah *in memoriam*. Another important example is Elsa Tamez's interpretation of the story of Hagar, a woman abused by a male and an elite female, Sarah.[13] The stories of women like Hagar, the Samaritan woman (John 4), and the Canaanite woman (Matt 15) disclose multiple oppressions. Religion, social position, ethnic origin, as well as their sex, mark characters as marginal.

2. Reconstruction of the historical and sociological background of the text with reference to the category of gender: rewriting the histories of Israel and the early church

Scholars have sought to do justice to the roles of women in history as the subjects or makers of history as well as the objects of oppression. Not only women leaders but also the everyday lives of "average" women are matters of concern. Taking as a given the past existence of both men and women, they have sought to give voice to the silenced. However, they have not been content simply to add what they can learn about women to previous interpretations of the biblical past. Feminist historians do not simply add women and stir. They have begun to rewrite the histories of Israel and the early church. They have begun to reconstruct the roles and relationships of men and women in the

12. Phyllis Trible, *God and the Rhetoric of Sexuality* (Philadelphia: Fortress Press, 1978), chapter 2.
13. Elsa Tamez, "Women and the Bible," *Lucha* 9 (1985): 54–64.

history of Israel and the early church. They have also started to write the history of gender ideologies, symbolic conceptions of maleness and femaleness. To do these tasks they have focused not only on the biblical text but also on archeological data and extracanonical writings. Biblical texts tell us what elite men thought about women and gender. They do not tell us directly what women were actually thinking and doing and how gender roles operated. Archeology and extracanonical texts add to the pool of data.

3. Recovering the history of women interpreting the Bible and rewriting the history of interpretation

One of feminist criticism's most exhilarating discoveries is the history of women interpreters of the Bible. This history extends from ancient women, to medieval women, to Reformation and Counter-reformation women, to nineteenth-century activists such as Sarah and Angelina Grimke and Elizabeth Cady Stanton, to contemporary members of the Society of Biblical Literature. Women have always interpreted the Bible. Their interpretations are not often found in academic tomes, but rather in letters, diaries, devotional literature, and speeches. Much work needs to be done in this area.[14]

4. Examining readers' responses: asking how gender and other historical and social variables shape the production of meaning

The previous activity, recovering the history of women interpreting the Bible, is actually a subset of this one. To answer the question, What difference does it make if a reader is a woman? interpreters have sought the history of women's interpretations of the Bible to compare to male interpretations.

What difference does it make if a reader of a text is a male or a female? As Robert Fowler explained in chapter 3, different interpreters stress the role of the author, text, reader(s), or context in creating meaning. Reader-response criticism stresses the role of the reader. Some reader-response critics write about the reactions of a first-time reader. Others write about an experienced or even an ideal reader who knows everything there is to know about the text. Some reader-response critics write about a hypothetical reader, others about actual readers, past or present. Sometimes critics call the various ways to describe the reading process *stories of reading*.

14. For sources, see Caroline Walker Bynum, *Fragmentation and Redemption* (New York: Zone Books, 1991); idem, *Jesus as Mother* (Berkeley: University of California Press, 1982); Ronald Kastner and Patricia Wilson Kastner, *A Lost Tradition: Women Writers of the Early Church* (Lanham, Md.: University Press of America, 1981); Alice Rossi, ed., *The Feminist Papers: From Adams to de Beauvoir* (Boston: Northeastern University Press, 1988); Elizabeth Cady Stanton et al., *The Women's Bible* (1895; reprint, Salem, N.H.: Ayer Company, 1988).

Feminist critics have asked, What difference does it make if the reader actual, ideal, or hypothetical is male or female, feminist or not?[15] They have created two new stories of reading. The first is the story of women reading androcentric and patriarchal texts. The second is the story of women reading women's writing and/or feminist writing. With the Hebrew and Christian Scriptures, we must deal with the first story. When a woman reads an androcentric/patriarchal text she is *immasculated,* that is, she reads and identifies as male.[16] Yet as the reader identifies with the male as universal and dominant, she knows she is a female. She constructs herself as Other.

Feminist biblical criticism documents this process. For example, in reading Matthew a woman might identify with Peter, who denies Jesus (Matt 26:33-35, 69-75) but who is also the rock upon which the church is founded (Matt 16:18-19). Peter is a universal model of Christian experience. She sees herself as someone who sometimes fails and denies Jesus, but who also can be a faithful rock. However, in the world of the Matthean text, only males are ruling authorities, rocks. Matthew excludes females and thus her from official authority. She is the Other, the maid in the courtyard to whom Peter lies. He should not fear a mere female servant. She is one of the women at the tomb. She fulfills the female role. She serves the disciples as she restores them as Jesus' brothers to him. She reads as a male who views women as weak and subservient. She also reads as a male in awe of female power. The women do remain at cross and tomb. Mary does give birth outside the normal patriarchal horizon.

However, that is not the end of this story of reading. Once a woman is aware of immasculation, she can read as a feminist. She recognizes the processes that are taking place. If she tells a story of reading that emphasizes the power of the text, she can describe how the text constructs gender. She can show what the text does to women and resist its gender ideology in her reading. She can help others do the same. If she tells a story of reading that emphasizes the reader, she can show how women immasculate themselves and how they can create readings in which they are not victims. Or perhaps a feminist can tell a third story of reading in which she recognizes the roles of both text and readers, male and female. As she reads, she recognizes the text immasculating her and the male reading strategies she uses. She also reads recognizing what the text does not allow or tensions within it. She recognizes what she and other feminists might do with the text. She can resist it, read it against the grain, or transform it for feminist use.

A particularly important question for many religious feminists is how the Bible has empowered women readers and hearers in the past and how it might

15. My discussion depends on many of the works on gender and reading cited in Diana Fuss, "Reading Like a Feminist," *differences* 1 (1989): 77–92 and Patrocinio P. Schweickart, "Reading Ourselves: Toward a Feminist Theory of Reading," in *Gender and Reading: Essays on Readers, Texts, and Contexts,* ed. Elizabeth A. Flynn and Patrocinio P. Scheickart (Baltimore: Johns Hopkins University Press, 1986), 31–62.
16. Judith Fetterley coined this term in *The Resisting Reader: A Feminist Approach to American Fiction* (Bloomington: Indiana University Press, 1978).

continue to do so, despite its patriarchy and androcentrism. Or, how have women read or heard the Bible so it has been a source of affirmation and power for them? When a feminist reader reads Matthew, how can she recover the power of identifying with Peter without reading herself as Other?

So far I have been mixing up what it means to be a woman, a female, and a feminist, *and* actual and hypothetical readers. Further, I have not asked what difference it makes if the reader is a black academic American woman or a Guatemalan peasant woman. Being a woman is a matter of biology. Being a female is a matter of a socially constructed gender. Being a feminist is joining a coalition based on politics; it is a position to act from politically. Other factors complicate all these categories. There is no essence of womanhood or even feminism. When I ask what difference it makes if the reader is a woman or a feminist, I can look at the interpretations of actual women of various races, classes, religions, sexual affiliations, and times. I can trace similarities and differences between them. I can also appeal to the experience of reading as a female or a feminist as a hypothesis. What if a woman or a feminist read this text? How might she/he respond? When I do this, I must construct what it means to be a woman or a feminist at the same time as I explore the gender ideologies the text constructs.

I agree with Elaine Showalter that when we speak of reading as a woman often what we mean is reading as a feminist.[17] As feminist readers, we appeal to the politics, values, and perspective of a class or coalition. We must. No one can speak for everyone. I can speak and read only as a white middle-class American heterosexual Christian feminist. Yet we must listen to, speak and read with and on behalf of one another. Although never fully achieved, we share bell hooks's commitment to resist the different forms of male domination and a commitment to respect our sameness and our differences. Admittedly, this view is optimistic. When we use the hypothesis of a feminist reader, we must always remember the challenge Audre Lorde poses: "Some problems we share as women, some we do not. You fear your children will grow up to join the patriarchy and testify against you, we fear our children will be dragged from a car and shot down in the street, and you will turn your backs upon the reasons they are dying."[18]

Doing Feminist Gospel Criticism

How does one begin a feminist analysis of a Gospel? A lot depends on your questions, methods, and goals. Let me suggest four steps that may help. These four steps are especially congenial to literary and some social approaches. They can, however, form a starting point for other approaches as well. They are not the only steps one could or should take.

17. Elaine Showalter, "Critical Cross-Dressing," in *Men in Feminism*, ed. Alice Jardine and Paul Smith (New York: Methuen, 1987), 124–27.
18. Audre Lorde, "Age, Race, Class and Sex: Women Redefining Difference," in *Sister Outsider* (Freedom, Calif.: Crossing Press, 1984), 119.

The first step is to look for male and female gender markers in the text, including descriptions of or prescriptions for gender roles and relationships, as well as analysis of male and female characters. One place to begin is with a concordance. There one can check for all references to gender-related terms such as *girl, woman, widow, son, father, sister, mother-in-law, prostitute, virgin, marriage, divorce, heir, birth, baby, and nursing.* Note that the Greek word for "woman" (*gunē*) can also mean "wife" and the Greek word for "male-man" (*ànēr*) also means "husband." Mark, for example, uses the term *gunē* in 5:25, 33; 6:17,18; 7:25, 26; 10:2,7,11; 12:19,20,22,23; 14:3; 15:40. You may also want to scan the Gospel to compile a list of passages that refer to clothing, hunting, agriculture, barter or sale of goods, food, childcare, battle, athletic competition, religious leadership, or other activities associated in some cultures with gender constructions. Another strategy that focuses on the text is to analyze male and female characters, including character groups. You can list all the male and female characters who appear in a text and the passages in which they appear. Not only how many times male and female characters surface, but also the content of the scenes in which they appear and their role in the plot are important. For each character ask the following questions and any others you think may be significant: Does the character have a proper name or other form of identification? How old is she or he? What is his or her ethnic or religious identity—Jew, Gentile, Samaritan? What is the character's occupation? family status? financial status? Does the character speak in direct or indirect discourse? Does anyone speak to him or her directly or indirectly? What does the person do as an actor? For what persons is he or she the object of actions? Is any of the narrative presented from his or her point of view within the view of the narrator? In what settings does he or she appear? What times does he or she appear—daytime, night, Sabbath? What is the character's relationship to Jesus?

The activities I have described will help you focus on the text using gender as an analytic category. After this initial investigation, you can describe any patterns that you see. Similarities and differences between genders as well as within genders are important. These activities can give rise to questions you would like to pursue further. The next three steps move outward.

A second step is to determine which passages are sites of interpretive arguments. One group is passages people use to oppress or liberate women. Passages about divorce or church leadership are examples.[19] Another site of arguments is passages scholars call interpretive cruxes. These are points in the text that are perennial puzzles.[20]

19. One place to identify such passages is *Religion Index One* under the headings "Women in Christianity" and "Women in the Bible" for the years 1970 to the present. Another source is Stanton, *The Women's Bible*, which confronted passages used to justify oppression.
20. One way to spot these is to check *Religion Index One* under the heading "Bible (NT)—name of Gospel" in the subject index and in the Scripture index. What passages are the subjects of articles over and over? Another way to find them is to leaf through the indexes, tables of content, and bibliographies of several

In the first case, the argument's focus on gender will be obvious. Examples in the Gospel of Mark are the discussion of divorce and marriage in 10:2-12 and the presence of the women at the cross and tomb in 15:40,47 and 16:1-8. In the second case, you will have to ask how gender figures into the puzzle. Two of the many interpretive cruxes in Mark are the meaning of the naked young man in 14:51-52 and the ending of the Gospel. What is a young man clothed only in a linen cloth doing in Gethsemane? What is the significance of the linen cloth and of his running away naked? Does the Gospel really end at 16:8 with the women saying nothing to anyone? If it does, why? The answers interpreters give to these questions reveal a lot about Mark's constructions of gender and those of the interpreters, both embedded in their social and historical locations.

A third step is to read several reconstructions of gender ideologies and the actual behaviors of men and women in the ancient Mediterranean world. This would suggest further avenues of investigation.[21]

A fourth step for those interested in the history of interpretation is to look for readings of passages you find interesting. One avenue of investigation is to compare various English translations. Translations are always interpretations. A translator's reading of a passage reveals something about the translator's own views and culture as well as about the text itself. Paraphrases and children's Bibles offer data on popular interpretations. For students with Greek, comparing different manuscripts' readings indicated in the notes that accompany the Greek text can also be interesting. Another avenue is to explore the views of various theologians or figures from religious history. Many works of theologians past and present contain scriptural indexes. Works of male theologians that mainstream religious traditions or scholarship consider important are readily available. Thus, finding out if Augustine or Luther commented on a passage is relatively easy. The works of women interpreters are becoming more accessible. Other avenues are interpretations offered in paintings, plays, movies, novels, letters, diaries, and devotional literature.

These four steps provide a starting point for further work. They can engage the interpreter in active thought about a Gospel and gender. The interpreter then must decide which of the types of feminist biblical criticism in the first section of this chapter to pursue, or whether to forge an entirely new path. Are you trying to discover what the Gospel might tell us about the actual roles of

---

standard commentaries on the Gospel such as Vincent Taylor's *The Gospel according to St. Mark*, 2d ed. (New York: St. Martin's Press, 1966) or Robert A. Guelich's *Mark 1–8:26*, vol. 34a of Word Biblical Commentary (Dallas: Word Books, 1989). Which passages do the authors single out for special comments or notes? Which passages provoke the longest bibliographies and the longest comments?

21. Unfortunately, this step is difficult because work in this area has only just begun. One place to start is with Bruce J. Malina's *The New Testament World: Insights from Cultural Anthropology* (Atlanta: John Knox, 1981). Another is with Elisabeth Schüssler Fiorenza's "The Jesus Movement as a Renewal Movement Within Judaism," in *In Memory of Her*. You will always have to keep in mind the presuppositions and ideology shaping any reconstruction.

women in early Christian history? Are you trying to place the Gospel's gender ideology in the context of first-century Mediterranean constructions of gender? Are you trying to show how interpretation of a Gospel has been androcentric and patriarchal? Do you want to compare how various modern male and female readers respond to the Gospel? Do you want to reconstruct how a first-century audience might have responded?

You must decide which historical, theological, literary, sociological, anthropological, or psychological methods or models to use. These methods and models can be those already developed or adapted by feminists. They could also be those you develop or adapt for feminist purposes. (One of the exciting things about feminist scholarship is that it is new and open to experiment.) You can critique or transform any of the other four approaches discussed in this book. You must subject whatever methods and models you use to a feminist analysis. You must ask yourself where you stand. You must recognize your historical and social location and political choices. In addition to many kinds of feminist biblical criticism, there are many feminisms, many theories of feminism. If all of this sounds complicated and hard, it is. Feminist biblical criticism is a revisioning of the whole critical enterprise. My recommendation is to start small and to rely on others to share in this group adventure. One of my contributions follows. I hope you will discuss, challenge, and extend it.

The Dancing Daughter

In Mark 6:14-29, King Herod orders the execution of John the Baptist. At his birthday banquet, Herod responds to his dancing daughter's request for John's head on a platter, a request prompted by Herodias, her mother. This story of the dancing daughter embodies a male construction of female gender. It has been a fertile site for further male constructions. Many theologians and scholars have commented upon it. It serves as the text for the Feast of the Decollation (beheading) of St. John the Baptist, celebrated on August 29 as part of the Roman Catholic liturgical calendar. It has provoked many interpretations. A 1912 German monograph contains 200 plates of paintings, sculptures, stained-glass windows, illuminations, engravings, and other art drawn from the story. The story also has given rise to numerous folk traditions, poems, plays, novels, and several operas. A version of a Strauss opera based on Oscar Wilde's play is even available on tape in my local video rental store.[22]

22. Works that discuss the use of the story in culture include Hugo Daffner, *Salome: Ihre Gestalt in Geschichte und Kunst* (Munich: H. Schmidt, 1912); Rama Kabbani, *Europe's Myths of Orient* (Bloomington: Indiana University Press, 1986); Blaise Hospodar de Kornitz, *Salome: Virgin or Prostitute?* (New York: Pageant Press, 1953); Ewa Kuryluk, *Salome and Judas in the Cave of Sex* (Evanston: Northwestern University Press, 1987), 189–258; Francoise Meltzer, *Salome and the Dance of Writing* (Chicago: University of Chicago Press, 1987), 13–46; Mario Praz, *The Romantic Agony,* 2d ed. (New York: Oxford University Press, 1970); Linda Seidel, "Salome and the Canons," *Women's Studies* 2 (1984): 26–66; and Helen Grace Zagona, *The Legend of Salome and the Principle of Art for Art's Sake* (Geneva: Librairie E. Droz, 1960).

Filippo Lippi, *Herod's Banquet*

Many interpretations of Mark 6:14-29 (= Matt 14:1-12) focus on the women characters, Herodias and her daughter. Although not named in the Bible, the daughter is usually called Salome, the name Josephus, the first-century Hellenistic Jewish historian, gives her in his *Antiquities* (18.5.4). Herodias and Salome evoke multiple examples of the varied male creation of woman as

Other, as Difference. The German poet Heine offers a particularly vivid example. In Heine's poem "Atta Troll," the narrator describes a wild goblin hunt on St. John's Eve. Three great dead women play a prominent role: the Grecian Diana, the Celtic Abunda, and the Jewish Herodias. They exude sexuality and violence. Herodias enthralls the narrator. He describes Herodias and woman as devil and angel:

> Whether she was saint or devil,
> I don't know. With women, never
> Can one know where ends the angel
> And the devil makes his entrance.
>
> On her fevered face lay glowing
> All the Orient's enchantment,
> And her dress recalled in richness
> Olden tales of Scheherazade.
>
> . . . .
>
> And in truth she was a princess,
> She was queen of all Judea,
> Lovely wife of Herod, she who
> Claimed the head of John the Baptist.
>
> For this bloody murder she was
> One accursed; a ghost of darkness,
> She must, till the Day of judgement,
> Ride on with the wild hunt's spirits.
>
> In her hands she holds forever
> That bright charger with the head of
> John the Baptist, which she kisses—
> Yes, she kisses it with ardor.
>
> For she loved him once, this prophet:
> It's not written in the Bible,
> But the people guard the legend
> Of Herodias' bloody passion.
>
> Otherwise there's no explaining
> The strange craving by the lady:
> Would a woman ask the head of
> Any man she does not love?[23]

23. Heinrich Heine, "Atta Troll," excerpt from Caput 19, in *The Complete Poems of Heinrich Heine: A Modern English Version,* trans. Hal Draper (Boston: Suhrkamp/ Insel, 1982), 458–59.

Some interpreters see Salome as Heine saw Herodias, embodying woman as purveyor of sex and death. Others see her as an innocent young girl used by her corrupt mother. The alternatives are pointedly embodied in the title of an obscure book, *Salome: Virgin or Prostitute?* (New York: Pageant Press, 1953). The author, Blaise Hospodar de Kornitz, wrote the book to reconstruct an historical Salome as innocent daughter and defend her honor.

I will look at this fertile story through the lenses of feminist reader-response criticism. I will examine it for the light it sheds on the gender ideologies—the social and symbolic constructions of gender—of Mark and his interpreters. First I will show how modern biblical scholarship usually treats the story. Second I will focus on the story itself and how it gives rise to various responses. Third I will look at the story against the backdrop of texts from its cultural palette. Finally, I will re-place the story in the context of the Gospel of Mark and its construction of male and female gender.

The Story in Modern Biblical Scholarship

The story of the dancing daughter has been a minor interpretive crux in Markan interpretation. Some scholars want to know how reliable it is as an historical account of the death of John the Baptist. They debate the significance of differences between Mark's account and that of Herod's execution of John in Josephus, the Hellenistic Jewish historian mentioned previously. They also debate the "legendary" character of story elements, that is, which details are historical and which are not. For redaction and narrative critics, the central question is, Why is this episode, a flashback, intercalated or inserted into the mission of the twelve apostles (Mark 6:7-13, 30)? These critics typically give one or more of the following answers:

(1) It provides an interlude to mark the period of time the mission took.
(2) It foreshadows the fate of Jesus, who like John will be executed and his body put in a tomb (6:29 = 15:5-46).
(3) It reinforces John as the prototype of Jesus: John preaches and is delivered up (1:7, 14); Jesus preaches and is delivered up (1:14; 3:19; 9:31; 10:33; 15:1, 10, 15).
(4) It serves to remove the blame for John's death from the Roman puppet Herod in the same way the Jewish crowds take responsibility for Jesus' death away from the Roman governor Pilate (15:6-15).
(5) It is ironic: it serves to undermine the insider status of the Twelve. The Twelve preach repentance as did John (1:4 = 6:12) and are warned about suffering rejection (6:11). However, in the midst of the successful mission of the Twelve, their failure is foreshadowed. John's disciples bury their master. Jesus' disciples forsake him and flee. An outsider, Joseph of Arimathea, buries Jesus. The stories of the mission and the death of John precede chapters 8–10, where the disciples fail to understand Jesus and his passion predictions.

The Story and Its Readers

Verses 14-20 set the stage for the story of the dancing daughter. In these verses the narrator presents the scene from Herod's perspective as well as his own. The narrator has Herod *focalize*; that is, the narrator tells what Herod hears and knows. He tells the story from Herod's point of view. The narrator also offers four explanatory comments beginning with "for" (*gar* in Greek, 6:14, 17, 18, 20), a typical narrative device in Mark. In these comments the narrator presents Herodias rather than Herod as the ultimate cause of John's death. Still, ambivalence remains: Why does Herod *himself* seize and bind John in prison? Why does he execute John when he does not want to do so? Why does he believe Jesus is John the Baptist raised from the dead? Verses 14-20 form the opening frame of the story of the banquet, presenting it in a certain light.

The narrator makes the transition from the mission of the Twelve to the episode of Herod, Herodias, and John the Baptist through Herod's focalization, "And King Herod heard [of Jesus]," (6:14a). The narrator then offers the first *gar* comment: "For his [Jesus'] name became known. Some said, 'John the Baptist has been raised from the dead; and therefore acts of power work in him.' But others said that he is Elijah; and others said that he is a prophet like one of the prophets" (6:14b-15).[24] The narrator then returns to Herod's focalization: "But hearing this, Herod said: 'John whom I beheaded, this one was raised . . .'" (6:16).

The narrator then begins a flashback with another *gar* explanation: "For Herod himself sending [representatives] seized John and bound him in prison because of Herodias, the wife/woman (*gunē*) of Philip his brother, because he married her (6:17)." The emphasis lies on Herodias as the cause of Herod's action. Attached to this comment is yet another *gar* comment: "For John said to Herod, 'It is not lawful for you to have the wife/woman of your brother'" (6:18). From the perspective of the implied author, this is a challenge to Herod's honor and the legality of the marriage. There are historical arguments about what actual first-century Roman or Jewish marriage and divorce laws and the practices of the descendants of Herod the Great were. Nonetheless, Mark tells us through a reliable character's speech, reported by the reliable narrator, that the marriage was illegal. Leviticus forbids marriage to one's brother's wife except to raise up sons to him through levirate marriage if he dies without an heir (Lev 18:16; 20:21.) In Mark 10:2-12, Jesus interprets Scripture as forbidding divorce of husband by wife and wife by husband. He labels subsequent marriage as adultery. In this light Herod and Herodias are committing adultery. The reader or listener's reaction depends in part upon the norms of kinship, status, marriage, and divorce common in his or her culture and knowledge of norms reflected in the Gospel. It also depends on his or her acceptance of the story's viewpoint. Readers who know Josephus's *Antiquities*—which includes most ancient and modern biblical scholars as well as writers such as Flaubert—can interpret the story as a rejection of endogamy, as well as of divorce. Endogamy

24. This and the following translations of Mark are the author's.

is the practice of marrying within one's extended family. It preserves or advances the wealth, status, and power of the family and of individuals within the family. Josephus's history tells the reader that endogamy and divorce (permissible under Roman and Jewish law) were frequent among the Herodian dynasty. There we learn, for example, that Herodias was not only the wife of Herod's brother but also niece to both of them. The Herod of our story, Herod Antipas, put away his first wife, a Nabatean princess—this marriage was exogamous, a marriage outside one's family—to marry Herodias. Herodias was the daughter of Aristobulus, son of Herod the Great and Mariammne II. Her two husbands were Herod Antipas, the son of Herod the Great and Malthace, and Herod (possibly Herod Philip), the son of Herod the Great and Mariammne II. Thus, the two husbands were half brothers.[25] The male and female forms of the same name, Herod and Herodias, emphasize the family ties.

After John's challenge of the marriage, the narrator introduces Herodias as an actor and announces her goal: "Now Herodias had a grudge against him and wished to kill him and could not" (6:19). Whereas more extended comments and inside views of Herod seem designed to win sympathy for Herod, this brief comment presents Herodias unsympathetically as a woman with a grudge. The narrator has already provided the motivation for her grudge in John's challenge. The narrator then offers yet another *gar* comment explaining why Herodias could not kill John. This comment again offers Herod's focalization of events as it describes what Herod knows and hears: "For Herod feared John, knowing him a just and holy man, and kept him safe, and hearing him was perplexed, but he heard him gladly." Herod properly recognizes John and protects him from Herodias. In protecting John, a holy man, Herod protects himself. According to the narrator, Herod as king and husband has control over Herodias's actions. Even queens cannot order an execution independently. However, the queen has some power because Herod must protect John from her. She focuses on the threat John poses rather than respecting or fearing any spiritual authority he possesses. The story of the birthday banquet begins in verses 21-23:

> But an opportune (*eukairou*) day came, when Herod gave a supper for his courtiers, and officers and the chief men of Galilee on his birthday, and the daughter of her/of him, Herodias, entered and danced. She pleased Herod and the ones reclining with him. And the king said to the young girl, "Ask me whatever you wish, and I will give it to you." And he swore to her, "Whatever you ask I will give up to half of my kingdom."

In verse 21 we find Herodias's perspective briefly embedded in the narrator's. The word *eukairou*, "well-timed" or "opportune," shows this. The view, however, is not flattering. The same word appears in 14:11, where Judas seeks an

25. Lev 18:16; 20:21 forbid marriage to a brother's wife. It is not clear whether and which first-century hearers would apply this to half-brothers. Leviticus does not prohibit uncle-niece marriages. See Josephus, *Antiquities*, 18.5.1–4; K. C. Hanson, "The Herodians and Mediterranean Kinship," parts 1 and 2, *Biblical Theology Bulletin* 19 (1989): 75–84, 142–51.

opportunity to betray Jesus. Herodias can use Herod's banquet to achieve her goal, the destruction of John. Women without direct power to achieve their goals may achieve them indirectly. In the patriarchal perspective presented, women's power comes from their ability to please men. The story moves in a progression of verbs. The well-timed day comes, the daughter enters, she dances. Verse 22 complicates the story. It reads differently in various early manuscripts and one can translate it in several ways:

> Entering, his daughter, Herodias, danced. . . .
> Entering, the daughter of Herodias herself, danced. . . .

Either way, because her name is the same or because the text identifies her as Herodias's daughter, the story associates the young girl with Herodias. In later verses the narrator identifies Herodias as the girl's mother. But is the girl Herodias's daughter from her previous marriage or Herod's own birth daughter? The text does not say.[26]

Whatever her name and exact relationship to Herod, the young girl's dancing elicits Herod's extravagant promise of up to half his kingdom. How does one understand the girl and her dance? How does one understand Herod and his guests' pleasure? The guests named are all elite males. Do we have a king and guests charmed by the innocent dance of his young daughter, the apple of his eye, or do we have a king and his guests aroused—incestuously in the king's case—and hypnotized by an erotic dance, a young nubile body offering an apple like Eve? Readers have answered the question in both ways. The daughter and her dance are not described. They are mirrors in which Herod, Herodias, and interpreters are reflected.

The answer of a father and guests charmed by the dance of an innocent girl depends in part on Mark's word for the girl, her subservience to her mother, and the word Mark uses for the pleasure of the king and his guests. It also depends on finding the honorable dance of a young girl at a male banquet a cultural possibility. The Greek word for "young girl" is *korásion*. This is the diminutive of the word for "girl," *kórē*. The word *kórē* also stands for the pupil or the apple of the eye. *Korásion* is the same word Mark uses to describe Jairus's twelve-year-old daughter who lives at home in 5:41, 42. It is the word used in the Septuagint, an early Greek translation of the Hebrew Scriptures, to describe the future Queen Esther and other beautiful girls, virgins (*parthénika*), who are gathered to King Artaxerxes's (Ahaseurus in the Hebrew version)

---

26. Various manuscripts read *autou* (of him) or *autas* (of her) in 6:22. If the original read *autou*, the little girl is Herod's daughter and her name is Herodias, like her mother's. If the original read *autas*, the girl is Herodias's daughter and Herod's niece. This relationship is further complicated by the extra-Markan information from Josephus that Herodias (the mother) was Herod Antipas's niece; and that Philip the tetrarch was not Herod Antipas's brother. Philip the tetrarch married Salome, Herodias's daughter.

harem as possible brides (Esth 2:2, 3, 7, 8, 9, 12).[27] Further, the girl does not make an immediate request. She seeks her mother's advise. She retains the child's obedience and unity with the mother. She reflects her mother's desire. The word for the pleasure of the king and his guests is *arésen*. According to many interpreters, this word does not refer to sexual pleasure. In the New Testament it refers to making someone happy, accommodating someone, or doing something that someone will approve or find pleasant (Mark 6:22 = Matt 14:6; Acts 6:5; Rom 8:8; 15:1-3; Gal 1:10; 1 Cor 7:33, 34; 10:33; 1 Thess 2:4, 15; 4:1; 2 Tim 2:4). Read in this light, the innocence of the dance is important. For some interpreters, it allows the end of the story to surprise. The haste of the girl and her demand in direct speech that Herod *immediately* give her John's head on a platter, as well as the transfer of the head from the girl to her mother, are shocking.

The construction of the daughter and the dance as innocent, however, has not been the construction of most scholars. Their answer to the question of Herod's response and the nature of the dance has been an aroused king and an erotic dance. Those interested in the historicity of the story see the dance of a princess at a male banquet as a legendary element scholars must justify. Vincent Taylor quotes Rawlinson: "It (the dance of Salome) is nevertheless not wholly incredible, however outrageous, to those who know anything of the morals of Oriental courts, or of Herod's family in particular."[28] Such reactions assume first-century elite patriarchal practices that seclude respectable women and carefully guard the modesty and virginity of daughters, especially royal daughters. The daughter's dance violates this norm. The definition of female it implies is of a being who desires sex and who is a temptation to males. The definition of male it implies is of one who is susceptible to female sexuality and who must protect the females of his family in order to preserve male honor. Women must be trained in the female virtue of shame; otherwise, they will become shameless.

This reaction also shares in the colonial and postcolonial Western male's tendency to view the Oriental, and especially the Oriental woman, as an exotic and often immoral Other. The very use of the term *Orient* invokes Otherness. Orient literally means East, that is, east of Europe. For nineteenth century Europeans the term Orient conjured up Middle Eastern bazaars and harems, but also by extension the Far East and even Africa—anything exotic and non-European. Rama Kabbani describes the male European view of the Oriental woman as the Other who attracts and repels:

> The eroticism that the East promised was mysterious and tinged with hints of violence. The Oriental woman was linked, like a primitive goddess,

27. The traditional age for marriage for females in Greco-Roman Palestine was probably about twelve. See Leonie J. Archer, *Her Price Is Beyond Rubies: The Jewish Woman in Greco-Roman Palestine*. Journal for the Study of the Old Testament Supplement 60 (Sheffield, Eng.: JSOT Press, 1990); Harold W. Hoehner, *Herod Antipas* (Cambridge: Cambridge University Press, 1972), 154–56.
28. Taylor, *The Gospel According to St. Mark*, 315.

Gustave Moreau, *L'Apparition*

with cycles of the supernatural. Cleopatra possesses knowledge of magic and poisonous prescriptions long before the need for death arises. Scheherazade lives on the edge of the sword, its blade is what her narrative must defeat, its shadow what makes her tale so captivating. Salome's dance is sexual and macabre at once. Her beauty is linked to the darker elements complicit with the corruption that John the Baptist's words uncover. Her dance is delirium inspiring, and causes the unleashing of evil. Oscar Wilde's interpretation of Salome's murderous desire for Jokanaan's head as the other side of her sexual passion for him indicates the treacherous nature of Eastern sexuality: Salome dances on blood, and kisses the severed head in a frenzy of brutish arousal: . . . . The dance became invested with an exhibitionism that fascinated the onlooker: he saw it as a metaphor for the whole East. In the Orientalist paintings of the nineteenth century, it often became a trope for the Orient's abandon, for it seemed to be a dramatically different mode of dancing from its Western counterpart.[29]

In addition to the Othering of the Orient, there is a presumption of the depravity of wealthy royals, the corruption of wealth and power. Often interpreters see a contrast between the ascetic John and the depraved Herodians. Chrysostom (ca. 347–407 C.E.) condemns the royal banquet for its drunkenness and luxury.[30] Calvin, (1509–64 C.E.) probably influenced by his view of contemporary royalty, praises John for reproving a king to his face and not "winking" at his faults. He warns those who sit at the tables of kings that although they may not end up watching severed heads made a matter of sport, they may partake of many crimes, at the very least debauchery.[31] Gustave Moreau, a nineteenth-century French Orientalist, paints Salome covered with jewels.[32]

As one can see from the previous references to Oscar Wilde and the European Orientalist painters, the answer of many men to the question of Herod's reaction and the nature of the dance has been an aroused king and an erotic dance. It is the answer of Flaubert's "Herodias," Huysman's *A Rebours*, Mallarmé's "Herodiade," Wilde's "Salome," and Richard Strauss's "Salome," and that of many paintings, stained-glass windows, sculptures, and carvings. Even children's Bibles portray the dance as erotic:

> Then, on the night of the banquet, the beautiful young Salome, daughter of Herodias, had taken up her beads, her bells and her veils, and she had performed an exquisite dance before all the company. It was late in the evening, and wine flowed freely, and Herod found himself overcome by Salome's charms. In his grandest manner, he proclaimed to her before all his guests, "Ask me for any reward, my dear! I will give anything in homage to such beauty, even half my kingdom.[33]

29. Kabbani, *Europe's Myths of Orient*, 68–69.
30. Chrysostom, "Homily XLVIII," in *A Select Library of the Nicene and Post-Nicene Fathers of the Christian Church*, ed. Philip Schaff. vol. 10, trans. George Prevost and M. B. Riddle (Grand Rapids: Wm. B. Eerdmans, 1956), 299.
31. Calvin, *A Commentary on a Harmony of the Evangelists*, vol. 1. trans. William Pringle (Grand Rapids: Wm. B. Eerdmans, 1949), 222–24, 228.
32. Kabbani, *Europe's Myths of Orient*, 76.
33. Sandol Stoddard, *The Doubleday Illustrated Children's Bible* (Garden City, N.Y.: Doubleday, 1983), 278.

Aubrey Beardsley, *The Dancer's Reward.*

Why the imagery of eroticism and excess? The text itself does not describe the dance. The dance does not even take up a whole sentence. One reason is Herod's response of offering up to half his kingdom. The readers can imagine no reason for it unless the young girl and her dance sexually entrance the king. A young virgin is sexually desirable. Herod's pleasure is sexual and corresponds to the pleasure King Artaxerxes finds in the *korasion* Esther. The word for this pleasure in the Septuagint of the book of Esther is the same one that Mark uses. Another justification given for this erotic and excessive imagery is the girl's haste to have the head of John. A third is her request in direct speech to have it on a platter, a detail not suggested by her mother. A fourth is the fact that Herodias uses her daughter to bring about John's death by decapitation. Both Herodias and her daughter speak in their own voices. Their desire for John's death is personally and vividly expressed. The girl serves her mother, however. The narrator makes this clear with the compactly described transfer of the head: "And [the executioner] brought his head on a platter and gave it to the girl, and the girl gave it to her mother" (6:28). There is a strange fascination with the detail of the platter. The head is like food on a platter at a banquet. A fifth reason for the imagery is: like mother, like daughter. The immorality of Herod and Herodias's liaison, which John condemned, marks them and their daughter. Herodias's desire is replicated in her daughter.

Both classes of readings—those that view the daughter and dance as innocent and those that view them as erotic—are male constructions of female gender: Salome, virgin and prostitute; Herodias, mother, procurer, and destroyer. Interpreters construct both readings from Herod's perspective. They also view the events from John's perspective, as condemner of immorality and victim. Herodias is universally condemned; Salome is sometimes seen as innocent. Few, if any, readings view the story from the perspective of the women.

In general terms, what is at play in the text and in readings of it? Conceptions vary, but sex, birth, death, food, and women are symbolic realms often associated in Western culture. Personhood is located in the head, the ruler of the body. To ask for a person's head is to ask for the person's death. The head is also a trope or figure of speech that represents the phallus. In patriarchal cultures the phallus often symbolizes male personhood and power. The severing of heads (decapitation or decollation) and castration are figures for one another. Males fear the power of women to control and thereby "castrate" them. Women are the source of life and nourishment as mothers or caregivers. They are a source of sexual pleasure and male identity as lovers, as the object of desire. If there is no Other, there can be no Self. The object of one's desire has control over one. Male orgasm is sometimes compared to dying or to lack of control. Men fear and label as dangerous and mysterious female powers they lack and need. They project upon woman what they fear or do not like in themselves, their own desire and violence. The standard, however, is always male. Women are what men are not, which sometimes takes the form of the oppositions discussed earlier in the chapter. In the context of Mediterranean conceptions of honor and shame, to die in battle at the hands of enemy soldiers is honorable. To be executed or to die at the hands of a woman is a mark of shame. For many Western readers, the race and class of the women plays an important role in their Otherness. Rich and powerful royal women are more feared and more desired. They are more dangerous than their poorer sisters. Wealthy royal women disturb the ordinary male/female paradigm of superior/inferior. Oriental women in general and Jewish (or Idumean, half-Jewish women as the Herodians were) are doubly Other for white gentile Western males. Even Origen, the third-century theologian who describes the daughter's dance as outwardly innocent, makes her movements an allegorical representation of the behavior of the Jewish people. Like Salome's dance, their behavior seemed according to the law up to the point that the grace of prophecy was taken away from them with the death of John the Baptist. Her dance cannot be a sacred Christian dance because it results in the death of John.[34]

Interpretations of this story split the "female" into depraved mother and innocent or depraved daughter as object of male desire. Herod and John are unified by male power and authority. However, the "male" is split into the deceived Herod and the righteous prophet. Both mother and daughter are feared—and victims. Both king and prophet are victims—and victors. By succeeding in her desire to have John beheaded, Herodias (and her daughter) defeat male/phallic power. However, the victory is only temporary.

There is also a question as to which man is actually rendered powerless, John or Herod. Herod is king, but fears and is puzzled by John. He succumbs to Herodias's wishes and the daughter's charms. Although dead, John retains his power because Herod fears Jesus as a John come back to life (6:14). In an ironic reversal in some interpretations, in death John's head born on a platter by a woman becomes food, the source of life. John is castrated, feminized, but thus assimilates the female power to give birth and nurture. In the Middle Ages veneration of *Johannisschüsseln*, devotional images of John's head on the platter, was popular in Europe. Herod's banquet foreshadowed the last supper, and John's head was a type of the eucharistic body and blood of Christ.[35] The veneration of John's head on the platter paralleled female imagery of Christ as the source of holy food. Through his death, Christ was the mother of the church on whose breast the faithful can nurse.[36] In a contrary move, in interpretations of the late nineteenth and early twentieth centuries, the food motif turns dark. John's head becomes the fetish of Herodias or Salome, depicted as the thwarted lover of John who could only taste his lips and possess (eat) him when dead.

Cultural Palette: Esther, Judith, Jezebel

Mark 6:14-29 evokes images of woman as deceiver and killer and as source of food and salvation alive in cultural tradition through intertextuality. It evokes images of man as wielder of authority, but susceptible to female charms. *Intertextuality* is the reference to or use of one text by another. The story directly cites the book of Esther.[37] It indirectly calls forth associations with the apocryphal

34. Allan Menzies, ed. *Commentary on Matthew, Book X,* vol. 10 in *The Ante-Nicene Fathers.* (Grand Rapids: Wm. B. Eerdmans, n.d.), 428–29.

35. Isabel Combs Stuebe, "The Johannisschüssel: From Narrative to Reliquary to Andachtsbild," *Marsyas* 14 (1968–69): 1–16; Seidel, "Salome and the Canons," 47.

36. Caroline Walker Bynum *(Fragmentation and Redemption: Essays on Gender and the Human Body in Medieval Religion* [New York: Zone Books, 1991], 151–65) describes males and females who use this imagery.

37. Roger Aus *(Water into Wine and the Beheading of John the Baptist,* Brown Judaic Studies 150 [Atlanta: Scholars Press, 1988] and Brenda Deen Schildgen ("A Blind Promise: Mark's Retrieval of Esther," *Poetics Today* 13 [1992]: forthcoming) discuss connections between Esther and Mark 6:14-29.

book of Judith and the story of Ahab, Jezebel, and Elijah in 1 Kings 19. Readers often read Mark's story in the light of these other stories.

The strongest tie with Esther comes from King Herod's offer of half his kingdom. This directly echoes King Artaxerxes's (Ahaseurus in Hebrew) repeated offer of half his kingdom to Esther in Esth 5:3, 6-7; 7:2-3. Esther, a beautiful young woman, becomes a candidate for queen after her predecessor, Vashti, an uppity woman, defies the order of the king to appear at a banquet as part of a display of his wealth and power. In the Septuagint, Esther and the other candidates are called *korasia*, the same term used of the dancing daughter in Mark. Esther's goodness and beauty win Artaxerxes, and she becomes queen. Esther, unbeknownst to the court, is a Jew. When her uncle and adopted father, Mordecai, learns about a plot to exterminate the Jews and confiscate their property, he calls upon Esther to prevent it. Although Esther is queen, her position is precarious. She does not want to be deposed, as her predecessor was, or killed. Her strategy is to make herself attractive and invite the king and the Jews' chief enemy, Haman, to a series of intimate banquets in her quarters. The king is pleased with her and makes the extravagant offer. He also is jealous of Haman, who attended the banquets and whom he catches leaning over Esther on her couch. Haman begs for his life, but Artaxerxes thinks he wants to violate the king's wife. Haman is executed.

Here again we have the indirect and cunning power of a wealthy royal woman in the context of sexuality, food, and execution. However, Esther stands in ironic contrast to Herodias and Salome, who split the roles of queen and young woman. Esther brings about the salvation of her people and the death of Israel's enemy rather than the death of God's prophet. Esther's story results in the celebration of Purim, Mark's in the Feast of the Decollation of John the Baptist. Female power, exercised through the ability to please men, is to be celebrated if it serves God and the salvation of God's people. It is tainted if it does not. In Esther the hand of a virtuous woman subverts unjust gentile male power. In Mark the hand of a corrupt woman makes a martyr of a prophet of Israel. "Salome" is the dark obverse of Esther—Esther's shadow sister. In the Septuagint version of Esther, Esther's prayer emphasizes her abhorrence of the bed of the foreigner and her position as his queen. It also emphasizes that she has not eaten his food. Herodias and Herod, in contrast, serve Rome.

Although not alluded to with a quotation, another biblical story also associates deceit, sexuality, food, the power of woman, male vulnerability, decapitation, and the salvation of Israel. In the apocryphal book of Judith, Assyrians, led by their commander Holofernes, besiege a key Israelite town. Judith, a beautiful, pious, rich, and chaste young widow, saves the day. Accompanied by a maid (protecting her reputation for chastity), she enters the camp of the enemy. Maintaining kosher by not eating the enemies' food, and regularly leaving the enemy camp to pray, Judith uses her sexuality to beguile and kill Holofernes. Holofernes invites her to a banquet for his personal attendants. She brings her own food in a bag. After he falls into a drunken stupor, she beheads him and places his head in her food bag (just as John's head is served up on a platter). The head of Israel's enemy replaces kosher food. She and her maid escape because the Assyrians are familiar with her bag and her departure from the camp to pray. The town is heartened and the enemy disheartened by Holofernes's head. Israel's enemy is defeated "by the hand of a woman" (Jdt. 9:10; 13:14; 16:5, echoing Judg. 5:24, where Deborah and Jael defeat Israel's enemy Sisera, again in a context where food, sexuality, and death are associated. Jael covers Sisera, feeds him milk, and kills him as he sleeps by driving a tent peg into his head). Judith exults:

> But the Lord Almighty has foiled them
> by the hand of a woman.
> For their mighty one did not fall by the hands of the young men,
> nor did the sons of the Titans strike him down,
> nor did tall giants set upon him;
> but Judith daughter of Merari
> with the beauty of her countenance undid him. . . .
> Her sandal ravished his eyes,
> her beauty captivated his mind,
> and the sword severed his neck! (16:5-6, 9)

The defeat of the Assyrians is even more remarkable because God uses a woman to accomplish it. The male is susceptible to female charm. Females can use their beauty and power to please against greater male authority and physical strength. Again the intertextual context is ironic. Judith beheads Israel's enemy, not one of its prophets. However, the food and castration motifs are more prominent than in Esther. Interpreters' tendencies to associate Salome and Judith have been strong. In European painting, sometimes the only way to tell a portrait of Judith with Holofernes's severed head from one of Salome with that of the Baptist is the presence of a sword in the woman's hand.

Margarita Stocker sees Judith and Salome as obverse sides of a male myth of the mysterious female Other: "For Judith with a sword is Judith; Judith with a severed head but no sword slides into Salome. She is the ambiguous Other, assimilating a Salome—whose own function is directly sensual and evil— to a more menacing, because sanctified destroyer."[38] In the history of the reception of the Salome story, we have seen the same kind of dual female nature constructed for Salome herself.

The third intertextual association is between Mark and 1 Kings 19–21 and 2 Kings 9. Mark closely associates John the Baptist with Elijah in 6:14-15 as well as in 9:11-13. Elijah's chief antagonist is Queen Jezebel, a Canaanite, who leads her husband to worship the baals, rival gods. Jezebel seeks to kill Elijah, although she is unsuccessful. She *is* successful in having Naboth, a faithful Israelite, killed so her husband can possess Naboth's vineyard, the inheritance given by God to Naboth's fathers. God punishes Ahab and Jezebel by cutting off their male descendants. Jezebel is thrown out of a window, trampled by horses, and eaten by dogs. Here we have a royal woman as a deceiver and as

38. Margarita Stocker, "Biblical Story and the Heroine," in *The Bible as Rhetoric*, ed. Martin Warner (London: Routledge, 1990), 94–95.

a threat to God's prophet. Unlike Esther and Judith, she is not a heroine. As God's opponent, she receives her just deserts.

Later interpreters' visions of the fates of Herodias and Salome, persecutors of the second Elijah, also reflect this concern with just deserts. Josephus recounts Herodias going into exile with her husband after reverses in dealings with Rome. Calvin views this as a proper punishment in his *Commentary on a Harmony of the Evangelists* (p. 223). Heine has her doomed to join a goblin hunt. Josephus does not recount Salome's death, but the popular male imagination has her falling through the ice up to her neck and dancing in the water until decapitated, committing suicide, or being trampled under the feet of soldiers by Herod's order.[39]

Wily female behavior with sexual overtones or undertones is judged appropriate if the results are approved. Feminine wiles are good if they further God's plans. Despite any human lords, is the woman faithful to the Lord? What the intertextual references to Esther and Judith do is to provide ironic commentary upon the Markan story. Both Esther and Judith as women are marginal and threatened. They personify the position of their people. Their stories are stories of the marginal and weak overcoming strong pagan empires. They succeed because they remain true to God and God to them. Their stories contrast with the stories of the pagan Jezebel and Herodias, who violate God's law and lead their husbands astray. Understood in this context, Mark 6:14-29 is part of the ambiguous portrayal of Rome in Mark. On the one hand, interpreters see a favorable view of Rome. They point to words borrowed from Latin and the shift of the blame for John's death from Herod to Herodias and that of Jesus from Pilate to the Jewish crowds (15:6-15). On the other hand, the unclean spirits cast from the Gadarene demoniac into the unclean pigs name themselves Legion (5:1-20), the name for a segment of the Roman army, and Herod is paralleled to the pagan Artaxerxes.

The Story in the Context of the Gospel of Mark

The reason I chose to examine the story of the dancing daughter was because it is the only story in Mark where a woman is *clearly* a "bad guy." Feminist critics have praised many women in the Gospel for their initiative and faith despite their unnamed and doubly marginal status as women who are poor (the widow who gives her mite, 12:41-44), gentile (the Syrophoenician woman, 7:24-30), or unclean (the hemorrhaging woman, 5:25-34). The woman who anoints Jesus for his burial beforehand (14:3-9) and the women at the cross and tomb (15:40-41,47; 16:1-8) have been contrasted favorably with the Twelve, who misunderstand Jesus and flee.

The story of the dancing daughter extends and complicates the picture of gender ideology in Mark. Women, like men, are "bad guys" as well as "good guys." The story highlights the complex and often contradictory character of symbols and assumptions about female and male gender. It also highlights the importance of variables like age, ethnicity, and class in constructions of gender.

39. Hospodar de Kornitz, *Salome*, 49–50.

The named adult royal woman Herodias is presented quite differently than the unnamed Syrophoenician gentile woman or the poor unnamed Israelite woman with her mite. As noted before, there is controversy over Mark's attitude to Rome. Nonetheless, royal women should be saviors of Israel and its prophet rather than aligned against them, just as the elite Pharisees and Sadducees should be. Here the cultural palette becomes significant for interpretation.

The cultural palette also reveals androcentric and patriarchal views of women—women's power is in their ability to please men, they bring blessing and threat to males and to male honor, the position of the *korásion* is dangerous, and so on—all replicated in Mark. A comparison with the other Markan story involving a *korásion*, the healing of Jairus's daughter (5:21-24, 35-43) emphasizes these views. Both Jairus's daughter and the dancing daughter are at a dangerous stage from a patriarchal perspective, between childhood and womanhood. Jesus saves the walking daughter (5:42) from corruption. The mother's corruption of the dancing daughter leads to the death of John. In the Jairus story, the daughter and mother are in the traditional cultural position, unnamed and embedded in Jairus, a synagogue ruler. They appear in the context of the home. The male healer returns this little daughter to life because of the faith of her father. Agency is in male hands. The story of Peter's mother-in-law (1:29-31) is similar. She is unnamed, embedded in a male, and healed in a house. Perhaps the strongest aspect of patriarchy is that, aside from Herodias, no women have positions of official authority and power, even those Mark implicitly praises. No women preach or heal. The only powerful woman in Mark is also, after Judas, one of its most reviled villains.

However, there are tensions in this androcentric and patriarchal perspective. Unnamed women not described as embedded in or protected by male fathers or husbands act boldly and are rewarded by Jesus. The first of these is the woman with the polluting female flow of blood (5:25-34). Jesus calls her "daughter" and praises her faith. Her story is intercalated in the healing of Jairus's daughter. The Syrophoenician woman comes to Jesus in a house and persuades him to heal her daughter, even though she is a Gentile (7:24-30). The poor widow with her mite exceeds the rich in her piety (12:41-44). In the house of Simon the leper, an unnamed woman anoints Jesus with costly oil beforehand for his burial. What she has done is to be remembered wherever the Gospel is proclaimed (14:9). The ambivalence is again seen in 15:40-41. Although it was not mentioned earlier, at the crucifixion, the reader is told about women who had come up with Jesus to Jerusalem and who had followed and served him all along. Above all, Jesus' rejection of traditional family ties introduces tensions. In 3:21, apparently his relations, including his mother, brothers, and sisters, think he is beside himself. Jesus is within a house with listeners encircling him. His family is outside (cf. 4:11). Doing the will of God rather than blood kinship constitutes his family, his brothers, sisters, or mothers. Again in 6:1-6, he confronts unbelief from those in his native place, his patrimony (*patrída*). They know him as the carpenter, the son of Mary. They know his brothers and sisters. Jesus responds to their being scandalized by him: "A prophet is not unhonored except in his native place (*patrídi*) and among his relatives and in his house" (6:4). Again in 10:29 he speaks of those who have left house or brothers or sisters or mother or father or children or lands, for his sake and for the Gospel. They will receive "a hundredfold now in this time, houses and brothers and sisters and mothers and children and lands, with persecutions, and in the age to come eternal life" (10:30). Jesus himself spends much time in houses, the private, domestic sphere, attempting to construct his new family. On one level, for Mark, gender and traditional kinship are irrelevant; on other levels gender *is* relevant and involves hierarchy. Perhaps this is the meaning of the saying that in heaven there will be no marrying or giving in marriage (12:25). As David Rhoads shows in chapter 6, the Markan Jesus breaks some cultural boundaries and transforms and forms others. Mark is full of reversals of insiders and outsiders, rich and poor, the first and the last, male and female. The key Markan distinction is between doing or violating the will of God, being on the side of God or of man (8:33).

What is a feminist Christian reader to make of the Herodias–dancing daughter story in the context of Mark and its interpretation? First, one sees different historical constructions of gender and contradictory constructions even within a single cultural moment. This shows that such constructions are not natural or unchangeable. Second, cultural definitions of female as different, as Other, as marginal, give witness to women's power. The need to assert marginality contradicts the assertion. Women provoke various male fears and desires. In the history of Western interpretation, this statement is true both of Herodias, who quite clearly is a villainess for Mark, and the daughter and the dance, whose sensuality and innocence are ambiguous in Mark. Third, Christian feminists could find an important clue for creating their own reading from the Markan emphasis on food and from medieval readings of the story, which emphasize the daughter bearing the head on a platter and the connection between John's head and the Eucharist.

Food is clearly an important topic in Mark, including the section in which our story occurs. The story of the dancing daughter is intercalated or inserted in the mission of the Twelve. The poverty and proclamation of the Twelve mirror the poverty and proclamation of the prophet John (1:4-6; 6:7-13). However, like Herod and the Pharisees, they do not correctly understand who Jesus is or that their mission will eventually involve shame/castration/martyrdom like that of John and Jesus (13:9 ff.). Jairus's daughter, healed, is to be given food (5:43). The disciples are not to take bread with them on their mission (6:8). It will be supplied. John's head becomes food on a platter. When the Apostles return, Jesus tells them to feed the male crowd of five thousand (6:34 ff.) He supplies the food. A short time later he again feeds a crowd of four thousand despite the disciples' skepticism (8:1-9). Finally, Jesus warns the dense disciples of the leaven of the Pharisees and of Herod, who both misunderstand who Jesus is (8:13-21). The disciples do not see Jesus as a source of food, as the source of bread. At the last supper (14:17-25), the Twelve (including the betrayer and the eleven who will flee) eat Jesus' bread (body) and drink his wine (blood), foreshadowed by John's head on the platter, which was recounted as the Twelve went on their mission. Herod's banquet gives way to Jesus' messianic banquet. Jesus, like John, is food.

Here is an answer to why the story of the dancing daughter is intercalated into the mission of the Twelve. Feasting and food link this intercalated episode to the bread of Mark's "sandwich." John, become food, is a type of Jesus, who will soon give his body to be eaten. But Jesus himself, in feeding the multitude, also prefigures his self-giving. As Peter's mother-in-law and the women who follow Jesus *serve* (1:31 and 15:41), so, too, Jesus serves. Jesus' own body is offered as nourishment—like that of a mother. So, too, is John's.

Jesus and John are female. They are sources of food who bleed and feed just as women bleed and feed. This upsets Western gender conventions. If one views this as simply assimilation and usurpation of female difference or even a simple reversal of value poles, it does not empower. It also posits a biological female essence. If, by contrast, we view it as the affirmation of the female body and common humanity along with human particularity—equality that does not destroy difference—it may.

FURTHER READING
Articles that Deal with Women in Mark

BEAVIS, Mary Ann. "Women as Models of Faith in Mark," *Biblical Theology Bulletin* 18 (1988): 3–9. Contrasts Markan pronouncement stories about women with others from Greco-Roman tradition.

MALBON, Elizabeth Struthers. "Fallible Followers: Women and Men in the Gospel of Mark." *Semeia* 28 (1983): 29–48. A narrative critical approach.

MUNRO, Winsome. "Women Disciples in Mark?" *Catholic Biblical Quarterly* 44 (1982): 225–41. An historical focus.

Bibliographical Articles

ANDERSON, Janice Capel. "Mapping Feminist Biblical Criticism: The American Scene, 1983–1990." *Critical Review of Books in Religion.* 1991:21–44. A bibliographical survey that includes references to books that introduce feminist theory and feminist scholarship in other disciplines, as well as references to works of feminist biblical criticism.

CULHAM, Phyllis. "Ten Years After Pomeroy: Studies of the Image and Reality of Women in Antiquity." In *Rescuing Creusa: New Methodological Approaches to Women in Antiquity.* A special issue of *Helios* 13 (1987): 9–30. Provides bibliographical information on the study of women in the classical Mediterranean world.

KRAEMER, Ross S. "Women in the Religions of the Greco-Roman World." *Religious Studies Review* 9 (1983): 127–39. Bibliographical information.

TRIBLE, Phyllis. "Five Loaves and Two Fishes: Feminist Hermeneutics and Biblical Theology." *Theological Studies* 50 (1989): 279–95. A bibliographical survey that focuses on the Hebrew Scriptures.

Monographs and Collections of Feminist Biblical Criticism

BAL, Mieke. *Murder and Difference: Gender, Genre, and Scholarship of Sisera's Death.* Bloomington: Indiana University Press, 1988. A literary critic explains how different disciplines look at Judges 4 and 5 and how gender is involved in interpretation. Included here as an example of a postmodern feminist approach.

CANNON, Katie Geneva, and Elizabeth Schüssler Fiorenza, eds. *Interpretation for Liberation. Semeia* 47 (1989). Six of the seven essays in this collection are by women of color. They all comment in one way or another on the way race, class, and gender shape interpretation. Clarice J. Martin's essay offers a history and critique of scholarship on Acts 8:26-40.

COLLINS, Adela Yarbro, ed. *Feminist Perspectives on Biblical Scholarship*. Chico, Calif.: Scholars Press, 1985. The essays in this volume focus on the tensions between historical criticism and feminist scholarship. One describes nineteenth-century feminist interpretation. Some focus on hermeneutics or the theory of interpretation, and others are examples of feminist exegesis.

EXUM, J. Cheryl, Johanna W. H. Bos, and Adela Yarbro Collins, eds. *Reasoning with the Foxes: Female Wit in a World of Male Power. Semeia* 42 (1988). Contains essays on woman as trickster in the Hebrew Scriptures and the Ancient Near East.

FIORENZA, Elisabeth Schüssler. *In Memory of Her. A Feminist Theological Reconstruction of Christian Origins*. New York: Crossroad, 1983. The major work of the best-known feminist New Testament critic. The first part of the book focuses on hermeneutics or theory of interpretation; the second offers a feminist reconstruction of early Christian history.

RUSSELL, Letty M., ed. *Feminist Interpretation of the Bible*. Philadelphia: Westminster, 1985. This collection of essays has three sections: Feminist Critical Consciousness, Feminists at Work, and Feminist Critical Principles. Only three of the essays are exegeses.

TOLBERT, Mary Ann, ed. *The Bible and Feminist Hermeneutics. Semeia* 28 (1983). Contains four exegetical essays on New Testament texts and two on texts from the Hebrew Scriptures. A concluding essay sharply outlines types of feminist criticism and future challenges.

TRIBLE, Phyllis. *God and the Rhetoric of Sexuality*. Philadelphia: Fortress, 1978.

———. *Texts of Terror: Literary-Feminist Reading of Biblical Narratives*. Philadelphia: Fortress, 1984. These two books are by a mother of recent feminist criticism of the Hebrew Scriptures. They involve literary methods. The second is especially accessible to students and others with little familiarity with biblical scholarship. It confronts texts that are very troubling for religious feminists, texts in which women are victims of male violence.

WEEMS, Renita J. *Just a Sister Away: A Womanist Vision of Women's Relationships in the Bible*. San Diego: Luramedia, 1988. Very accessible to beginning students because it was written for use in home or church group Bible study. Weems approaches a number of biblical passages from a womanist perspective.

6

Social Criticism:

Crossing Boundaries

DAVID RHOADS

The New Testament is a profoundly social document. Each writing in the New Testament emerged from a community. Each writing addressed specific people with a unique message for a given time, place, and circumstance. Each writing was deeply embedded in a particular culture and history. Each writer shared a common social system with readers that enabled communication to take place. The writings of the New Testament were social acts.

Our reading of the New Testament is also a social act. For us, however, reading the New Testament is a cross-cultural experience. The writers of the New Testament were first-century people; we are from the late twentieth century in the West. Our language, customs, economy, political order, social system, values, cultural knowledge, and ethos are very different from the cultures of the first-century. We tend to project our urban industrial society back onto writings that are from a preindustrial peasant society. We read into the writings our modern Western cultural assumptions about life—our notions of individualism, progress, freedom, class structure, time, mobility, and so on. We have our twentieth-century "cognitive maps" by which we select, sort, and comprehend the material we read in the New Testament. In so doing, however, we misunderstand writings addressed to first-century people.

A text from the first-century is like a keyhole, an opening through which to look into another culture, a different world. However, if we look at the keyhole without looking through it, we see only how the space fits into the decor on our side of the door. We see it only in the context of the world we inhabit. Instead, we need to look through the opening into the world on the other side of the door, into the very different cultures of first-century Palestine and the Roman Empire. The question is, How can we understand the New Testament as a collection of writings from the eastern Mediterranean world of the first-century rather than impose the meanings we bring to the text from our time and place? The social study of the New Testament addresses this question.

In recent years, there has been an explosion of social studies of the New Testament. During the last fifteen years, seminars in scholarly societies have appeared under such titles as The Social Description of Early Christianity, Social Sciences and the New Testament, The Social Facets Seminar, and The Context Group. All these groups are devoted to sharing and promoting scholarship on the social study of the New Testament. Biblical scholars are eager to understand the society, the culture, and the communities in and behind the New Testament writings.

As a way to describe this emerging social study of the New Testament, we identify four approaches that have emerged: (1) social description, (2) social history, (3) the sociology of knowledge, and (4) the use of models from the social sciences, particularly cultural anthropology. These approaches overlap and depend upon each other.

Social Description

Social description draws upon all the information we have from the ancient world: literature, archeological excavations, art, coins, inscriptions, and so on. Scholars gather, analyze, and organize this information to describe every aspect of the social environment of the New Testament in its original setting: occupations, tools, houses, roads, means of travel, money, economic realities, architecture, villages and cities, laws, social classes, markets, clothes, foodstuffs, cooking practices, and so on. Such social description enhances our understanding of the daily cultures and customs in Palestine and in the Roman Empire at the time of Jesus and the early Christian movement.

One way to think about social description is to imagine you are the director of a film portraying scenes from the life of Jesus. For example, take the story about Jesus healing the man with the withered hand (Mark 3:1-6). What information do you need in order to make this scene authentic? For example, what did a synagogue look like? Was it a stoa (porch) in a market area, a free-standing building, or a room in another structure? Who went there? What did they do? Did they read from the Torah (the first five books of the Hebrew

Bible)? Was it a papyrus book or a parchment roll? How did they dress? What was the Sabbath? What were the practices and the prohibitions related to the Sabbath at that time? How did people treat a man with a "withered hand" in that culture? What Sabbath laws were at stake? How serious were penalties for violation of the Sabbath? Who were the Pharisees? How would they bring charges against Jesus? Why in the end did they not indict him? Why did they seek to meet with the Herodians? If you were a director staging such a drama, you would develop a passion for such questions as a means to comprehend fully this scene.

Understanding such a story is like understanding a joke from another culture. You have to know what ideas and information are being assumed before you can "get" the meaning. For example, the Pharisees were watching to indict Jesus because it was illegal to work on the Sabbath, and healing was considered to be work. Such a situation was serious because observing the Sabbath was a solemn religious obligation and because penalties for flagrant offenses could be severe. Synagogues likely also functioned as courts of law, which is why this setting was so threatening to Jesus. And the key question is, Why did the Pharisees not indict Jesus when he healed the man? The reason is that Jesus cleverly evaded indictment by avoiding any real "work." He does not touch the man or command him to "be healed" but only tells him to "stretch out the hand!" No wonder the Pharisees went off in frustration to plot with Herod to destroy Jesus. They went to Herod because Herod alone had the right to carry out capital punishment in Galilee under the Romans. Such information is essential for readers to "get" the story.

Many fine studies describe daily life in the social worlds of the first-century. In New Testament studies, Abraham Malherbe, John Stambaugh, David Balch, Eric Meyers, James Strange, and many others describe the material and social life of the first-century. In so doing, they provide vital means for us to understand people, events, and stories from that time.

Social History

Social historians seek to understand the broad sweep of change in history. This approach applies a comprehensive knowledge of social description through time to produce a social history of the period. Scholars such as Gerd Theissen, Wayne Meeks, and Martin Hengel have sought to answer critical questions of social history. For example, How did Christianity develop in the rural areas of Palestine? How did Christianity develop in the urban areas of the ancient world? How did the Greek culture and the Jewish culture interrelate in the period of Roman domination? What were the social causes and dynamics of the Roman-Jewish war of 66 to 70 C.E., and how did this war affect the early Christian movement? Then the question becomes, How do these developments fit into the social movements of the larger Greco-Roman world of that time? Regarding the study of biblical literature, those who take this approach might ask how the Gospel of Mark fits into the social and political history of the times, much as we might ask the place of Franklin's *Poor Richard's Almanac* in preindustrial

America or the relation of Steinbeck's *The Grapes of Wrath* to the Great Depression.

To deal with social history in relation to Mark, we might pose the following questions: What were the social forces behind the writing of the Gospel of Mark? What political conditions prevailed in that time and place? How did the Roman-Jewish war of 66 to 70 C.E. affect the writing of the Gospel? What was Mark's community like, and how did they spread the good news? How much did the expectation of an imminent end to the world impel the writing of this Gospel? Did the Gospel serve lower classes, upper classes, or both? Were the readers Jewish? If not, how much did they know of or identify with the Jewish people? What groups persecuted Mark's community? What was the fate of Mark's community in the context of the Roman Empire? Although one cannot do a broad social history based on one writing, nevertheless social historians can seek to explain the appearance of Mark's Gospel in the sweep of the social history of the time. Unfortunately, the task is difficult because Mark refers to his own time only indirectly in the story.

As an illustration, we might ask how the Roman-Jewish War of 66 to 70 C.E. affected the writing of Mark's Gospel. In 66 C.E., the Jews expelled the Roman troops from Palestine and rallied for independence. Diverse groups from all over Israel joined the war movement—lower class groups resisting economic oppression, sectarian groups fighting for the first commandment prohibition against any lord but God, and high-priestly groups seeking better terms in the Roman relationship. The war ended in disaster for the Jews. The Romans returned, defeated the nation, destroyed Jerusalem, and razed the Temple in 70 C.E.. Writing his Gospel during or just after the war, Mark told a story about events preceding the war. The Jewish Messiah had already come in the person of Jesus, who preached to his disciples that they should be like servants and not like the leaders of the gentile nations who lord over people (10:42-45). The leaders of Israel rejected Jesus. Jesus in turn predicted their downfall and that of the Temple (12:9; 13:2; 14:62). At the trial scenes, the high priests stirred up the crowd to call for Jesus' execution and to choose freedom for Barabbas, a prisoner who had committed murder in an insurrection (15:6-15). When Jesus died, God split the curtain and left the Temple and Israel to destruction (15:38). We can see how Mark wrote this story in part to reveal what he considered to be the destructive attitudes in Israel that led to the Roman-Jewish war. He also showed how Jesus' point of view differed from those of other Jewish groups.

With this approach, we can see how the sociopolitical history of the time shaped the Gospel of Mark. In turn, we can also see how this early Christian writing fit into the broader social history of the Roman period. Recently, some social historians have reconstructed the past from the perspective of the oppressed, seeking to unmask the dynamics of oppression and to recover the lives of the poor, outcasts, slaves, and women from all social strata of ancient cultures. The Gospels are prime sources for such social histories, as Elisabeth Schüssler Fiorenza and Ched Myers have shown in their studies of Mark.

Sociology of Knowledge

This approach offers the insight that different worldviews support different social orders. The first aspect of this approach is to reconstruct the worldview, the everyday assumptions, of a given culture or group. The second aspect is to see how this worldview gave legitimacy to and maintained the particular social order of the group or society from which it emerged.

First, sociology of knowledge deals with what people in a particular culture take for granted in their understanding of the world, their "social construction of reality."[1] Whereas social description focuses on the material realities of a society, sociology of knowledge deals with how that society organizes and interprets those realities. Each society interprets, organizes, and experiences life in its own way. Each society has sets of common values and customary ways in which people interact. Each society has shared beliefs about time, space, and the meaning of life. All these facets make up the common sense of a given culture. Such beliefs and understandings constitute the fabric of meaning without which a society does not exist. People seldom question these assumptions. People simply grow up taking the world of shared meanings for granted.

If we are to understand the first-century cultures and subcultures, we should be aware of the assumptions we make from our own cultures and subcultures. Otherwise, we will unconsciously project them onto our reading of a writing such as Mark's Gospel. To see and judge other societies by our own assumptions is cultural ethnocentrism. The first-century Mediterranean cultures would consider "the way things are" to be quite different from the dominant United States culture. For example, many people in the United States may assume that it is good for an individual to "get ahead," but some cultures, including the peasant cultures of the first-century, view "getting ahead" as dishonorable and destructive of the social order. Thus, the sociology of knowledge is about the everyday understandings of the world that people in a culture take for granted, what everyone in that culture "knows" to be true. If we are to understand the cultures of the first century, we need to appreciate how their cultures are different from our own.

When children grow up enculturated into a particular society, sociologists refer to this process as "primary socialization." When people enter another society and take on the basic assumptions of this other culture, sociologists refer to this process as "resocialization at the primary level." Such resocialization in primary assumptions is also a way to understand conversion. The Christian movement arose in particular cultures and led people to change the way they thought about some assumptions of those cultures and to abandon other assumptions. It called them to inhabit the world in a different way, to convert.[2]

1. Peter Berger and Thomas Luckman, *The Social Construction of Reality: A Treatise in the Sociology of Knowledge* (Garden City, N.Y.: Doubleday, 1963). On worldviews, see Michael Kearney, *World View* (Novato, Calif.: Chandler & Sharp, 1984).
2. Beverly Gaventa, *From Darkness to Light: Aspects of Conversion in the New Testament* (Philadelphia: Fortress Press, 1986).

Thus, from the perspective of sociology of knowledge, early Christianity offered an alternate world of meaning for those who chose to inhabit it. Reading or hearing a narrative like Mark can be a way to enter such a new symbolic universe. We might ask, What assumptions about life does the author of Mark take for granted with the readers? What assumptions does the author lead the readers to abandon? What new views does the author want the readers to adopt?

Consider, for example, the strange world of space and time in the narrative world of Mark's Gospel. Early in the story, the narrator tells us that Jesus saw "the heavens being torn open" and "the Spirit of God coming upon him" (1:9-11).[3] After this, "a voice from the heavens" addressed Jesus. Immediately, the Spirit drove Jesus to the desert to be "tested by Satan," and "angels" served him (1:12-13). Subsequently, Jesus appeared in Galilee where he "drove out many demons" (1:39). When we combine these and other clues, we see that the author holds a Hebrew conception of the cosmos. There is no notion of a universe infinite in time and space, but a limited and flat earth with a canopy over it, heavens reaching from earth up to where God dwells, and Satan dominating an earth populated by angels and demons. Many other elements of the story fill out this spatial picture of the cosmos, such as Jesus going "up onto a mountain to pray" (6:46), the promise to gather disciples "from the four winds" (13:27), and the prophecy that Jesus would "come on the clouds of heaven" (14:62). The author does not argue for this view of the cosmos but simply assumes that the audience shares the same worldview. At the same time, Mark wants to change the reader's temporal view of the cosmos. Mark wants to convince readers that God's kingdom began with the baptism of Jesus (1:14-15) and that the fulfillment of that kingdom would come before the end of Jesus' generation (9:1; 13:30).

To ferret out a comprehensive picture of how Mark imagines the world, we might consider his views about nature and history, past and future, laws and customs, the human condition, sin and illness, purity and pollution, death and the afterlife, and so on. By culling details from the narrative, we can put together cultural assumptions the author makes about the world. In this way, we can sort out which primary cultural assumptions the author takes for granted and which primary assumptions the author wishes to challenge and change—such as purity rules, ethical values, and attitudes toward death.

The second facet of the sociology of knowledge correlates such worldviews with particular social organizations. Here sociologists make the argument that a mutual relationship exists between the assumptions of a given culture or group and the social organization of that group. How does the worldview of a group generate, legitimate, and maintain the particular social order of the group? In turn, how does the social order of a group influence the worldview of that group? There is no "necessary" correlation between worldview and social order, but efforts to make correlations are illuminating.[4]

3. All translations from Mark in this chapter are the author's.
4. Richard Rohrbaugh, "'Social Location of Thought' as a Heuristic Construct in New Testament Studies," *Journal for the Study of the New Testament* 30 (1987): 103–19.

For example, Wayne Meeks argues that the symbolic universe expressed in the Gospel of John supports a certain kind of social group.[5] The Gospel of John portrays Jesus as "the man from heaven" who brings knowledge of God to the world, yet only some people understand him while most people do not grasp him at all. Such a belief system about Jesus, Meeks argues, supports a small, tight-knit group of people who understand Jesus, but who are isolated and alienated from the general society of people who do not understand. As such, the belief system in the Gospel of John gave religious legitimacy to the group's isolation from the world.

Similarly, in the narrative world of Mark's Gospel, there is a correlation between the worldview held by the characters in Mark's story and the social organization of the Jesus movement depicted there. The worldview Jesus teaches his followers involves these assumptions: God's kingdom has begun (1:15); followers are to cross boundaries to proclaim the good news to the ends of the earth (13:10, 27); and the mission is urgent because the end of history will come soon (13:5-37). This missionary commitment to spread the good news to all nations before the world ends supports a social organization very different from that of John's Gospel. Instead of fostering a tight-knit group isolated from the world, Mark depicts a loose-knit social network based on hospitality as disciples go from place to place proclaiming the Gospel (1:17; 6:7-13; 10:29-30).[6] Thus, the sociology of knowledge helps one to see how the group's "knowledge" relates to the social order of that group.

Models from Cultural Anthropology

A fourth area of social study of the New Testament involves the use of models from cultural anthropology. From the study of many cultures, anthropologists formulate models to map the dynamics of a culture and to describe certain phenomena that occur in many cultures. Models deal with such matters as kinship systems, power relations, rituals, purity-pollution rules, economies, and so on.

A model is a simplified description of like events or interactions drawn from the study of many cultures or groups. Models are not a tool to research historical information. Rather, they aid in the process of interpretation. Models help to overcome ethnocentrism by providing a framework different from our own cultural maps with which to organize and assess information. The point of using a model is not to fit facts into an abstract paradigm. Rather, a model serves as a heuristic device to probe and to question, to notice details we might have ignored, and to see connections that explain dynamics and relationships. For example, if we understand the characteristic features of demonic possession from the study of many cultures, we will know better how to investigate and

---

5. Wayne Meeks, "The Man from Heaven in Johannine Sectarianism," *Journal of Biblical Literature* 91 (1972): 44–72.

6. Howard Kee, *Community of the New Age: Studies in Mark's Gospel* (Philadelphia: Westminster, 1977).

understand demonic possession in first-century Israel. Biblical scholars draw upon the models of anthropologists whose work is especially helpful in the study of early Christianity. They change and adapt the models to the specific historical situations in New Testament times.

For example, Robin Scroggs drew a model from the work of Max Weber and Ernst Troeltsch on the characteristics of religious sects.[7] Scroggs applied the model to the early Christian church to show in what ways it was indeed a typical religious sect. John Gager drew upon the work of anthropologist Leon Festinger about religious sects that expected the end of the world.[8] Gager applied the model to the earliest Christians because they expected that Jesus would return within their own generation. Gager argued that when this did not happen the early Christians responded like other such sects: they intensified their missionary activities rather than give up their beliefs.

Bruce Malina has made the most comprehensive effort to map the framework of first-century culture by using models drawn from the study of modern Mediterranean society.[9] As such, he interprets the New Testament with models drawn from societies that are in historical continuity with those of the first-century Mediterrean region. He provides the following models. In contrast to our social preference for economic gain, first-century Mediterranean people sought above all else to gain honor. In contrast to our quest for individual freedom, people got their identity from group participation and conformity. In contrast to our assumption that economic acquisition can be unlimited, people held to the peasant notion that all goods are limited and in short supply. Also, they had a patrilinear kinship system in which people married within their own group. Finally, society was organized according to rules for purity and pollution. Malina's work lays out the dynamics of each of these models and applies them to the New Testament writings. Other scholars have developed cross-cultural models for the study of healing, demonology, deviance, and so on.

Cultural anthropologists may take one of three approaches to analyze a society or group:[10]

1. Models may come from a structural-functionalist approach, which assumes that social forces work together to create a balance. Here the problem is to see how different parts of a society work together. This approach tends to see society in terms of how it preserves the status quo.
2. Models may come from a conflict framework of analysis, which assumes that different parts of society are in conflict with each other. Here the

7. Robin Scroggs, "The Earliest Christian Communities as Sectarian Movement," in *Christianity, Judaism, and Other Greco-Roman Cults: Studies for Morton Smith at Sixty.* Part 2: *Early Christianity,* ed. Jacob Neusner (Leiden, Neth.: E. J. Brill, 1975), 1–23.
8. J. G. Gager, *Kingdom and Community: The Social World of Early Christianity* (Englewood Cliffs, N.J.: Prentice Hall, 1975).
9. Bruce Malina, *The New Testament World, Insights from Cultural Anthropology* (Atlanta: John Knox Press, 1981).
10. Bruce Malina, "The Social Sciences and Biblical Interpretation," *Interpretation* 37 (1982): 229–42.

problem is how the conflicting dynamics will be worked out. This approach tends to see society in terms of changes that take place in struggles over power and oppression.

3. Models may come from a symbolic framework of understanding, which focuses on the meanings people assign to social interactions. Here the problem is to discern the symbolic meanings that members of the society share and to determine how those symbols change.

Several scholars have applied models from cultural anthropology to the Gospel of Mark. Vernon Robbins analyzed the social roles of the teacher Jesus and his disciples.[11] John Pilch has studied Markan assumptions about the nature of illness, healing, and exorcism.[12] Herman Waetjen employed a model about millennarian sects to highlight the new social order that Jesus announces in his establishment of the kingdom.[13] Jerome Neyrey applied a model from the work of anthropologist Mary Douglas to display the dimensions of purity and pollution in Mark's narrative.[14] I will elaborate this last example here in my case study of Mark.

The four approaches to the social study of the New Testament outlined above interrelate with and depend upon one another. They may be used together with great profit. In fact, John Elliott has developed a method that combines several social approaches in the service of interpeting a New Testament text, a method he calls Social-Scientific Criticism.[15] Such an approach draws upon social description and models from cultural anthropology to reconstruct the sociopolitical situation of the audience and the author's strategy for dealing with it. Elliott analyzes The First Epistle of Peter as a letter written to Christians who were displaced aliens in Asia Minor. This approach works especially well with letters in which the author, readers, and social situation are identified directly in the letter. There are, however, many ways to combine these methods with benefit. In the case study that follows, I will draw upon social description, worldview, and models from cultural anthropology to study one facet of the narrative world of the Gospel of Mark.

A Case Study: Purity and Boundaries

In order to illustrate the social study of the New Testament, I will analyze the dynamics of clean and unclean in the Gospel of Mark. In this study, I am

11. Vernon Robbins, *Jesus the Teacher: A Socio-Rhetorical Interpretation of Mark* (Philadelphia: Fortress Press, 1984).
12. John Pilch, "Healing in Mark: A Social Science Analysis," *Biblical Theology Bulletin* 15 (1985): 142–50.
13. Herman Waetjen, *A Reordering of Power: A Socio-Political Reading of Mark's Gospel* (Philadelphia: Fortress Press, 1989).
14. Jerome Neyrey, "The Idea of Purity in Mark's Gospel," *Semeia* 35 (1986): 91–128.
15. John Elliott, *A Home for the Homeless: A Sociological Exegesis of 1 Peter, Its Situation and Strategy,* 2d ed. (Minneapolis: Fortress Press, 1990).

assuming that Mark was written in Galilee or rural Syria around 70 C.E. and that his audience shared a social world similar to that of Jesus' time depicted in the narrative.[16] After briefly introducing the case of Mark, I will describe the social phenomenon of purity and pollution in first-century Israel and then show its relevance to the narrative world of Mark. In order to clarify the issues at stake, I will then apply models from the symbolic approach to cultural anthropology.

It is easy to see how this case study relates to several other disciplines we have been presenting in this book. First, the analysis will focus on the narrative world of Mark's Gospel. Thus, it will not deal with the historical Jesus or with Mark's community, but with the society and the Jesus movement portrayed in Mark's narrative. Second, the description of purity and pollution in the social context of the first-century is the kind of information that enabled first-century readers to make an informed response to the Gospel. Finally, it will be clear from the subject matter itself how relevant the study of purity is for feminist concerns.

When we read Mark, we come across phenomena that are strange to us. Jesus drives out "unclean spirits" (1:23; 5:2); he "cleanses a leper" (1:40-45). Pharisees accuse Jesus' disciples of eating bread with "defiled hands" (7:1-23). These notions of clean and defiled have nothing to do with our modern ideas of sanitation. Rather, they are forces capable of making things pure or polluted, holy or defiled, clean or unclean. When we investigate the Jewish society of Palestine in the first-century, we realize that issues of purity and pollution pervaded the whole culture. When we come to understand Mark, we see that the forces of purity and defilement relate to many aspects of the story: holiness, graves, corpses, Gentiles, Sabbath, foods, hearts, and so on. The issues of purity are writ large across the pages of Mark's story.

Social Description and Worldview in First-Century Palestine

In the first century, the Jewish nation was a temple state under the control of the Roman Empire.[17] For Jews living there, religious, political, and economic

16. There is disagreement about the location and date of Mark's Gospel. For the view expressed here, see Kee, *Community of the New Age*. For the traditional view, which places the Gospel in Rome during the 60s, see Martin Hengel, *Studies in the Gospel of Mark* (Philadelphia: Fortress Press, 1985).

17. In addition to Neyrey's work, I am especially indebted in this section to the following works: Jacob Neusner, *The Idea of Purity in Ancient Israel* (Leiden, Neth.: E. J. Brill, 1973); Jacob Milgrom, "Purity and Impurity," *Encyclopedia Judaica* (Jerusalem: Keter, 1971), 1405–14; idem, "Israel's Sanctuary: The Priestly Picture of Dorian Grey," *Revue Biblique* 93 (1976): 370–99; Baruch Levine, *In the Presence of the Lord* (Leiden, Neth.: E. J. Brill, 1974); Marcus Borg, *Conflict, Holiness, and Politics in the Teaching of Jesus* (New York: Edwin Mellon, 1984). For further bibliography, see Jerome Neyrey, "Unclean, Common, Polluted, and Taboo: A Short Reading Guide," *Foundation and Facets Forum* 4 (1988): 72–82.

life centered around the Temple in Jerusalem. This Temple was a huge complex that dominated the city. It housed more than two thousand priests at a time. During religious festivals, the Temple teemed with tens of thousands of Jews from all over the known world. The Jewish people believed that God dwelt on earth in the inner sanctuary of the Temple. God's presence there and proper worship in the Temple would guarantee the prosperity of the nation, the productivity of the land, and the security of the nation from foreign domination. Israel was a theocracy, a form of government in which God is considered to be the origin and head of state. Within the nation, the high priests had the actual task of leading the nation (within Roman parameters) and providing proper worship in the Temple, the Sanhedrin was the administrative and judicial council, and the Pharisees and scribes were experts in the interpretation of the law or Torah, the five books of Moses. As the people of God, the Jews believed they were set apart to be holy, dedicated to the Lord, to worship God faithfully, and to follow God's laws.

What gave this whole system coherence was the concept of holiness. Holiness was a core value of the Jews, as stated (by God) in the law : "You shall be holy, for I the Lord your God am holy" (Lev 19:2). God was holy and the people were to be holy. Because God was holy, God would not tolerate immorality. And God wanted people to worship rightly. The law of Israel therefore dealt with holiness. The law contained the moral codes for holy behavior among people in the nation. The law contained the regulations for the observance of holy times and holy festivals to guarantee prosperous life on the land. The law contained the regulations for proper worship in the Temple. The law contained the holiness codes about those animals people were permitted to eat and those animals that would defile them, the definitions of leprosy, the rituals for cleansing, and so on. Moreover, the law prescribed rituals and sacrifices as means to purge any defilement from the land, the Temple, and the people. Hence, Jews in Palestine were devoted to preserving God's holiness and to preserving their own holiness.

First, most Jews were devoted to preserving God's holiness. They protected God's dwelling in the Temple from unclean people and defiled things. For example, only priests in a state of purity could enter the Temple court to offer sacrifices, and they offered there only animals classified as pure and without blemish. All Israelites were to be in a state of purity when they came to worship in the Temple. Otherwise, they would defile the Temple. In turn, God might destroy the unclean person who came into God's presence in the Temple. If people defiled the sanctuary in a flagrant way, God might withdraw from the sanctuary, thereby removing the protection and the benefits that God's presence there secured. Also, the effects of flagrant immorality committed outside the Temple could reach into the Temple and violate God's presence.

Second, Jews in Palestine were concerned to preserve the holiness of God's people. For example, Jews avoided contact with unclean people and things— lepers, menstruating women, corpses, and Gentiles, among others. Such contact defiled a person for a period lasting from one to seven days. Such a state of defilement prohibited people from participation in festivals, certain meals, and Temple functions. To become pure again, the defiled person was required by the law to do ritual washings, endure a waiting period, and/or make an offering to God. In addition to ritual purity, Jews were to avoid immorality and idolatry.

We can see how Jews in Palestine organized their world to preserve their holiness. Jerome Neyrey has demonstrated the structures of holiness by reference to "cultural maps" of places, people, things, and times that served to organize Jewish life.[18] Although these maps of holiness come from later writings, they nevertheless reflect an earlier time and are helpful in understanding the mentality of holiness that prevailed in the first century.

Take first the map of places from the Mishnah, the early third-century collection of oral commentary on the Torah. It offers a geographical listing (*Kelim* 1.6-9) cited in ascending order of holiness:

1. The land of Israel is holier than any other land. . . .

2. The walled cities of Israel are still more holy. . . .

3. Within the walls of Jerusalem is still more holy. . . .

4. The Temple Mount is still more holy. . . .

5. The rampart is still more holy. . . .

6. The Court of Women is still more holy. . . .

7. The Court of the Israelites is still more holy. . . .

8. The Court of Priests is still more holy. . . .

9. Between the porch and altar is still more holy. . . .

10. The sanctuary is still more holy. . . .

11. The Holy of Holies is still more holy. . . .

Notice that the Holy of Holies, where God resides on earth, is the holiest place. At all costs, the Jews must protect this inner sanctuary of the Temple from defilement. The degree of holiness outward from the sanctuary corresponds directly with the nearness to or distance from this sanctuary. In this listing, certain people belong in certain spaces. Each group is holy enough to attain their proper place, but not pure enough to penetrate closer to the sanctuary without bringing defilement. Notice that the territory of gentile (non-Jewish) nations is outside the map and is not holy at all. In general, the Jews avoided contact with Gentiles because they represented immorality, idolatry, and ritual impurity.

Neyrey also presents the purity map of people from the later Jewish Tosefta (*t. Meg*), cited in descending order of holiness:

1. High priest

---

18. Jerome Neyrey, "The Idea of Purity in Mark's Gospel," *Semeia* 35 (1986): 91–128. See also idem, "A Symbolic Approach to Mark 7," *Foundations and Facets Forum* 4 (1988): 63–91; John Pilch, "Biblical Leprosy and Body Symbolism," *Biblical Theology Bulletin* 11 (1981): 102–6.

2. Priests

3. Levites

4. Israelites

5. Converts

6. Freed slaves

7. Disqualified priests

8. Temple slaves

9. Bastards

10. Eunuchs

11. Others with physical deformities

Note how some of these people correlate with places on the geographical map. Only the high priest can enter the Holy of Holies. Only priests and levites can enter the Court of the Priests. Only male members of groups 5 through 7 can enter the Court of the Israelites, and so on. Again, the map does not include Gentiles, because they are not holy. Also, the map excludes women from the scheme of holiness. As we shall see, women bear a perpetual threat of defilement and are therefore treated as unclean.

Neyrey presents other maps. One such list specifies who can marry whom. Another map lists the degrees of defilement attached to people and to things that will defile by contact, such as a leper, the corpse of an animal or a human, body fluids out of place, or persons considered defiled. Another map lists the hierarchy of holy times not to be defiled by certain prohibited behavior, such as the Sabbath days and the Passover festival.

Holiness was a core value of the society. It was the major concept by which the nation-culture structured and classified everything in its world—people, places, objects, and times. All groups and sects agreed on the importance of purity. However, various Jewish sects in Palestine understood purity in different ways and applied the regulations about it in different ways.

1. The sect of the Sadducees included mainly chief priests and other aristocrats. They believed that proper worship in the Temple was essential to the holiness that preserved the life of the nation. As such, they applied the strict purity regulations only to life at the Temple. Lower priests and levites needed to be pure only when they took their annual two-week stint of service in the Temple. Ordinary Israelites needed to preserve their purity only when they entered the Court of the Israelites to offer sacrifices. Jews were to offer at the sanctuary only pure, unblemished animals. As Sadducees, the high priests guarded everything and everyone who entered the Temple in order to ensure the purity of this holy place.

2. The Pharisees were a group of Jews who studied the written law and also passed down oral traditions of their interpretation and application of the

law. Like the Sadducees, they applied purity regulations to the Temple. However, they went further and applied the purity regulations to all Israelites and to all times, not just when people were at the Temple. Pharisees believed that all Israel was a kingdom of priests. Just as priests kept themselves pure while doing service in the Temple, so all Jews should at all times observe the purity regulations. Just as the priests performed ritual washings before meals as a removal of defilement from contact with that which was unclean, so all Jews should wash hands and food and utensils before eating. They should do this in order to cleanse themselves from direct and indirect contact they may have deliberately or inadvertently had with unclean things or people. The Pharisees promoted these measures as a "fence" or margin to protect people from defilement due to contact with Gentiles.

3. The sect of Essenes had the strictest purity regulations.[19] The Essenes had withdrawn from the life of the nation and the Temple in the second century b.c.e. and established a monastic community at Qumran on the shores of the Dead Sea. They believed that the Maccabean high priests of that time were not legitimate and as such had defiled the Temple and the whole land by their presence there. In their view, God had withdrawn from the Temple because of these violations. So, too, the Essenes withdrew. At Qumran, the Essenes carried out the strictest holiness codes as if for the Temple. They did so on the conviction that their community was now the Temple, the only place holy enough for God to dwell on earth. The Essenes offered no sacrifices, but they preserved holiness for the presence of God on earth in the hope that God would soon inaugurate a new order in Israel and the world.

4. Most Jews in Palestine were peasants who followed the regulations when they went to the Temple for festivals. Few of them, however, had the time or the resources to carry out the ritual prescriptions the Pharisees advocated. Furthermore, many Jews ignored other laws as well, such as the regulations of the Sabbath and the requirements for tithes due the Temple. Many Jews had direct contact with Gentiles in the marketplaces of the cities and indirect contact through Jewish tax collectors. The Pharisees looked upon ordinary Jews who disregarded the law as "sinners."

This system of holiness served Israel well throughout its history, preserving a minority culture from absorption into dominant cultures. At the time of Jesus, the culture and religion of the Jews were threatened with absorption into the dominant Greek culture and the imperialism of the Roman Empire. The Jewish structures of purity protected the people from these threats of cultural domination. By keeping themselves separate from Gentiles, the Jews maintained their beliefs and practices. At the same time, they sought to be an example of

19. Michael Newton, *The Concept of Purity at Qumran and in the Letters of Paul* (Cambridge: Cambridge University Press, 1985).

purity for the nations. The Jewish nation hoped that eventually the gentile nations would be drawn to Jerusalem as the place of justice and true worship.

When we turn to the depiction of the Jewish nation in the Gospel of Mark, we see issues of purity and defilement throughout: the Holy Spirit, lepers, work on the Sabbath, corpses, unclean spirits, Gentiles, sinners, unclean foods, and so on. As portrayed in Mark's story, the leaders of the nation uphold the laws of ritual purity as we have outlined them. By contrast, Jesus makes an onslaught against these purity rules and regulations. In Mark's view, Jesus is indeed holy, for the "Holy Spirit" comes upon Jesus at his baptism (1:10) and he is called "the Holy One of God" (1:24). Nevertheless, Jesus counters the purity rules that preserved the holiness of the nation.

- He encounters "unclean spirits" (1:21-28).

- He touches a leper (1:40-45).

- He heals Simon's mother-in-law on the Sabbath (1:29-31).

- He pardons sinners (2:1-12).

- He calls a tax collector to follow him (2:13-14).

- He eats with tax collectors and sinners (2:15-17).

- His disciples pluck grain on the holy Sabbath (2:23-28).

- He heals an impaired man on the Sabbath (3:1-6).

- He drives unclean spirits from a man at a graveyard in gentile territory, and they go into a herd of swine (5:1-20).

- He heals a woman with a flow of blood (5:25-34).

- He touches the corpse of a little girl (5:35-43).

- His disciples eat bread with defiled hands (7:1-15).

- He declares that all foods are clean (7:17-23).

- He heals a gentile woman in Tyre whom he calls a "dog" (7:24-30).

- He uses spittle in the act of healing (7:31-36; 8:22-26).

- He feeds and eats with Gentiles in a desert (8:1-10).

Instead of using purity regulations to protect, the Markan Jesus trangresses the boundaries of purity. Through the agency of the Holy Spirit upon Jesus, God enters the arena of impurity without regard to the risk of defilement.

In Mark's portrayal, the leaders of the nation protect the boundaries of ritual purity that Jesus violates.

- They accuse Jesus of blasphemy for claiming the right to pardon sins (2:1-12).

- They challenge his eating with tax collectors and sinners (2:15-17).

- They challenge the disciples' plucking grain on the Sabbath (2:23-28).

- They seek charges against Jesus for healing on the Sabbath and they plot to destroy him (3:1-6).

- They say Jesus is possessed by Satan, not the Holy Spirit (3:22-30).

- They accuse Jesus because his disciples violate the traditions of the elders by eating bread with unwashed (defiled) hands (7:1-15).

- They condemn him to death for blasphemy against God (14:53-65).

Cultural Anthropology: Models, Explanations, and Insights

What is going on here? How can we make sense of the issues of purity? How do the notions of purity and pollution work? What is the difference in the two approaches to purity between Jesus and the Jewish leaders? How can we unpack the dynamics of Mark's story? To deal with these questions, we can turn to explanations, insights, and models from cultural anthropology.

For example, we can understand better the concepts of purity and pollution by making use of a model from the British cultural anthropologist Mary Douglas.[20] In her view, purity represents the notion that there are places for things and things are in their place. By contrast, pollution represents the notion that some things have no place or that things are out of their place. Purity and pollution imply, therefore, an ordered classification of things and people with corresponding boundaries. Thus, if we observe what a culture considers to be pure and polluted, we can see how that culture gives order to the world.

As Douglas points out, dirt or that which pollutes is "matter out of place." Soil belongs in a garden, but soil does not belong in a house. When soil is in a house, we consider it to be "dirt" because it is out of place. This is an analogy for the whole purity-pollution system. The assumption is that there are "places" for things and people and animals and behaviors—a place for everything and everything in its place. We have already seen how thoroughly Israel had classified people, places, objects, and times in terms of holiness. Purity occurs when something or someone has a place and is properly in place. Pollution occurs when something or someone is out of place or when something or someone has no place in the system. Purity rules of avoidance and cleansing are ways of dealing with things and people that are out of place or do not belong. Such regulations serve to make the world conform with the structure of ideas. By keeping the purity rules, people impose order on experience and achieve harmony or consonance between worldview and behavior.

Douglas's analysis of the ancient Hebrew system of purity-pollution illustrates the model clearly. The ancient Hebrew culture as reflected in Leviticus is a

---

20. See especially Mary Douglas, *Purity and Danger: An Analysis of the Concepts of Pollution and Taboo* (London: Routledge & Kegan Paul, 1966); idem, "Pollution," *The International Encyclopedia of the Social Sciences*, vol. 12, ed. David Stills (New York: Macmillan, 1968), 336–42; idem, *Implicit Meanings: Essays in Anthropology* (London: Routledge & Kegan Paul, 1975); idem, *Natural Symbols: Explorations in Cosmology* (New York: Pantheon, 1982).

purity-pollution system based on "holiness." The notion of holiness is rooted in two concepts: wholeness and set-apartness. First, holiness has to do with what is whole. That which is pure and holy is that which conforms wholly to its classification. Now we can see why human beings with "deformities" were considered marginal and unclean and why animals with blemishes were considered unclean and were not to be offered at the Temple. They were not considered to be whole and therefore did not fit wholly within their class. Also, we can see why fish and cattle and doves are clean animals and do not defile people who eat them. These animals fit the Israelite classification of "normal" animals. Conversely, eels and pigs and ostriches do not fit the Hebrew classification of normal or whole animals. These animals are therefore not clean and will defile those who eat them. In light of these explanations, we can now understand the list of holy places cited previously and the list of those people who belong in each place. We can see also that Gentiles are unclean because there is no place for them in the system.

Second, holiness has to do with things and people that are set apart, things which by virtue of being in their place are kept away from certain other things; that is, things are holy when they are in their place, when they are not where they do not belong. Now we can understand why blood, spit, or semen are unclean. They belong inside the body. When they come out of their place, such as in a menstrual flow, they are unclean and will defile people. Lepers are unclean because they have boils or breaks in the skin where pus or fluid comes out. Also, we can see how important it was for certain people to stay apart from certain places. No one can enter the Holy of Holies except the high priest. Women who go beyond their place into the Court of the Priests will defile it. Gentiles were prohibited from entering the Temple on penalty of death. Thus, in the Hebrew culture, there was an ordered classification of the world with proper places for people and things. Things or people that did not fit the classification or that were out of place were considered to be unclean and capable of making other things unclean.

In Mark's depiction of the Jewish nation, the authorities support this system. But in Mark's portrayal Jesus has a very different Jewish approach. Jesus does not reinforce the purity system of the authorities. He crosses boundaries, redraws them, or eliminates them. As a result, he has contact with all types of unclean people and objects. He goes to places that are out of bounds. He violates holy times. What is the key to this clash between the authorities and Jesus? How can we explain these two very different approaches to purity?

We can get insight into the different approaches of the leaders and Jesus by delineating their differing attitudes toward boundaries. We have already seen the connection between purity and boundaries. In his work on boundaries, Jonathan Smith helps us see the fundamental difference between these two approaches to purity depicted in Mark's Gospel.[21] Smith would argue that the

---

21. Jonathan Z. Smith, "Animals and Plants," *Encyclopedia Britannica*, 15th ed., vol. 1, 911–18; "The Influence of Symbols upon Social Change: A Place on which to Stand," *Worship* 44 (1970): 457–74; "The Wobbling Point," *Journal of Religion* 52 (1972): 134–49.

difference between the authorities and Jesus is so dramatic as to represent polar opposites. One approach erects boundaries and preserves holiness by guarding against that which would defile. The other approach crosses boundaries and risks defilement to make what is unclean pure.

The one choice is "the affirmation of one's place" within the order of certain boundaries. Here, "each person is called to dwell in a limited world in which everything has its given place and role to fulfill. To be sacred is to remain in place. To break out, to cross boundaries, is to open the world to the threat of chaos, to commit transgression."[22] In this approach, the hero is one who discerns order and helps people fulfill their roles within that order. We can see that the leaders of Israel in Mark embrace this stance.

The other choice expresses a desire "to be unbounded, to be liberated." In this view, boundaries have become oppressive and restrictive or are simply limiting. Here people do not define themselves "by the degree to which they harmonize themselves and their society to the cosmic patterns of order, but rather to the degree to which they can escape that order."[23] Here, "positive sacred power [is] to be gained from the violation of the given boundaries of the world, from the transcendence of the way things ordinarily are."[24] In this approach, the heroic figure is the one who enables people to escape the bounds. We can see that Jesus and his followers in Mark embrace this stance, not so much to attain liberty as to bring to outcasts the reign of God.

These stances, Smith argues, are "the two basic existential options" open to human beings. A total worldview is implied in each of these stances. Smith resists giving a higher value to one stance or the other. Order can be creative or oppressive. The transgression of order can be creative or destructive. Yet the two options represent such fundamentally different worldviews that "to change stance is to totally alter one's symbols and to inhabit a different world."[25]

How then can we bring these two different worldviews into sharper focus? To help us, we can now turn to another model from the work of Mary Douglas. She argues that a given culture or group tends to have a uniform approach toward all boundaries. She shows how people in the same culture have a similar attitude toward boundaries at several levels of experience. One can see this "unity of experience" in the attitude toward boundaries at three levels:

1. The social boundaries of the group or culture.

2. The bodily boundaries of individuals within the culture.

3. The cosmological boundaries that the people project through their belief systems about God and the world.

Douglas argues that the attitude toward boundaries tends to be the same at each of these levels. For example, if a society is anxious about what goes in

22. Jonathan Z. Smith, "Animals and Plants," 914.
23. Jonathan Z. Smith, "Influence of Symbols," 467.
24. Jonathan Z. Smith, "Animals and Plants," 914.
25. Jonathan Z. Smith, "Influence of Symbols," 467.

and out of the orifices of the bodily boundary, then this society will probably also guard the social boundary carefully to protect who goes in and who goes out of their social group. Regarding the cosmological level of beliefs in such a society, one would expect to find a dualism with a distinct boundary separating the good from the evil, the holy from the unclean. "Conversely," Douglas says, "if [in another culture] there is no concern to preserve social boundaries, I would not expect to find concern with bodily boundaries."[26] And in a culture with little concern to guard social boundaries, the beliefs about God and the world will show ambiguity and interaction around the boundary between good and evil.

We can see how the system works when we notice how the view of boundaries in the Jewish culture of the first-century is the same at the cosmological, bodily, and social levels.

1. *Cosmological boundaries.* At the cosmological level, the dominant motif is the pursuit of holiness by separation from what is unclean. There is a boundary around God to protect God's holiness and to separate God from all that would defile. People are to guard this boundary in order to keep God from withdrawing. On earth, God is located in the holiest place in the Temple. As we have seen, many boundaries surround this place. The cosmic order also includes boundaries for people and animals. Cosmological lines separate Israel from the Gentile nations. Other lines separate animals into clean and unclean. Thus the boundaries in the cosmology separate the clean from the unclean. As we have seen, people are to guard these boundaries in order to keep what is holy separated from that which defiles.

2. *Bodily boundaries.* Similarly, the skin of the body is a boundary to be guarded. The skin makes a person a bounded system. The skin keeps certain things in place inside the body, such as spit, blood, or semen. When out of place, these things will make a person unclean. Similarly, people can guard the skin from unclean things going in from outside the body, for example, by refusing to eat the meat of an unclean animal. Such unclean food taken in from the outside will defile a person. Hence, people guard the boundary of the body to avoid contact with what is unclean, because what comes out and certain things that go in will pollute people.

3. *Social boundaries.* The boundary of Israel distinguishes Jew from Gentile. Only male Jews who are circumcised and without blemish are considered pure. Jews who have contact with Gentiles become unclean, and intermarriage is strictly prohibited. At the same time, Gentiles who come among Jews are "out of place" in the Jewish community and, as we have seen, are prohibited from entering the sanctuary on penalty of death. Generally speaking, Jews guard the social boundary to keep Jews in and Gentiles out.

26. Mary Douglas, *Natural Symbols*, 70.

In this scheme, the most important level is that of the social group. The bodily boundaries and the cosmological order protect and maintain the social boundaries of the group or society. Thus, Douglas notes, "Israel is the boundary that all other boundaries celebrate and that gives them their historic load of meaning."[27] The whole classification system existed in order to protect and sustain the group. The avoidance of unclean food and of marginal people within the nation was a hedge against the outer boundary that separated Jew from Gentile. Thus, according to Douglas's model, there was a coherence of attitudes toward boundaries at several levels, and the coherence served to reinforce the group's experience of its social boundary.

As we have seen, this system is reflected in the depiction of the authorities in Mark's story. They separate from the unclean in Israel (2:15-17), guard the holy Sabbath from defilement (2:23—3:6), guard God from blasphemy (2:1-12; 14:53-65), guard the Temple from unclean people (11:15-18) and blemished sacrifices (12:32-33), and guard the body from impure food (7:1-23).

By contrast, the Jewish movement of Jesus in Mark illustrates a contrasting attitude toward boundaries, the effort to be "unbounded" in order to overcome obstacles in the service of the kingdom of God. Here we see what happens when people abrogate purity rules, cross boundaries, or redraw them. Whereas the authorities in Mark's story guarded boundaries, Jesus and his followers transgressed boundaries. Whereas the leaders saw boundaries as means of protection, the Jesus movement saw boundaries as oppressive and limiting. Whereas the leaders withdrew from uncleanness, the Jesus movement attacked or ignored uncleanness. Whereas the Pharisees avoided contact with that which defiled, Jesus and his followers sought contact. The leaders had power by staying within the ordered boundaries, whereas the Jesus movement expressed power by crossing boundaries. The Jesus movement, as depicted by Mark, treated boundaries as lines to cross, redraw, or eliminate.

In Mark's depiction of the Jesus movement, we see again a consonance, albeit of a very different character, in the attitude toward boundaries at the cosmological, the social, and the bodily levels.

Cosmological Boundaries

Mark's narrative shares the core value of the Jewish society in depicting God as holy. The empowering force behind the activity in the kingdom of God is the "Holy Spirit" (1:8-10), and Jesus is the "Holy One of God" (1:24). However, in contrast to the view that people are to attain holiness by separation from the threatening force of impurity, Mark presents the view that people are to overcome uncleanness by spreading wholeness. Here God does not withdraw because of the threat of defilement by contact with the unclean. Rather, God's holiness is an active force that expands and invades in order to remove and to overcome uncleanness. Thus, in contrast to the view that God is to be protected within the confines of the Temple, the Markan God spreads the life-giving

27. Mary Douglas, *Implicit Meanings*, 269.

power of the kingdom through Jesus and his followers into the world wherever people are receptive to it.

In Mark, God's holiness spreads even into the territory of Satan. Satan is the adversary of God, and Mark refers to the demons under Satan's authority as "unclean spirits." Before the kingdom arrived, the world was Satan's house (3:23-29). Now, however, God breaks out of the confines of heaven, rips apart the boundary between heaven and earth, and invades Satan's territory (1:9-13). To establish rulership over the world, God crosses into Satan's arena. God sends down the Holy Spirit upon Jesus at his baptism (1:10-11). Immediately, the Spirit drives Jesus to confront Satan in the desert. Through the agency of Jesus, God binds Satan and plunders Satan's house (3:22-30). As such, God reclaims people from the destructiveness of the "unclean spirits" (1:12-13; 5:1-20; 9:14-19). The "holy" work of God is that which brings life and overcomes the destructive work of Satan (3:4; 9:42-49).

Also, in Mark, God breaks out of the confines of the Temple to be available everywhere. The Jewish leaders know that God resides on earth in the Temple, and they protect God from what is unclean. Jesus condemns the Temple as holy space because the leaders use it to set boundaries and prohibit the Gentile nations from worshiping there (11:17). God therefore leaves the Temple in order to spread out over the earth. At the death of Jesus, God rips apart the curtain of the sanctuary and breaks out of the confines of the sanctuary (15:38). God leaves the Temple and becomes available anywhere on earth to grant blessings and to pardon sins. The Temple is no longer needed for rituals and sacrifices because God is now accessible wherever people offer prayers of faith and forgiveness (11:20-25).

Furthermore, Mark eliminates the cosmological boundaries that would identify people or things as unclean in and of themselves. For example, Mark eliminates the notion that animals might be unclean in and of themselves, for the Markan Jesus declares all foods clean (7:19). Also, Mark eliminates the notion that Gentiles are unclean in and of themselves. Mark rejects the boundary line distinguishing pure Jews from impure Gentiles. In Mark's view, any Jew or Gentile may be on God's side or against God based on faith and moral behavior rather than on ritual purity (3:29; 7:29). Also, gentile territory is not unclean in and of itself (4:1-20; 7:24-8:10).

Mark's Jesus does not eliminate the line distinguishing God's people from others. He redraws the boundary line in terms of moral behavior rather than ritual impurity.[28] He eliminates dietary boundaries and "ritual defilements" that come by external contact with unclean things, but he does not abrogate purity notions altogether. Rather, he redefines purity of people and times in terms of faith and moral behavior enjoined by the Law and the Prophets (7:14-23; 12:28-34). Those who respond favorably to Jesus and his teaching are on the inside; those who reject him and his teaching are on the outside (3:31-35; 4:10-13). Those who do the will of God are Jesus' "brother and sister and mother," whereas those who do not do the will of God are in opposition to Jesus and are on the outside (3:31-35). In order to give all people an opportunity

28. See Neyrey, "Idea of Purity," 15.

to be on the inside, the followers of Jesus are to proclaim to all people, Jew and Gentile alike, without respect to ritual purity or impurity (13:10, 27). Thus, Jesus redraws the line distinguishing God's people without respect to "ritual" purity or impurity.

As portrayed in the narrative, God is spreading holiness throughout the earth. Followers are also to spread out in order to tell others the good news. They are not to avoid people or animals or things that are considered unclean by society.

Social Boundaries

The attitude toward social boundaries in Mark's narrative world reveals the same expansiveness. The Jesus movement described in the narrative of Mark is not a stationary community that seeks to protect its boundaries but a network going out from Jesus like branches on a tree: first Jesus, then the disciples he sends out (6:7-13), and then those who receive the disciples by hospitality (9:37) and pass the word on (1:28, 45; 5:20). The people in the network expand in outreach and influence.

Relationships in the network are based on reciprocity between those who proclaim and heal and those who give them hospitality. Jesus offers no provisions for establishing stationary communities—no ongoing rituals such as baptism or Eucharist and no directions for communal organization or discipline. Jesus tells disciples to leave their families and property and to receive new familial relations in the hospitality offered them from one village to the next. The person who is at the extremity of the network—one who simply offers a cup of water to someone who bears the name of Christ—is fully part of the network and will receive a reward (9:41). Solidarity in this network is based, therefore, not on relationships in a stationary community, but on the hospitality that followers receive from sympathizers as they move from place to place—"houses, brothers, sisters, mothers, children, and fields" (10:28-30). In contrast to a stationary and protectionist culture, the Jesus movement in Mark is a loose-knit network comprised of people who are reaching out.

Like God, Jesus and his followers are "boundary-crossing" figures. They cross the boundaries established by the culture that protect people from ritual uncleanness. Instead of preserving holiness by avoiding contact, the Markan movement spreads holiness by making contact. Instead of avoiding contact with all people outside the group, Jesus' followers give all people the chance to experience the good news of the reign of God (13:10). In every case, instead of Jesus being defiled by the contact, Jesus makes clean that which was unclean by spreading purity, forgiveness, and wholeness.

Nor does the Jesus network depicted in Mark guard boundaries to protect those who are inside from those who are outside. The people in the network sow the seeds of the good news everywhere (4:13-20) and exclude no one from the network or from its benefits. Jesus eats with tax collectors and sinners. Jesus heals all who request healing, including a gentile woman in Tyre (7:24-30). He feeds four thousand people in gentile territory who have followed him into the desert (7:31—8:10). The narrative explicitly rejects exclusion. At one point, the disciples prevent a man from exorcising a demon in Jesus' name because he "was not following us." In response, Jesus tells them, "Do not stop him . . . for whoever is not against us is for us" (9:38-40). As such, those inside the network are to do nothing to set the limits of the community. Rather, they simply spread the influence of the network. Those outside the network who reject the followers of Jesus are the ones who set the limits of the network by their acts of rejection. Jesus tells the disciples that if others do not welcome them they are to leave that locale and shake the dust off their feet as a witness to the rejection (6:11). However, they do so only to confirm a decision already made by the outsiders rejecting them.

Furthermore, Jesus gives no directions for expulsion from the network. In fact, he strictly prohibits any attempt to dominate or exclude "the little ones who have faith" (9:42). Jesus himself, knowing that one of the Twelve is about to betray him, nevertheless offers the cup at the last communal meal, and they all drink from it—including Judas (14:23). The Markan Jesus sets the boundary lines, but he prohibits the people in the network from guarding these lines. And because followers do not guard or protect the boundary lines, there is no margin to the boundary. People can get in easily, and once inside they can be at various levels of commitment or betrayal. This prohibition against guarding boundaries serves to prevent anything or anyone from inhibiting the expansion of the network. It is also in conformity with Jesus' moral injunction not to lord over anyone (10:41-45).

Bodily Boundaries

Similarly, the followers of Jesus do not guard the body against things going in from the outside. Jesus says, "'There is nothing from outside that by entering people is able to defile them, because it does not enter into the heart, but goes into the stomach and on out into the latrine'—thus he declared all foods clean" (7:17-19). Therefore, there is no need to wash the hands before eating or to protect the body from taking in certain foods or to be concerned about the waste that goes out into the latrine, because Jesus declared all foods to be clean (7:1-23). This attitude toward the bodily boundary replicates the attitude toward the social boundary. As anyone may enter the network without making the group unclean, so anything may go into the body without making it unclean. There is no need to guard the boundaries from what is outside the person or the group.

There are two exceptions to the prohibition against guarding the boundary of the body. In Mark, demons are "unclean spirits" who enter and possess people. Unlike foods, they do not enter the stomach and go on out. Rather, they affect the whole person, including the heart, making faith impossible. To drive out an unclean spirit by the power of the "Holy" Spirit is thereby to render a person clean. Also, people are to guard the bodily boundary against fornication and adultery. Here the focus is not so much on guarding physical boundaries. Rather, the focus is on guarding to ensure that immoral and destructive behavior will not come out from the heart (10:1-12).

In Mark, what renders one clean or unclean is the behavior that comes out from the heart. As God spreads the kingdom and as the Jesus movement spreads holiness, so the individual spreads love for God and neighbor outward from the whole heart (12:29-31). However, immoral behavior that goes out from the heart can make that person unclean (7:20-23). Jesus says, "For from inside, from the hearts of people come the evil designs: fornications, thefts, murders, adulteries, acts of greed, acts of malice, deceit, licentiousness, envious eye, blasphemy, arrogance, reckless folly. All these wicked things come out from within and defile the person" (7:21-23). Thus, Mark eliminates ritual purity-defilement as a demarcation and draws a line between moral and immoral behavior as that which determines purity or pollution. Mark honors moral behavior coming from the inside rather than guarding against unclean things from the outside.

In the same way, the Markan Jesus gives place to moral behavior over against physical wholeness. Mark shows through the many healings that it is God's will to make people whole. Yet, rather than cause someone else to sin, it is better to cut off one's own hand and to enter the rule of God maimed than to have two hands and be thrown into Gehenna (9:42-49). Thus, physical wholeness is not a criterion for being acceptable to God; it is what comes out of the heart. This concern for morality over ritual purity and physical wholeness is evident in the "wise" statement of the scribe that loving God and the neighbor with the "whole" heart is more important than all the "whole" burnt offerings and sacrifices (pure animals without blemish, 12:32-33).

As such, the only maintenance Jesus recommends for the bodily boundary is for followers to do whatever they must do in order not to let harmful actions come out from the heart. One guards not the body but the heart so that what comes out of the heart is life-giving for others rather than destructive.

In summary, in Mark's narrative, the Jewish leaders erected and maintained boundaries to preserve holiness, and the Jewish followers of Jesus spread holiness outwardly—the good news of the kingdom, the power of the Spirit, and the loving deeds that come from within. In Mark's narrative, the leaders guarded the boundaries to prevent what was unholy from coming in, and the followers of Jesus overcame boundaries until they should reach the ends of the earth, a goal that Mark considered to be attainable within a generation after the death of Jesus (13:26-31).

We do not know how much Mark's portrayal accurately depicts the historical Jesus. Nor do we know if Mark's approach to boundaries reflects the realities of his own community. The approach to boundaries in Mark is somewhat unusual, even in early Christianity. Just as there were differing approaches to purity among groups in Judaism, so the early expressions of Christianity differed. For example, many early Christian communities considered baptism to be an important ritual of entrance. Also, both Paul (1 Cor 5:3-5) and Matthew (18:15-18) have procedures for expelling people from a Christian community. Thus, even if Christianity did begin as a movement of Jews who were boundary-crossing figures, the early churches soon consolidated and organized in order to survive as they spread into the larger Greco-Roman world. Nevertheless,

Mark offers the vision of a radical attitude toward boundaries inspired by the mission to bring the good news of healing and wholeness to all.

Conclusion

The extended example given here illustrates the various approaches presented at the beginning of this chapter.

1. *Social description.* We identified many customs, laws, and practices related to pollution and purity in first-century Palestine.

2. *Social history.* We saw to some extent how the approach to purity in Mark related to the social history of the times. We might also have shown how the conceptions of purity developed in the course of Israel's history and how they related to the social history of the larger Roman world.

3. *Worldview and social structure.* We showed "maps" that reveal how the ancient Jews organized their life together in terms of holiness and defilement. Also, we saw how the Markan Jesus sought to "convert" followers from their primary socialization regarding purity, defilement, and boundaries. Furthermore, we saw how the Markan attitude toward boundaries supported a social network oriented to mission.

4. *Cultural anthropology* We employed models to help us interpret the social phenomena and to clarify the different attitudes to purity and boundaries evident in the narrative of Mark's Gospel.

The social study of the first-century seems like an overwhelming task. If you wish to pursue it, begin with one event or a single text, such as the Gospel of Mark. Find something there that puzzles and fascinates you—demons, tax collectors, the Temple, fasting, marriage and divorce, leprosy, attitudes to Gentiles, and so on. Then begin to explore this problem with the methods presented here. Many books available on daily life in the first century give extensive social description. Many of the books cited here bring insights from cultural anthropology to bear upon the dynamics of first-century culture. You will discover other resources. Soon you find yourself unraveling a mystery or putting the pieces of a puzzle in place. Then you can go on to the next problem. Soon you find how pieces of the puzzle fit together into a larger picture. You are doing detective work on the first century. Although the task may seem endless, the delight comes from the process of exploration into another world and from the illumination of the biblical stories that results along the way.[29]

29. I am grateful for a summer grant from the National Endowment for the Humanities that enabled me to do the initial research for this article. I am grateful to the following people for reacting to a draft of the manuscript: Joanna Dewey, Edgar Krentz, Wilhelm Linss, Jerome Neyrey, John Pilch, Jonathan Smith, and Herman Waetjen.

FURTHER READING

BALCH, David, ed. *Social History of the Matthean Community*. Minneapolis: Fortress Press, 1991. Contributors investigate various facets of Matthew's community, such as social status, urban environment, economic level, and gender relations.

ELLIOTT, John H. *A Home for the Homeless: A Sociological Exegesis of 1 Peter, Its Situation and Strategy*. 2d ed. Minneapolis: Fortress Press, 1990. Combines social description, models from the social sciences, and interpretation to show how 1 Peter addresses Christians who are resident aliens in Asia Minor.

——— ed. *Social-Scientific Criticism of the New Testament*. Semeia 35, 1986. A collection of articles that explore the use of the social sciences in biblical interpretation.

HARRINGTON, D. J. "Second Testament Exegesis and the Social Sciences." *Biblical Theology Bulletin* 18 (1988): 77–85. A comprehensive bibliography of books and articles on the social study of the New Testament.

HOLMBERG, Bengt. *Sociology and the New Testament: An Appraisal*. Minneapolis: Fortress Press, 1990. A summary of key issues and a critique of various approaches.

HORSLEY, Richard. *Sociology and the Jesus Movement*. Philadelphia: Fortress Press, 1989. A critique of Gerd Theissen's structural-functionalist study of the Jesus movement and an alternative approach through conflict analysis.

KEE, Howard. *Knowing the Truth: A Sociological Approach to the New Testament*. Minneapolis: Fortress Press, 1989. An approach informed especially by sociology of knowledge.

MALHERBE, Abraham. *Social Aspects of Early Christianity*. 2d ed. Philadelphia: Fortress Press, 1983. Contains excellent examples of social description and analysis.

MALINA, Bruce. *The New Testament World: Insights from Cultural Anthropology*. Atlanta: John Knox Press, 1981. Introductory text using models from anthropology to map the framework of first-century cultures.

———. *Christian Origins and Cultural Anthropology: Practical Models for Biblical Interpretation*. Atlanta: John Knox Press, 1986. Comparison of New Testament cultures with modern societies by means of a group/grid model from anthropologist Mary Douglas.

MEEKS, Wayne. *The First Urban Christians: The Social World of the Apostle Paul*. New Haven: Yale University Press, 1983. A description and analysis of the social dynamics of Pauline churches.

MYERS, Ched. *Binding the Strong Man: A Political Reading of Mark's Story of Jesus*. Maryknoll, N.Y.: Orbis, 1988. Interprets Mark from a liberation perspective in the context of other first-century political options.

MYERS, Eric and James Strange. *Archaeology, the Rabbis, and Early Christianity*. Nashville: Abingdon, 1981. A good example of the use of archeology in the social description of villages, languages, burial practices, synagogues, and art in ancient Galilee.

NEYREY, Jerome, ed. *The Social World of Luke-Acts: Models of Interpretation*. Peabody, Mass.: Hendrickson, 1991. Uses models from the social sciences to provide a comprehensive analysis of the social world in the narrative of Luke-Acts.

OSIEK, Carolyn. *What Are They Saying about the Social Setting of the New Testament?* New York: Paulist Press, 1984. Readable summary and analysis of this field of study.

———. "The New Handmaid: The Bible and the Social Sciences." *Theological Studies* 50 (1989): 260–78. A recent survey and evaluation of the social study of the whole Bible.

PETERSEN, Norman. *Rediscovering Paul: Philemon and the Sociology of Paul's Narrative World*. Philadelphia: Fortress Press, 1985. An analysis of the cultural assumptions and social roles in Paul's Letter to Philemon.

SCHÜSSLER FIORENZA, Elisabeth. *In Memory of Her: A Feminist Theological Reconstruction of Christian Origins*. New York: Crossroad, 1986. Exposes the oppressiveness of texts and interpreters to recover the presence and activity of women in the early Christian movement.

STAMBAUGH, John, and David Balch. *The New Testament in Its Social Environment*. Philadelphia: Westminster, 1986. Social description of many facets of daily life in the New Testament world.

THEISSEN, Gerd. *The Sociology of Early Palestinian Christianity*. Philadelphia: Fortress Press, 1978. Social analysis of the Jesus movement in the context of first-century Palestine.

WAETJEN, Herman. *A Reordering of Power: A Socio-Political Reading of Mark's Gospel*. Minneapolis: Fortress Press, 1989. Draws upon studies of apocalyptic sects to unpack the meaning of Mark's story.

WILSON, R. R. *Sociological Approaches to the Old Testament*. Philadelphia: Fortress Press, 1984. A general survey and critique of the social study of the Old Testament.

GLOSSARY

Allegory–a text that has hidden, often spiritual, meanings lying behind its literal sense.

Anachronism–reading the Gospels through the lenses of one's own time, ignoring the historical gap between "then" and "now," e.g., reading Mark as a twentieth-century text.

Anagogy–the spiritual or mystical level of interpretation in the fourfold levels of meaning sought by interpreters in the Middle Ages. The other levels were the literal, the allegorical, and the moral. Anagogy is often related to the heavenly, transcendent realm.

Analepsis–the narration of an event *after* its ordinary chronological order in the narrative world; a flashback. A term introduced by Gerard Genette in *Narrative Discourse*.

Androcentrism–treating males as the universal human norm; a male-centered worldview.

Binary opposition–pairs of concepts placed in opposition to one another. One of the pair is often considered to be superior to the other. Key binary oppositions in Western culture are male/female, white/nonwhite, pure/impure, and presence/absence.

Canon–a list of works accepted as authoritative and normative by a particular group—the canon of English literary classics, for example. The New Testament canon consists of twenty-seven early Christian writings accepted as authoritative by all Christian traditions.

Character–the persons in a narrative, the participants in its action or plot. E. M. Forster distinguished "flat" and "round" characters in *Aspects of the Novel*. Flat characters are simple, constructed around a single idea or trait, and static. Round characters are complex. They cannot be summed up in a single sentence, and sometimes develop over the course of a narrative. Two methods of characterization are sometimes also distinguished: showing and telling.

The narrator may "show" a character through the character's words and actions; the narrator may also "tell" about the character, describing and evaluating him or her directly.

Cultural anthropology—in Gospel studies, the use of anthropological models that organize information about a culture, such as a model of a kinship structure, to illuminate the cultural context of the Gospels.

Deconstructive criticism—a flexible and inventive strategy of reading that seeks to highlight troubling aspects of texts that more traditional readings have tended to repress (e.g., logical contradictions), or that highlights seemingly unimportant details of texts that traditional readings have ignored or failed to notice but that can yield important insights into the workings of the text. Deconstruction is associated with the work of such philosophers and critics as Jacques Derrida, Paul de Man, and Barbara Johnson.

Demythologizing—Rudolf Bultmann's attempt to translate the myths of the New Testament into existentialist expressions about the truth of what it means to live as an authentic human being in this world.

Endogamy—the practice of marrying within one's family or clan. It preserves or advances the wealth, status, and power of the group and of individuals within the group.

Ethnocentrism—reading a Gospel through the lenses of one's own culture and imposing those categories on a text from a different culture.

Evangelist—the writer of a Gospel. The term comes from the Greek *euangelion* or "good news," which was translated into Old English as "Gospel."

Exogamy—the practice of marrying outside one's primary family or clan as defined by one's culture. It is often used to prevent conflict and cement alliances between groups.

Feminism—a term that probably should appear in the plural as feminisms. There are liberal, cultural, socialist, existentialist, radical, psychoanalytic, and other forms of feminism. What most feminists share is resolute opposition and resistance to the various forms of male domination faced by women. They also share the conviction that women can and should create their own gendered identities and take responsibility for their own choices, political and personal.

Feminist criticism—in Gospel studies, any approach to the text that begins with a commitment to feminism. It can involve a critique of previous interpretations of a text; it can seek to reconstruct the history of women in the cultural context of the text; or it can offer a feminist reader-response analysis, among other perspectives.

Focalization—a technical term some narrative theorists use to refer to the perspective from which a narrative event (scene or speech) is presented, that is, who sees and hears. In the Gospels the narrator may present a scene from his or her own perspective or from the perspective of a character. See *point of view*.

Form criticism–a scholarly method that traces the history of the Gospels to an oral stage lying behind the written Gospels. It seeks to classify small units of tradition, of which the Gospels were thought to be composed, into categories or "forms," such as controversy story, parable, legend, and so on. It assigns each of these units a *Sitz im Leben*, a setting and function in the life of the early Christian communities, such as preaching, teaching, or baptismal ceremony.

Gender–the social construction of persons as male or female. Often contrasted with *sex*, which is considered as a biological designation for men and women distinguished in terms of genetic structure and reproductive organs.

Immasculation–a term coined by Judith Fetterley in *The Resisting Reader*. It refers to what can happen when a female reads an androcentric or patriarchal text: she reads and identifies as male, identifying against herself.

Implied author–the author implied by the totality of a work. The implied author is distinguished from the flesh-and-blood real author. The implied author is the persona and the set of values that the reader experiences as the implicit creator and controller of the work. Wayne Booth coined and popularized this term in *The Rhetoric of Fiction*.

Implied reader–This term was originally coined by Wolfgang Iser in *The Implied Reader*. Iser defined the concept as one that "incorporates both the prestructuring of the potential meaning by the text, and the reader's actualization of this potential through the reading process."

Intentional fallacy–seeking to interpret a text by imagining what the real author's intentions were.

Intercalation–inserting or sandwiching one story inside another.

Intertextual–between texts.

Intratextual–within a text.

Irony–incongruity between the literal meaning and another meaning. Verbal irony involves an utterance that cannot be taken at face value. Dramatic irony is an ironic incongruity in situations or events in a narrative. In theater, dramatic irony occurs when the audience recognizes something that a character or characters in the play do not. In Mark, the readers often understand something that characters, such as the disciples, do not.

Markan hypothesis–the hypothesis that Mark is the earliest Gospel. Proponents of the hypothesis often argue that Mark, therefore, preserves the most accurate historical record of the life of Jesus. They view Mark as the most realistic and least theological Gospel. These views were strongly challenged by Wilhelm Wrede in *The Messianic Secret*.

Narratee—the persona in the text to whom the story is addressed. In some narratives the narratee is a character. In others, as in the Gospels, it is difficult to distinguish the narratee from the aspect of the implied reader that is internal to the text.

Narrative criticism—a term coined by New Testament critics to refer to analysis of each Gospel as a literary whole. Deeply influenced by secular narratology, it focuses on character, plot, setting, and point of view.

Narratology—narrative theory. Typically, narratology searches for the general principles that manifest themselves in individual narratives.

Narrator—the person who tells the story. In some works this is a character (e.g., John in Revelation). In the Gospels, the narrator is not a character. The reliable third-person omniscient narrator of each Gospel is the voice of the implied author.

New Criticism—The dominant mode of Anglo-American literary criticism in the 1940s and 1950s. It focused on the literary work itself (its language and internal structures) rather than on the historical background of the text, the biography of the author, or the effect on the reader.

Parousia—the Greek word for "coming" or "presence," it refers to the second coming or return of Jesus clothed with power to judge and redeem.

Passion—When used of Jesus, this term refers to his suffering and death. The passion narrative in a Gospel consists of those portions of the Gospel that narrate the crucifixion and the events leading up to it.

Plot—the arrangement of the episodes of a story; the structure and relations between its actions. Often motivation and conflict are considered central elements of plot.

Point of view—the perspective from which a story is told. It includes both visual and aural perspectives as well as evaluative or ideological perspective. The size of a character may be presented through a child's eyes, for example. A character may be viewed as wicked, a servant of Satan. Narrators tell the story from their own perspectives and may incorporate the perspectives of characters within their perspectives. Traditionally, a distinction has been made between first- and third-person point of view. A first-person narrator is an "I" who is also a character in the story. A third-person narrator stands outside the story and refers to characters as "he" or "she." Point of view is further classified according to the degree of knowledge possessed and reliability. An omniscient point of view, for example, knows everything about characters and events. It has privileged access to the minds of characters. A reliable point of view is aligned with the point of view of the implied author. In the Gospels, Jesus' point of view is aligned with that of the implied author, whereas that of the Jewish authorities is not.

Prolepsis—the narration of an event *before* its logical order in the narrative world; foreshadowing. A term introduced by Gerard Genette in *Narrative Discourse*.

Reader-response criticism–a pragmatic approach to criticism that focuses on the role of the reader. It privileges the reader over the author and the text in the creation of meaning. Some versions of reader-response criticism focus more on the "reader-in-the-text"—the role of the reader encoded or implied in the text—and others emphasize the various responses of actual readers as individuals or as members of interpretive communities.

Redaction criticism–a scholarly method that treats each evangelist as an editor or redactor of traditional material. It seeks to separate tradition (materials the evangelist inherited) from redaction (how the evangelist edited and shaped tradition). It uses editorial material to reconstruct the evangelist's community—the situation he (or she?) sought to address—and unique theology.

Self-consuming artifact–Stanley Fish's term for literature that says something and then takes it back or does something to the reader and then undoes it in the course of the temporal experience of reading.

Septuagint–the Greek version of the Hebrew Scriptures. It contains Greek translations of Hebrew and Aramaic texts as well as some material composed only in Greek.

Settings–Temporal, spatial, and social locations of narrative events. In the Gospels location may have important symbolic significance. In Matthew, for instance, Galilee is associated with the Gentiles. The events of the passion take place in a social setting where a Roman governor has the final say over Jesus' fate.

Social criticism–an umbrella term we have chosen to cover approaches to the Gospels influenced by sociology, anthropology, and social history. The focus is "social," that is, less on the individual and the unique than on the group and the general.

Social description–the reconstruction of the material culture, customs, and everyday life of the first-century Mediterranean world.

Social history–the history of groups, movements, and institutions, it charts broad historical changes.

Sociology of knowledge–the study of the relationship between a group's worldview and its social organization.

Source criticism–a scholarly method that seeks to determine the sources of the Gospels and especially to explain the literary relationships between them. The majority explanation is the two-source hypothesis.

Story and discourse–terms introduced to Gospel critics by Seymour Chatman. Story is the *what* of the narrative, its plot, characters, setting, and the like. Discourse is *how* the narrative is told, including the ordering of the events in the plot, comments by the narrator to the narratee, point of view, and so on. Story and discourse are separable only in theory; what we have in narrative is the story-as-discourse.

Structuralism—a multidisciplinary approach arising out of linguistics. It views language as a system of signs that have meaning only in relation to other signs. It tends to analyze texts in terms of the systems of rules, codes, and conventions that govern their production. It may view the text as a complex communication between a sender and a receiver. Bracketing historical questions, it studies the text "synchronically," that is, as it appears at a given point in time. It may seek to uncover the "deep structures" of the text. These structures are often seen in terms of binary oppositions such as good and evil, order and chaos, and light and dark and mediations between these oppositions.

Synoptic Gospels—The Gospels of Matthew, Mark, and Luke. They are called synoptic (from the Greek word *synopsis*, meaning "a viewing together") because of the similarities between them in wording and content in contrast to the Gospel of John.

Two-source hypothesis—the hypothesis that Mark was the first written Gospel and that Matthew and Luke used Mark and a second source called Q (for the German word for source, *Quelle*) to compose their Gospels. It attributes passages common to all three Gospels to Mark and passages common only to Matthew and Luke to Q. To round things out, scholars often label material peculiar to Matthew as *M* and material peculiar to Luke as *L*.

INDEX OF ANCIENT SOURCES

Hebrew Bible (Old Testament)

GENESIS
1   107–8
2   107
2:7,23   100
2-3   108
3:16   108
3:17-19   108
3:20   100
4:1   100
11–23   106

EXODUS
3:14   41
3:14ff   100
4:21ff   90 n.9
16:13-30   41

LEVITICUS
18:16   119, 120 n.25
19:2   145
20:21   119, 120 n.25

NUMBERS

5:23-24   100
27:17   41

JUDGES
4-5   108
5:24   129
19:1-30   109

1 SAMUEL
1   106

1 KINGS
1:19   128
19–21   129
22:17

2 KINGS
9   129

ESTHER
2:2,3,7,8,9,12(LXX)   122, 125
5:3,6-7   128
7:2-3   128

JOB
38:28-29   108

PSALMS
22   64, 96
22:9   108
107:23-32   38
123:2   108

ISAIAH
6:9-10   37
42:14   108
66:7-14   108

JEREMIAH
31:15-22   108

EZEKIEL
2:8—3:3   100–1
34:5   41

JOEL
2:28-32   108

Apocrypha

JUDITH
9:10   129

13:14   129
16:5-6, 9   129

New Testament

MATTHEW
1:18   86
3:13-17   2
4:1-11   4
4:12   62
8:28   38
12:15   62
13:1   62
13:31-33   108

14:1-12   116
14:6   122
14:12   62
14:13   62
15   109
16:18   101
16:18-19   111
17:1-8   2
18:15-18   158

21:12-17   4
26:33-35   111
26:69-75   111
27:45-56   2
27:62-66   76
27:62—28:20   75, 79
28:1-10   2
28:2   77
28:2-4   77

Rabbinic and Other Ancient Jewish Materials

Patristic and Other Early Christian Writers

INDEX OF TOPICS AND NAMES

CONTRIBUTORS

JANICE CAPEL ANDERSON is Assistant Professor of Philosophy at the University of Idaho, Moscow, Idaho. She is the author of "Matthew: Gender and Reading" in *Semeia* 28: 3–27 and "Mapping Feminist Biblical Criticism: The American Scene, 1983–1990" in *Critical Review of Books in Religion* 1991.

ROBERT M. FOWLER is Associate Professor of Religion and Chair of the Department of Religion at Baldwin-Wallace College, Berea, Ohio. He is the author of *Loaves and Fishes: The Function of the Feeding Stories in the Gospel of Mark* (Chico, Calif.: Scholars Press, 1981) and *Let the Reader Understand: Reader-Response Criticism and the Gospel of Mark* (Minneapolis: Fortress Press, 1991).

ELIZABETH STRUTHERS MALBON is Professor of Religion at Virginia Polytechnic Institute and State University, Blacksburg, Virginia. She is the author of *Narrative Space and Mythic Meaning in Mark* (Sheffield: Sheffield Academic Press, 1991) and *The Iconography of the Sarcophagus of Junius Bassus* (Princeton: Princeton University Press, 1990).

STEPHEN D. MOORE is Assistant Professor of Religious Studies at Wichita State University, Wichita, Kansas. He is the author of *Literary Criticism and the Gospels* (New Haven: Yale University Press, 1989) and *Mark and Luke in Poststructuralist Perspectives* (New Haven: Yale University Press, 1992).

DAVID RHOADS is Professor of New Testament at the Lutheran School of Theology at Chicago, Chicago, Illinois. He is the author of *Israel in Revolution: 6–74 C.E.* (Philadelphia: Fortress Press, 1976) and with Donald Michie, *Mark as Story: An Introduction to the Narrative of a Gospel* (Philadelphia: Fortress Press, 1982).